ACKNOWLEDGEMENT

My thanks are due to Volkswagen for their unstinted co-operation and also for supplying data and illustrations.

Considerable assistance has also been given by owners, who have discussed their cars in detail, and I would like to express my gratitude for this invaluable advice and help.

Kenneth Ball
Associate Member, Guild of Motoring Writers
Ditchling Sussex England.

Volkswagen Beetle 1968-77 Autobook

By Kenneth Ball

Associate Member, Guild of Motoring Writers
and the Autobooks Team of Technical Writers

Volkswagen 1200 1968-77
Volkswagen 1300, 1300A 1968-75
Volkswagen 1500 1968-70
Volkswagen 1302 (1285cc) 1970-72
Volkswagen 1302S, LS (1584cc) 1970-72
Volkswagen 1303 (1285cc) 1972-75
Volkswagen 1303S, LS (1584cc) 1972-77
Volkswagen Karmann Ghia 1968-74

Autobooks Ltd. Golden Lane Brighton BN1 2QJ England

The AUTOBOOK series of Workshop Manuals is the largest in the world and covers the majority of British and Continental motor cars, as well as the majority of Japanese and Australian models.

Whilst every care has been taken to ensure correctness of information it is obviously not possible to guarantee complete freedom from errors or omissions or to accept liability arising from such errors or omissions.

CONTENTS

ISBN 0 85147 797 6

First Edition   1970
Reprinted   1970
Reprinted   1970
Second Edition, fully revised   1971
Third Edition, fully revised   1972
Reprinted   1972
Fourth Edition, fully revised   1973
Reprinted   1973
Fifth Edition, fully revised   1974
Reprinted   1974
Sixth Edition, fully revised   1975
Seventh Edition, fully revised   1978
Eighth Edition, fully revised   1978

© Autobooks Ltd 1978

760

Printed in Brighton England for Autobooks Ltd by G. Beard and Son Ltd
Bound in Hove England for Autobooks Ltd by Jilks Ltd

E

INTRODUCTION

This do-it-yourself Workshop Manual has been specially written for the owner who wishes to maintain his vehicle in first class condition and to carry out the bulk of his own servicing and repairs. Considerable savings on garage charges can be made, and one can drive in safety and confidence knowing the work has been done properly.

Comprehensive step-by-step instructions and illustrations are given on most dismantling, overhauling and assembling operations. Certain assemblies require the use of expensive special tools, the purchase of which would be unjustified. In these cases information is included but the reader is recommended to hand the unit to the agent for attention.

Throughout the Manual hints and tips are included which will be found invaluable, and there is an easy to follow fault diagnosis at the end of each chapter.

Whilst every care has been taken to ensure correctness of information it is obviously not possible to guarantee complete freedom from errors or omissions or to accept liability arising from such errors or omissions.

Instructions may refer to the righthand or lefthand sides of the vehicle or the components. These are the same as the righthand or lefthand of an observer standing behind the vehicle and looking forward.

CHAPTER 1

THE ENGINE

1:1 Description

In such an unconventional car as the Volkswagen 'Beetle' it would be reasonable to expect an engine of equally unconventional design and this is the case. Examination of **FIG 1:1** will enable the component parts to be identified. The flat-four arrangement of the cylinders is such that pairs of cylinders face each other horizontally on either side of the crankshaft. The four finned cylinder barrels are identical and interchangeable and closely resemble their motorcycle counterparts, being cooled by air, flowing over the fins. Cylinder heads are provided by a single aluminium alloy casting to each pair of cylinders, the casting being secured by eight long studs and nuts. To give more durable working surfaces there are pressed-in valve guides and valve seat inserts.

The engine has inclined valves 8 and pushrods 20 in **FIG 1:1**. The inner ends of the rods register in separate bucket-type cam followers 22. Oiltight pushrod covers are ribbed to accommodate changes in length due to expansion and contraction. The slope on the covers enables lubricating oil from the valve gear to drain back into the crankcase.

The two pairs of cylinders 9 are mounted on a crankcase which is split vertically on the centre line. During manufacture the two halves of the crankcase are machined as an assembly and only a complete crankcase can be supplied as a spare part. It is not possible to renew one half of the case by itself.

The crankcase carries the crankshaft 26 in four bearings, No. 1 bearing at the front being a light-alloy bush with flanges to take end thrust. No. 2 bearing is of the split light-alloy type although some engines may have steel-backed lead-alloy shells. Nos. 3 and 4 are light-alloy bushes. The bearing surfaces of the crankshaft are hardened.

The short and very sturdy connecting rods 15 are fitted with thinwall lead-bronze bearing shells in the big-ends and there is a bronze bush for the gudgeon pin in the small-end.

The light-alloy pistons 10 carry fully floating gudgeon pins which are retained by circlips and there are three piston rings, the bottom one being of the oil control type.

The short, stiff, camshaft 28 runs in bearings fitted with renewable liners. The rearmost bearing liners are flanged to take care of end thrust due to the helical timing gear. There are only four cams because each one operates two valves, one on each side of the engine. The large single helical timing gear is made from light-alloy and is riveted to the camshaft. It engages with a smaller gear which is keyed to the crankshaft between the rear bearings. The rear end of the camshaft drives an orthodox gear-type oil pump 27.

The pump draws lubricating oil from a strainer 29 in the ribbed sump and passes it to a vertical oil cooler 3 positioned in the air flow from the cooling fan. From here the cooled oil passes through drilled passages to the main

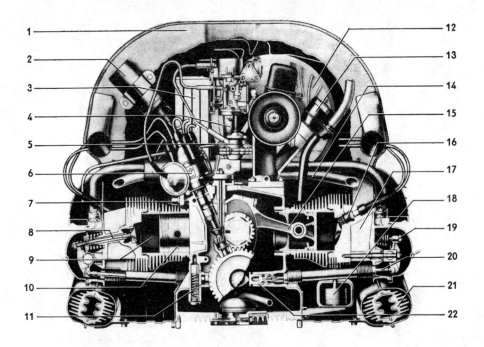

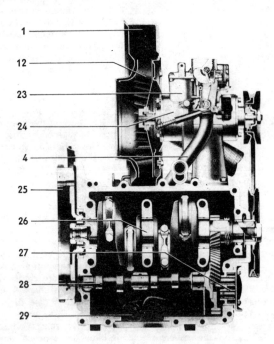

FIG 1:1   Sectional views of the engine. Note the inclined valves, the separate cam followers and the position of the fuel pump, with vertical pushrod operation. Later engines differ in detail but the basic design is unchanged

Key to Fig 1:1   1 Fan housing   2 Ignition coil   3 Oil cooler   4 Intake manifold   5 Fuel pump   6 Distributor
7 Oil pressure switch   8 Valve   9 Cylinder   10 Piston   11 Oil pressure relief valve   12 Fan   13 Oil filler and breather
14 Preheating pipe   15 Connecting rod   16 Spark plug   17 Cylinder head   18 Thermostat   19 Rocker arm
20 Pushrod   21 Heat exchanger   22 Cam follower   23 Carburetter   24 Generator   25 Flywheel   26 Crankshaft
27 Oil pump   28 Camshaft   29 Oil strainer

and big-end bearings, to the camshaft bearings and up the hollow pushrods to the rockers and valve gear. From here the oil drains down the inclined pushrod covers back to the sump. The cylinder walls, pistons and gudgeon pins are lubricated by splash. In cold weather, when the oil is of high viscosity a pressure relief valve 11 allows oil to pass directly to the engine without passing through the cooler.

The distributor 6 is driven by a spiral gear keyed to the crankshaft just in front of the rear bearing.

The generator 24 is belt driven from a pulley on the rear end of the crankshaft. The forward end of the generator shaft carries a fan 12 which supplies the large volume of cooling air required. Some of this air, when heated by the exhaust system is used for the car interior heating. The flow of air through the engine cooling ducts is thermostatically controlled by flaps. Heated air for the car interior is obtained by passing air over finned heat exchangers 21.

The complete engine is not attached to the chassis but is secured by four bolts to the transmission flange which is in-line with the rear face of the flywheel 25. The transmission and final drive case is flexibly mounted in a cradle formed at the rear end of the chassis backbone. The engine is thus cantilever mounted and can be withdrawn from the transmission simply by detaching the wiring, the carburetter controls and the fuel pipe and undoing the four bolts. It will be noted that the sump is part of the crankcase so that it is impossible to service the camshaft and crankshaft components without removing the engine and splitting the crankcase.

Table of models:

The following specifications will help the reader to identify the models being discussed in the servicing instructions.

Model			VW '1200'
Cylinder bore	..	..	77 mm
Stroke	..	..	64 mm
Capacity	..	..	1192 cc
Compression ratio	..		7.0:1
Power output (DIN)	..		34 bhp at 3600 rev/min

Model			VW '1300' (till August 1970)
Cylinder bore	..	..	77 mm
Stroke	..	..	69 mm
Capacity	..	..	1285 cc
Compression ratio	..		7.3:1
Power output (DIN)	..		40 bhp at 4000 rev/min

Models			VW '1300', '1302', '1303'
Cylinder bore	..	..	77 mm
Stroke	..	..	69 mm
Capacity	..	..	1285 cc
Compression ratio	..		7.5:1
Power output (DIN)	..		44 bhp at 4100 rev/min

Model			VW '1500'
Cylinder bore	..	..	83 mm
Stroke	..	..	69 mm
Capacity	..	..	1493 cc
Compression ratio	..		7.5:1
Power output (DIN)	..		44 bhp at 4000 rev/min

FIG 1:2   Using feeler gauges to adjust the valve rocker clearance

Models			VW '1302S', '1303S', '1600', 'GT'
Cylinder bore	..	..	85.5 mm
Stroke	..	..	69.0 mm
Capacity	..	..	1584 cc
Compression ratio	..		7.5:1
Power output (DIN)	..		50 bhp at 4000 rev/min

1:2 Servicing without engine removal

Apart from adjustments to the fuel and ignition systems, and these will be found in the appropriate chapters, the most likely operation to be tackled without removing the engine is that of adjusting the rocker clearance. Adjustment of fan belt tension is covered in **Chapter 4, Section 4:6**.

Adjusting the rocker clearance:

Valve clearance increases when the engine is hot, so all adjustments must be made with the engine cold. Excessive clearance leads to noisy operation and performance suffers because the timing will be wrong. Insufficient clearance will also affect the timing. If the clearance is very small the valves will not be seating when they are supposed to be closed and this will cause burning of both valves and seats. The reduced compression will then lead to poor performance.

FIG 1:2 shows the method of making clearance adjustments. Before removing the covers to gain access to the rockers it is essential to clean all dirt from the covers and surrounding parts. Then prise off each spring clip and remove the covers. If the gasket sticks firmly to one surface, leave it in position, but if there has been obvious leakage from the cover joint be prepared to renew the gasket.

Adjustment should be made in a cylinder sequence of 1, 2, 3 and 4. Viewing the cylinders from the rear of the car,

FIG 1:3 Finding TDC when adjusting valve clearances. Pulley notch in line with crankcase joint (righthand dotted line), and rotor arm in line with notch on distributor body (lefthand dotted line)

FIG 1:4 Oil strainer cover removed from underside of sump to reveal strainer gauze and gaskets

No. 1 is right front, No. 2 is right rear, No. 3 is left front and No. 4 is left rear. Start with No. 1 cylinder. The two valves will be fully closed on the compression stroke when the piston is at TDC. This position is found quite simply by turning the engine over by pulling on the fan belt. Alternatively use a spanner on either of the pulley nuts. Remove the distributor cap and turn the engine anticlockwise. Watch the front rim of the crankshaft pulley for a notch, and when this is in-line with the vertical joint between the crankcase halves, the rotor arm of the distributor should be in the position shown in FIG 1:3. Note that the righthand notch in the pulley is used as a datum and the rotor is in-line with a small nick on

the face of the distributor body. In this position the rotor indicates TDC for No. 1 cylinder on the compression stroke. To arrive at the same position for No. 2 cylinder turn the engine anticlockwise 180 deg. so that the rotor arm turns through 90 deg. Two further rotor movements of 90 deg. each will give the TDC positions for cylinders 3 and 4.

With No. 1 cylinder correctly set, check the clearances between No. 1 rocker arms and valve stems with feeler gauges. If incorrect, adjust as shown by loosening the locknut and turning the adjuster until the correct feeler just slides between the surfaces. Hold the adjuster with the screwdriver and tighten the locknut, then check the clearance again. With all clearances adjusted, see that the cover joint faces and gaskets are clean and dry and fit the covers, renewing the gaskets if there has been leakage. The inlet and exhaust valve clearances (cold) on all models is .004 inch up to 1971, later engines require a clearance of .006 inch.

Lubrication servicing:

Renew the engine lubricating oil every 3000 miles. Drain the sump and remove the strainer cover (see FIG 1:4). Clean the strainer gauze with a brush and petrol, not a fluffy rag. Install with new gaskets and new copper washers. Do not overtighten the nuts. With the car standing on level ground put in $4\frac{3}{8}$ pints of fresh oil of the correct grade.

1:3 Removing and replacing the engine

With the exception of valve clearance adjustment, and removal of the oil pump, all further engine overhauling must be done with the engine out of the vehicle. Fortunately the engine is light enough for two men to be able to remove it providing they have adequate clearance under the vehicle. This can be arranged by working over a pit. The alternative is to raise the vehicle on a hoist, or jack-up and support the rear of the vehicle until it is about three feet off the floor. **At this point we must emphasize the great importance of ensuring the safety of operators by arranging suitable supports under the car in the absence of a pit or hoist.** These supports must be capable of remaining firm under all stresses and may be placed under the crossmember or floor pan just behind the front axle and at the rear axle under the torsion bar.

Remove the engine as follows:

1 Disconnect the battery earthing strap.
2 Open the rear hood and remove the air cleaner as described in **Chapter 2.**
3 Disconnect the cable from terminals 51 and 61 of the regulator box if mounted on the generator. Also disconnect the cables from ignition coil terminal 15, from the automatic choke, from the electro-magnetic pilot jet if fitted and from the oil pressure switch behind the distributor.
4 Disconnect the accelerator cable from the carburetter. The cable is shown in **Chapter 2, FIG 2:15.** On some models, a throttle positioner is fitted and this will have to be removed before disconnecting the cable (see **Chapter 2, FIG 2:17**).
5 Pull off the fuel hose and seal it. Detach the flexible heater pipes.

6 Move round to the front of the plate separating the engine from the transmission casing underneath the car and remove the two lower nuts from the casing flange. Another pair will be found on top behind the fan housing, the nuts facing to the rear. Do not remove these until the weight of the engine has been taken on a jack, preferably a trolley jack which can be wheeled about. With the jack in position remove the nuts from the two upper mounting bolts behind the fan housing. An assistant will be useful to hold the bolts while the nuts are removed. Withdraw the accelerator cable and the fuel hose forward (away from the engine).

7 **The next operation needs great care to avoid damage to the drive shaft or the clutch driven plate and release bearing.** Whilst being withdrawn rearwards a matter of four inches, the engine must be kept perfectly square with the transmission casing and its weight completely supported until the clutch driven plate and the release plate are clear of the drive shaft, see **Chapter 5. Serious damage can be caused by allowing the engine to tilt or by letting its weight hang on these components.** When the parts are clear of the drive shaft the engine can be tilted down at the rear and lowered away. Keep an eye on the distributor while doing this.

Replace the engine as follows:

These operations are described on the assumption that the clutch has not been disturbed. If the clutch has been dismantled refer to **Chapter 5** for instructions on centring the clutch driven plate. This is essential because the splined hub of the driven plate must accept the splined drive shaft and allow the spigot of the shaft to enter the central bearing in the flywheel retaining nut as can be seen in the section in **FIG 1:20**.

1 Put $\frac{1}{3}$ oz of Universal grease in the bearing in the flywheel retaining nut. Lubricate the starter shaft bush, the starter drive gear and the flywheel ring gear. Use heavy-duty grease on the splines of the drive shaft or dust with molybdenum disulphide powder applied with a brush or piece of clean cloth.

2 Clean the mating flanges of the engine and transmission. Engage a gear to stop the drive shaft from turning.

3 Pay particular attention to the warnings in preceding Operation 7 and proceed to fit the engine. **Never at any time let the weight of the engine hang on the drive shaft.** To engage the splines of the clutch plate and the drive shaft turn the engine by means of the fan belt. Press the engine home, guiding the lower mounting studs into the corresponding holes in the transmission flange. Partly tighten the upper mounting nuts, fully tighten the lower nuts and then return to the upper nuts.

4 Adjust the accelerator cable, refit the cables and pipes and adjust the ignition timing as instructed in **Chapter 3.** Check the sump oil.

1:4 Dismantling the engine

1 Remove the coverplate in front of the engine, take off the fan belt and disconnect the wire between the coil and distributor.

2 Take off the two large hoses between the fan housing and the heat exchangers. Remove the preheater pipe

FIG 1:5 Rocker shaft mounting showing the split mounting block

sealing plate. Remove the generator with fan housing and control flaps.

3 Remove the rear air deflecting plate and the lower part of the warm air duct. Pull off the crankshaft pulley with an extractor. Disconnect the fuel pipe.

4 Remove the induction manifold and the preheater pipe, the silencer and heater assembly. Remove the heating channels and the cylinder coverplates, also the plate under the fan pulley.

5 Remove the clutch. Remove the cylinder head covers and the rocker shafts.

6 Remove the cylinder heads, the pushrod tubes and the pushrods.

7 Remove the deflector plates and then the cylinders, followed by the pistons. Remove the oil cooler and the oil pump. Remove the fuel pump.

8 Remove the distributor and lift out the drive gear. Remove the flywheel.

Finish dismantling by splitting the crankcase for access to the camshaft and crankshaft.

More detailed instructions on the various operations will follow. For those which concern the engine cooling and heating system refer to **Chapter 4.**

1:5 Servicing cylinder heads

If necessary, the rocker gear can be removed from the heads without detaching the heads from the cylinders. The type of rocker shaft mounting is shown in **FIG 1:5.** The removal of two nuts will enable the shaft to be lifted off. Note the split mounting blocks which fit over the studs, together with the oil seals on the studs.

Before removing the cylinder heads devise some means of stopping the cylinder barrels from lifting off the crankcase. Loops of wire or rope attached to some convenient point could be arranged or make up a clamp to fit between the fins. Care must be taken however not to stress the fins, which are brittle. Remove the cylinder head nuts and tap the head fins with a soft-faced hammer used squarely on the edges of the fins to avoid breakage. This should loosen the heads and they can then be lifted off. Note that there is no gasket between the head and barrel mating faces.

Removing the valves:

Use a valve spring compressor to compress the valve springs and so release the two split collets from each

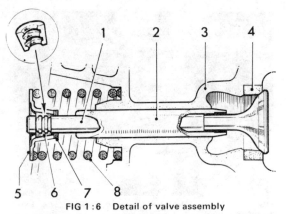

FIG 1:6   Detail of valve assembly

Key to Fig 1:6   1 Valve   2 Valve guide   3 Cylinder head
4 Valve seat insert   5 Spring cap   6 Split collet   7 Oil
deflector ring   8 Valve spring

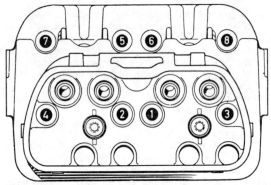

FIG 1:7   Sequence for preliminary tightening of
cylinder head nuts

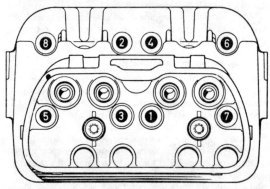

FIG 1:8   Sequence for final tightening of cylinder
head nuts

valve stem 6 in **FIG 1:6**. Remove the compressor and
lift off the spring cap 5 and spring 8. An oil deflector ring 7
is fitted on the valve stem below the cap. Remove any
burr from the cotter grooves in the valve stems and push
out the valves, keeping them in the correct order for
reassembly or mark them on the head. Note that the
springs have close-wound coils at one end. This end is
always fitted adjacent to the cylinder head.

Servicing valves, seats and springs:

If decarbonization is intended, scrape the carbon from
the head before removing the valves. This will protect the
valve seats. Use a piece of wood or a soft tool when cleaning the carbon from the alloy head to prevent scratching.
Remove the valves and check the stems and seats.
Renew the valves if the stems are worn or bent, or if the
seats are deeply pitted and burnt. Light marking can be
removed by grinding-in but heavier defects should be
removed by a garage equipped with a valve-refacer.
Clean and polish the valve heads before grinding.

Clean all carbon from the ports and have the valve
seatings reground by a VW agent if they are deeply pitted
or burnt. Remove the carbon from the counterbore at the
inner end of the valve guide. It is not possible to renew
the valve guides or the seat inserts because of the high
interference fits in the head. **Any serious defects are
best overcome by exchanging heads for factory-
reconditioned parts.** Clearances between valve stems
and guides should be, inlet .002 to .003 inch and exhaust
.0032 to .0045 inch. Clearances should not exceed
.0065 inch for either valve. Valve seat widths should be,
inlet .05 to .06 inch and exhaust .06 to .08 inch. Seat
widths can be reduced by a VW agent using special
grinding tools.

Grind in the valves with a suction cup tool, putting a
light spring under the valve head so that the valve will
lift off the seat when pressure is released. Use coarse
paste if the seats are fairly deeply pitted and finish off
with fine. Spread the paste lightly round the valve seat and
use a semi-rotary grinding action, letting the valve rise
off the seat now and then to help the distribution of the
paste.

When the seats are a smooth matt grey without any
signs of pitting, clean every trace of grinding paste from
both head and valves. A useful check of the accuracy of
the grinding can be made by marking the valve seat with
several pencil lines across the face. If the valve is then
rotated on the head seating all the lines should disappear.

Before refitting the valves examine the springs for cracks
and check the length against the figures given in **Technical Data**. Coat the valve stems with oil or molybdenum-
disulphide paste and insert in the guides. Replace the oil
deflector rings on the stems and install the springs and
caps. Remember to fit springs with close-coiled ends so
that the close coils are adjacent to the cylinder head.
Compress the springs and replace the cotters, using a little
grease to hold the cotters in place while the compressor
is released. Press down on the valve stem to check that the
assembly is correct.

Refitting cylinder heads:

Before fitting the heads, check the tightness of the
securing studs. If they cannot be firmly tightened because
of defective threads in the crankcase it is possible for
special inserts to be fitted by a VW agent.

When replacing the heads, note that there is no gasket
between the top of the barrel and the register in the
cylinder head.

Before actually placing the heads on the barrels check
the pushrod tubes for length. As shown in **FIG 1:9** the
dimension over the corrugations should be $7\frac{1}{8}$ inches on
1192 cc engines and $7\frac{1}{2}$ inches on subsequent engines.
Tubes can be stretched carefully if they are not up to

length. When fitted, the tube seams must face upwards. Also check that the seals shown in **FIG 1:10** are in good condition and properly seated on the ends of the tubes.

With the head in place and the pushrod tubes correctly seated, fit the washers and nuts, coating the threads with graphite paste, and tighten down in the two sequences given in **FIGS 1:7** and **1:8**. During the first sequence use a torque wrench set to break at 7 lb ft. Final tightening should be to a figure of 22 to 23 lb ft, using the second sequence.

1:6 Servicing the rocker gear

To dismantle the rocker shaft, remove the spring clips at each end. Mark the rockers to ensure correct reassembly and pull off the washers, rockers, spacing tube and spring, or the bearing supports according to model. Check the rocker arms and the shaft for wear. Undue wear of the adjusting screw faces which bear on the valve stems will make accurate clearance setting impossible. Also check the pushrod sockets of the rocker arms for wear.

Reassemble the parts, lubricating the shaft and rockers. Slacken off all the adjusting screws. Before finally tightening the rocker shaft securing nuts, check the point of contact between each adjusting screw and valve stem. A small offset as shown at 1 in **FIG 1:12** is correct and it is possible to move the rocker shaft axially to achieve this result, due to some clearance on the securing studs. Ensure that the rocker shaft-mounting blocks are fitted with the chamfered faces outwards and the slots upwards, as shown in **FIG 1:11**. The shaft securing nuts are of a special grade, and are copper-plated so that they can be readily recognized. Tighten them to 18 lb ft. If no more work on the engine is intended, adjust the rocker clearances and replace the covers.

1:7 Cylinder barrels and pistons

With the heads off, the cylinders can be removed. The pushrods must be extracted and the deflector plates removed from under the cylinders. Pull off the cylinders and mark the piston crowns for correct reassembly if they are to be removed.

Removing and servicing pistons:

Remove one gudgeon pin circlip and heat the piston to 80°C (176°F) in an oil bath. The expansion will free the gudgeon pin which can then be pushed out. Piston rings must be removed with a ring tool, but if removal is not strictly necessary they can be left in the grooves to avoid breakage.

Clean the piston crown and ring grooves free from carbon but use a soft tool and take great care not to damage the alloy surfaces. Rough treatment of the ring grooves will result in increased oil consumption. When the pistons are clean, check them for clearance in their respective cylinder barrels, but first look on the piston sides for unbalanced wear indications. Carbon or wear at the top on one side of the piston and at the bottom of the skirt on the other side is a sign that the connecting rod is bent.

Piston clearance cannot be checked with feelers, but only by measurement with precision instruments. The clearance between piston and cylinder bore should be between .0015 and .0024 inch measured at right angles

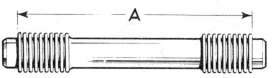

FIG 1:9 Check pushrod tube length at **A**. Dimension should be $7\frac{1}{8}$ inches on 1192cc engines and $7\frac{1}{2}$ inches on subsequent engines

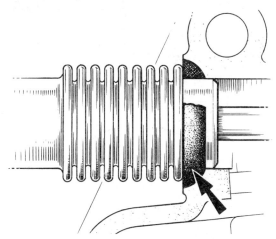

FIG 1:10 Sealing washers on pushrod tube ends must be in good condition and seated correctly

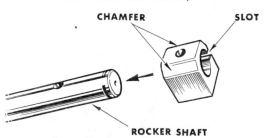

FIG 1:11 Fit mounting blocks to rocker shaft with chamfer outwards and slot facing upwards

to the gudgeon pin about $\frac{1}{2}$ inch below the piston crown. If the clearance reaches the figure of .008 inch replace both piston and cylinder by a pair of the same size and weight grading. If the cylinder of a damaged piston shows no signs of wear it is sufficient to renew the piston alone, making sure that it is of the correct grade. Only cylinders and pistons of the same size and weight grading should be installed in an engine. If the oil consumption has reached one pint in 300 miles the cylinders and pistons need renewal. Measure the cylinder bore $\frac{1}{2}$ inch below the top edge. Measure the piston at the bottom of the skirt, at right angles to the gudgeon pin axis.

Piston crowns are marked in various ways to indicate size and weight grading (see **FIG 1:13**). They are also stamped with an arrow which should point to the flywheel when installed. Paint spots are used to indicate both size grading (blue, pink and green) and weight grading (brown for —weight and grey for +weight). In this way it is possible for the VW Spares Department to match pistons and cylinders exactly.

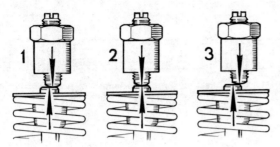

FIG 1:12 Rocker adjusting screw should contact valve stem slightly off-centre as at 1. Positions 2 and 3 are incorrect.

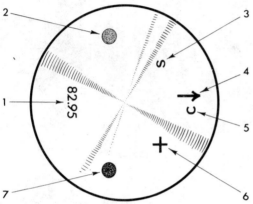

FIG 1:13 Grading marks on a piston crown

Key to Fig 1:13   1 Piston size in mm   2 Paint spot indicating matching size (pink, blue or green)   3 Gudgeon pin bore size grading (S=black, W=white)   4 Arrow must point towards flywheel when piston is fitted   5 Index letter for piston Part No.   6 + or — indicates weight grading   7 Weight grading by paint spot. Brown= —weight, grey= + weight

Gudgeon pins should normally be a light push fit in the piston bosses at room temperature (20°C), or with the piston heated to a temperature of 80°C (176°F) in an oil bath. If the pin fits loosely in the piston, renew both. Clearance between the pin and the connecting rod bush should lie between .0004 and .0008 inch. If the clearance reaches the wear limit of .0016 inch renew the pin and the connecting rod bush. **Do not try to install an oversize pin in a worn bush.** When fitting gudgeon pins, oil them and push them into the heated pistons without stopping.

Piston rings:

When fitting new rings check the gaps and file the ring ends if necessary. Use a piston to push the ring about ¼ inch up the cylinder bore from the bottom. Using feeler gauges the gap should be .012 to .018 inch for compression rings and .010 to .016 inch for the oil control ring

which is fitted in the bottom groove. The wear limit is .037 inch. Also check the side clearance in the grooves. For the top compression ring this should be .003 to .004 inch with a wear limit of .005 inch. For the lower compression ring the figures are .002 to .003 inch with a wear limit of .004 inch. For the oil control ring the clearance should be .001 to .002 inch with a wear limit of .004 inch. Note that the two compression rings are marked 'TOP' or 'OBEN' for correct fitting.

Fitting pistons and cylinders:

Insert the gudgeon pin circlip at the flywheel end of the piston boss. If the pin is tighter than a light push fit, heat the piston. Fit the lubricated pin in one steady movement. Fit the second circlip. **Make sure that the arrow or the word 'VORN' on the piston crown points towards the flywheel.**

The cylinder flange, the gasket, and the mating surface of the crankcase must be perfectly clean. Remove all traces of the old gasket and use a new one for each cylinder. Oil the piston and set the rings so that the gap in the oil ring is uppermost. The gaps in the other two rings should be evenly spaced 120 deg. apart. Oil the cylinder bore, compress the rings and slide the cylinder into place. The head studs must not contact the cylinder fins. When installing the deflector plates seat them correctly and ensure that they cannot rattle by bending them until they bear tightly on the studs.

1:8 The lubricating system

We propose to deal with the lubricating system before discussing the crankcase because the component parts can all be serviced with the engine in situ.

The system:

The gear-type oil pump is bolted to the rear of the crankcase below the fan pulley and is driven from the rear end of the camshaft. It lifts oil from a strainer in the sump and pumps it under pressure to the oil passages, to an oil pressure relief valve and to an oil cooler bolted on top of the engine where it is cooled by ducted air from the fan.

When the oil is cold and thick, pressure is high and to avoid restricting the flow to the bearings by passing it through the oil cooler, the oil is bypassed direct to them. This is done by the relief valve plunger lifting as shown on the left in FIG 1:14. As the oil warms up the pressure drops so that the relief valve plunger moves to the left to allow oil to pass both through the cooler and direct to the engine. When the oil has reached operating temperature the pressure has dropped. The relief valve plunger then routes all the oil through the cooler. At all times any excess pressure of oil will pass the relief valve and fall back into the sump.

A bypass valve is fitted to the strainer. Under normal conditions this valve remains closed, but should the strainer become blocked, the bypass valve opens and allows oil to flow to the engine.

FIG 1:14 Operation of lubricating system. On left, engine cold, oil thick, relief valve plunger right back against spring Oil goes direct to engine but excess pressure relieved by oil return to sump. Centre, oil thinning, plunger partially returned to block relief to sump. Some of main supply to engine goes by way of cooler. Right, oil at running temperature and much thinner. Plunger returned by spring, all oil to engine goes through cooler

The strainer:

The strainer is illustrated in **FIG 1:4.** When servicing the strainer, clean off all old gasket material from the joint faces and scrub the gauze clean with a brush and fuel. **Do not use fluffy rag as fibres may adhere to the gauze.** When refitting the strainer make sure that the suction pipe in the sump enters the strainer and is a snug fit. The bottom end of the pipe must be clear of the domed base of the strainer. Measure the distance between the crankcase face and the tip of the suction pipe. The dimension should be .39 ± .040 inch. It is also necessary to check the measurement from the strainer flange to the bottom domed face of the strainer to ensure clearance for the drain plug. The dimension should be .236 ± .040 inch.

On 1200 cc engines the suction pipe is .47 inch diameter, and on larger engines .55 inch diameter. The strainer for 1300 cc, 1500 cc and 1600 cc engines is identified by a circular depression at the top of the mesh. It is important that the correct strainer is used, in order to prevent damage to the engine due to insufficient oil flow.

Check the joint faces for flatness, use a new gasket and fit new washers under the securing nuts. Do not overtighten.

The oil pressure relief valve:

This will be found under the rear of the engine on the lefthand side (see 11 in **FIG 1:1**). Always check this valve first if there are oil circulation problems, such as a leaking oil cooler or oil starvation causing engine seizure, as these might be due to a sticking plunger in the valve.

Remove the plug and gasket and withdraw the spring and plunger. If the plunger sticks, pull it out with a 10 mm metric tap, which can be lightly screwed into place. Check the surface of the plunger for signs of seizure. If these are evident, also check the bore in the crankcase. Polish out the scores but do not remove any metal otherwise. Renew the plunger if its condition is doubtful. Check the spring for wear and settling. The free length of the spring should be 2.44 to 2.52 inches. Renew a spring if it is curved along its length and shows signs of the coils rubbing in the bore. Renew the plug gasket when re-installing.

Some late models have a second, similar valve at the opposite end of the crankcase.

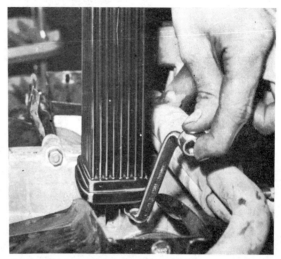

FIG 1:15 Removing oil cooler with cranked spanner

FIG 1:16 Component parts of oil pump

Key to Fig 1:16
1 Pump housing   2 Cover
3 Gasket for housing   4 Gasket for cover   5 Driving gear
6 Idler gear

FIG 1:17 Removing the screws securing the rear cover plate

FIG 1:18 Location of distributor drive shaft arrowed. Note offset driving dogs on end of distributor shaft

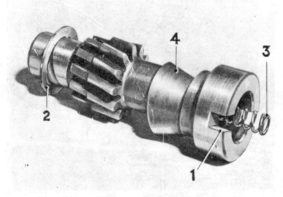

FIG 1:19 Distributor drive shaft

Key to Fig 1:19 1 Offset dogs driving distributor 2 Thrust washer(s) 3 Spring 4 Fuel pump operating eccentric

The oil cooler:

This can be removed as shown in **FIG 1:15** but note that it can also be taken off with the engine in the vehicle by removing the fan housing. The two outer nuts are best unscrewed with the type of cranked spanner shown. If the cooler has been leaking first check the oil pressure relief valve and then, if necessary, subject the cooler to a test pressure of 85 lb/sq in. The ribs of the cooler must not touch each other and the partition plate must not be loose. Renew the two gaskets when re-installing the cooler and make sure the retaining nuts and the bracket are tight.

The oil pump:

The location of the pump can be seen as item 27 below the crankshaft pulley in **FIG 1:1**. To remove the pump:

1 Remove the engine rear coverplate as indicated in **FIG 1:17**.
2 Remove the fan pulley with an extractor, using the slots provided.
3 Remove the sheet metal pulley cover. Remove the oil pump cover nuts and take off the cover and gasket. Lift out the gears. The parts are shown in **FIG 1:16**.
4 To withdraw the pump housing make up a bridge piece from flat steel so that the two ends are bent down at right angles and straddle the pump flange. Make a threaded bolt with prongs which fit inside the pump housing passages and have the bolt long enough to protrude through a central hole in the bridge piece to take a nut. Tighten the nut and draw the pump housing out of the crankcase.

Wear will result in loss of pressure. Check the backlash between the gear teeth with feeler gauges. The permissible backlash is .001 to .003 inch. With the gears in position and the housing face free from old gasket material, place a straightedge across the face and measure the clearance between the straightedge and the gear faces. This should not exceed .004 inch. Wear of the coverplate face will make this clearance excessive so renew all the parts needed to reduce the clearances. The idler gear pin must not be loose in the housing. If peening will not lock it in place, renew the housing and also the pin if worn. The outer end of the pin must be .02 to .04 inch below the housing face.

To install the pump turn the engine until the pump driving slot in the end of the camshaft is vertical. Fit the pump housing and gears, using a genuine .003 inch gasket without jointing compound. Fit the cover with a similar gasket without compound. Run up the cover nuts finger tight. Turn the engine over for two complete revolutions. This will centre the driving slot and tongue. Make sure the housing does not move and tighten the cover nuts.

Automatic transmission models have a dual pump, one half of which circulates the torque converter fluid. The two sets of gears are separated by a plate sandwiched between the pump housing and cover.

1:9 The distributor drive shaft

The location of the drive shaft is indicated by the arrow in **FIG 1:18**. Note the offset driving dogs on the distributor shaft. Assuming that the distributor has already been removed, remove the fuel pump. Remove the pushrod housing **after** the pushrod has been lifted out. In this case blank off the hole so that nothing can be dropped into the crankcase. Adhesive tape will do.

1 Extract the small spring 3 from the top of the drive shaft (see **FIG 1 : 19**).

2 Set No. 1 cylinder to the firing point on the compression stroke and devise an expanding tool which will grip the bore of the shaft and enable it to be turned to the left and lifted out at the same time. It might be possible to tap a piece of hardwood into the slot and use it to lift out the shaft.

3 There are two washers under the drive shaft. Hook these out or use a magnet if the engine is installed. If the engine is out of the vehicle turn the crankcase upside down so that the washers fall out. Be very careful not to drop these washers into the crankcase. During reassembly a piece of rod is used as a guide to ensure that this cannot happen.

4 Check the drive gear and fuel pump eccentric for wear. If the gear teeth are worn it will be advisable to check the drive gear on the crankshaft as well. Renew the washers under the drive shaft gear if they are worn.

Set the pulley notch in-line with the crankcase joint as shown in **FIG 1 : 3**, that is with No. 1 piston at the top of its compression stroke, with both valves closed. Fit the two washers by sliding them down a piece of rod which locates in the housing. Install the driving shaft in the correct position: looking down on the end of the shaft the large offset should be at the front, that is, with the smaller segment of the head nearest the pulley and the slot should be at right angles to the crankcase joint line. Insert the small spring, guiding it down a piece of rod to ensure that it locates in the shaft recess. Install the distributor and set the ignition timing as instructed in **Chapter 3**. Refit the fuel pump.

Remember that if the engine is completely dismantled, the oil pump, the coverplate under the pulley and the crankshaft pulley itself must be fitted before the distributor shaft.

1 : 10 Removing and refitting the flywheel

Refer to **FIG 1 : 20** for details of the flywheel assembly. The flywheel is located on crankshaft 9 by four dowel pins 11 and secured by the large central gland nut 2. Inside the nut is a needle roller bearing 7 which supports the rear end of the transmission drive shaft. An oil seal 13 is fitted into a recess in the crankcase 8 and has a lip which seals on the flywheel flange.

Before removing the flywheel it is a good plan to check the crankshaft end float so that adjustment can be made if necessary. Set up a dial gauge so that the plunger bears on the flywheel face. Drive the crankshaft backwards and forwards to the limit of its movement, using a soft-faced hammer, and record the total float indicated. Adjustment is needed if the float exceeds .006 inch. The correct figure is between .002 and .005 inch. The flywheel must be removed to gain access to the adjusting shims.

Removing the flywheel:

If the manufacturer's balance marks are not clear, mark the clutch, flywheel, and one of the dowels so that the parts can be refitted in the same relative positions.

Remove the clutch and clutch driven plate. Prevent the flywheel from turning. The official VW tool spans several starter gear teeth and is bolted to the casing: alternatively,

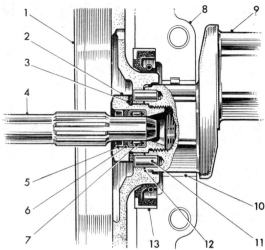

FIG 1 : 20   Section through flywheel mounting

Key to Fig 1 : 20   1 Flywheel 2 Gland nut, securing flywheel 3 Gland nut lockwasher   4 Main drive shaft   5 Retainer 6 Felt sealing ring   7 Needle roller bearing   8 Crankcase 9 Crankshaft   10 Crankshaft bearing   11 Flywheel locating dowels   12 Sealing ring   13 Crankshaft oil seal

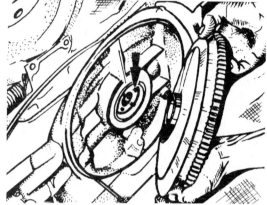

FIG 1 : 21   Flywheel removed showing dowels and sealing ring

attach a length of bar or angle iron with two of the clutch mounting bolts. Remove the nut, which is extremely tight, and pull off the flywheel.

Check the starter gear teeth for damage. A VW Service Station can have the teeth re-machined by removing up to .08 inch on the clutch side of the teeth and re-chamfering them. Check the dowels for wear and looseness. Wear in the dowel holes can be cured by having new holes drilled by a Service Station. Check the needle bearings in the gland nut for wear. A section through the nut is shown in **FIG 1 : 20**.

Adjusting the end float:

On removing the flywheel, note that there is a sealing ring 12 fitted over the dowels. The ring and dowels are clearly shown in **FIG 1 : 21**.

Always use a genuine replacement ring. Note also the adjusting shims for end float, usually three in number.

FIG 1:22　Fitting a new crankshaft oil seal

FIG 1:23　Separate pushrod and cam follower

Shims are available in various thicknesses and, knowing the dial indicator reading for excessive end float and using a micrometer on the shims it is possible to calculate the thickness required to bring the end float to the correct figure. Subtract the required end float from the measured float. Do not use more than three adjusting shims and never use more than one sealing ring. Remember that the thickness of the ring will affect the end float.

Renewing crankcase to flywheel oil seal:

While the flywheel is off, examine the seal and the flywheel flange for signs of damage and leakage. Polish the flywheel flange if there is any roughness where the seal lip contacts it. To renew the seal, prise out the old one and clean out the crankcase recess. It helps to chamfer the outer edge of the recess with a scraper to facilitate fitting the new seal.

Coat the recess with sealing compound and press the seal into place with the lip facing inwards. **FIG 1:22** shows the operation, the centre bolt of the VW tool being screwed into the crankshaft. The seal must bed down squarely in the recess.

Replacing the flywheel:

Clean the mating surfaces thoroughly and smear the oil seal contact surface with oil. Fit a new sealing ring over the dowels. Look for the out-of-balance marks on the crankshaft, flywheel and clutch. The crankshaft mark is a paint dot on the side of the hole for the gland nut. The flywheel has a paint dot and a small hole on the clutch face. The clutch has a paint line on the outer edge of the pressure plate. Not all three components need have out-of-balance marks. Using the crankshaft mark as a datum, fit the flywheel and clutch with their marks spaced out 120 deg. apart. If only two components are marked space them 180 deg. apart.

Before fitting the gland nut smear 1 gram of universal grease in the roller bearing. If a check of the bearing and

the spigot on the end of the transmission shaft reveals excessive clearance it is possible to obtain undersize bearings which have a bore .0032 inch smaller than standard. Excessive clearance may be responsible for chatter on clutch take-up. Tighten the nut with a torque wrench set at 217 lb ft.

Check the flywheel for runout. Maximum runout of the face when measured on the greatest diameter should not exceed .012 inch.

It may be of interest to owners to know that on some models a thrust piece and spring were fitted between the crankshaft and the rear end of the transmission shaft to eliminate noise when idling. The cone-shaped spring has its large coil against the crankshaft, in the bore for the gland nut. The thrust piece seats on the small end of the spring and in the recess in the end of the transmission shaft.

1:11 Dismantling the crankcase

1 Remove the oil pump, the oil strainer, the oil pressure switch and the oil pressure relief valve if not already removed.

2 Remove the oil filler.

3 Unscrew the crankcase nuts and tap on the righthand half of the case with a rubber hammer. **Do not attempt to drive a screwdriver between the joint faces.** There are six 12 mm and twelve 8 mm studs and two 8 mm through-bolts. On either side of the front camshaft bearing are two 8 mm studs with nuts tightened on the outside.

Before parting the crankcase halves it will also be useful to consider making some spring clips to hold the cam followers in place. This will stop the followers from falling out and will be particularly useful when reassembling. The clips are coiled up from stout wire like the spring end of a safety pin and the two legs span a pair of followers to grip and hold them in place.

4 Lift out the camshaft and crankshaft, the crankshaft oil seal and the blanking plug at the flywheel end of the camshaft. Lift out the cam followers. The pushrod and follower are shown in **FIG 1:23**.

5 Lift out the camshaft bearing shells and the main bearing shells for No. 2 crankshaft bearing, which is the second from the flywheel end. Lightly mark the backs of the shells so that they can be restored to their original positions if they are not renewed. Do not mark in such a way that burrs are raised.

6 Clean the crankcase halves, removing old jointing compound with a solvent. Be particularly careful not to raise burrs on the mating faces through careless handling. These faces must be absolutely flat and true. Examine the halves for cracks or damage. The bores of the camshaft and crankshaft bearing housings can be measured with precision instruments to check for wear. The 'crush' on the main bearing shells should be about .002 inch to ensure that they are tightly gripped when the crankcase is assembled. It is possible to obtain factory-reconditioned crankcases fitted with main bearing shells which are oversize on the outside diameter. These crankcases are stamped 'P' when the mating surfaces have been planed to bring them closer together. Crankcases with oversize bores for the main bearings are stamped 'O'. Further checks on the crankcase would include the condition of the bores

for the cam followers, and the tightness of studs. The tapped holes for studs can be restored by fitting Helicoil inserts. Also check the fit of the main bearing locating dowels. If the suction pipe to the oil pump is loose, peen round the hole to tighten it. Finally, clean out all oilways with compressed air. If any bearing metal has 'run' it is essential to clean out all particles of alloy from every oil passage. Finish off by injecting clean engine oil before reassembling. The operation of reassembling the crankcase is covered later, after the crankshaft and camshaft have received attention.

1:12 The crankshaft and connecting rods

Checking crankshaft end float has been covered in **Section 1:10**. When the crankshaft is lifted out complete with connecting rods, it can be seen that, counting from front or flywheel end, Nos. 1, 3 and 4 main bearings are one-piece bushes, the flanges on No. 1 bearing taking end thrust. No. 2 bearing is of the split type. A limited number of engines were made with all the bearings of the split-type and some with No. 2 bearing taking crankshaft end thrust. At the rear end the shaft carries a concave oil thrower, No. 4 main bearing, a retaining ring for the distributor drive gear, which is keyed to the shaft with a Woodruff key and then a spacing ring followed by the small timing gear also keyed with a Woodruff key. Lastly comes No. 3 main bearing bush. Remove all these parts after prising out the fan pulley key from the extreme rear of the crankshaft. Observe the fit of the gears, as these should be a press fit on the shaft. To facilitate removal, heat the gears to about 176°F. Remove the front main bearing bush.

Removing and servicing connecting rods:

Refer to **FIG 1:24** which shows the connecting rod. The rod has bolts which are captive in the cap, together with securing nuts. Note that identification numbers are stamped on both rod and cap. If in doubt, mark the rods lightly so that they can be restored to their original positions on reassembly. Remove as follows:

1 Unscrew the clamping nuts and remove the caps. Lift out the bearing shells, noting the locating tags and notches. If it is likely that the same shells will be used on reassembly, mark them very lightly on the back for correct location.
2 Check the weight of the rods. Any variation should not exceed 10 grams. Any rod which is outside the weight limit should be taken to an authorized VW agent for attention, as metal should only be removed at precise locations.
3 Check the fit of the gudgeon pin. It should be a light push fit at room temperature. Normally the clearance should be between .0004 and .0008 inch, with a wear limit of .0016 inch. Do not try to fit an oversize pin to overcome excessive clearance but have a new bush fitted and reamed to suit.
4 Check the connecting rod alignment. One of the signs of a bent rod is offset marking of the piston skirt. If there is bright wear above the gudgeon pin hole on one side and similar marking below the hole on the other side the piston has been tilted in the bore due to a bent connecting rod. In expert hands a bent rod can be straightened, but the alignment check needs very accurate mandrels and gauging equipment.

FIG 1:24 Connecting rod showing fixed bolts, and nuts. Arrow indicates mark which must be upwards on installation

5 Assemble each rod in turn on its crankpin, tightening the bolts to a torque of 32 ± 4 lb ft, using Plastigage for checking the running clearance. While assembled, check the end float, which should be .004 to .016 inch. Dismantle the rod and measure the thickness of the Plastigage. The running clearance should be .0008 to .003 inch. Worn shells can be renewed, but it is also essential to check the crankpins for wear and ovality if clearance is excessive. Nominal diameter is 2.1654 inch.
6 Maximum permissible ovality of the crankpins is .0012 inch. The same figure also applies to the main bearing journals. Anything in excess of this calls for a new or reground crankshaft and bearings. Regrind undersizes are approximately the equivalent of —.010, .020 and —.030 inch.
7 Renew all bearing shells which are scored or have bearing metal breaking away. **Never try to adjust the running clearance by filing the caps or the shells.** It is not necessary to scrape the bearing surfaces of the shells. Make sure the tags on the shells fit into the notches in the connecting rod and cap.
8 When refitting connecting rods, oil the bearing surfaces liberally. When the nuts are tightened to the correct torque figure the rods should fall from the horizontal position under their own weight. **Light taps with a hammer** on the outer faces of the cap will help to settle the parts into their correct relationship and may help to ease a tight bearing. Refer to **FIG 1:24** and note the forged marks arrowed on the shank of each rod. These marks must face upwards in an assembled engine.

FIG 1:25 Crankshaft removed, showing front bearing drilled for dowel

The crankshaft and main bearings:

At one time all the main bearings were of aluminium-alloy but engines now have a No. 2 main bearing of steel-backed lead-alloy. This is the one which is split. Check journals and bearings as follows:

1 Look for scored journals on the crankshaft and check that ovality does not exceed .0012 inch. If the shaft can be supported in V-blocks for a check on runout, this must not exceed .001 inch at the 2nd and 4th journals with the other two supported in the blocks.
2 Measure the bores of the bearing bushes and the corresponding journals. Running clearance when new is .001 to .004 inch **after** allowing for the .002 inch by which the crankcase halves 'crush' the bearings. The wear limit is .0072 inch. The most effective way to measure the bores is to assemble the bearings in the crankcase with the nuts fully tightened.
3 Worn crankshafts can be reground as indicated in the preceding notes on worn crankpins. It is best to fit a factory reground shaft as the dimensions for the fillet radii joining the journals to the crank webs are very important. The crankshaft will also be carefully tested for cracks.
4 The diameters of the connecting rod journals and main bearings 1 to 3 are 2.1650 inches and that for No. 4 is 1.5748 inches.
5 Before refitting a crankshaft, check the following points. Make sure the bearing shell dowel pins are tight. If they are loose, new holes can be drilled by a VW Service Station. Any foreign matter embedded in the working surfaces of the bearing shells should be carefully scraped out without removing any bearing metal. Radius the sharp edges of the oil holes in the crankshaft, especially after a regrind. If it was obvious when removing the drive gears that they would not be a tight press fit on the crankshaft when they were replaced it will be necessary to check whether new gears would be a cure or whether the crankshaft ought to be built up and ground to the correct size. Clean out

all oilways with compressed air or by forcing paraffin through under pressure and then inject clean engine oil. Reassembling the crankshaft in the case will be covered in **Section 1:14.**

1:13 The camshaft and followers

When the crankcase was split, removal of the camshaft was possible. Note that the camshaft journals run in replaceable bearing liners located by tags and notches. No. 3 liner has flanges to take camshaft end thrust. The large timing gear is riveted to the camshaft permanently. **FIG 1:23** shows the pushrod and cam follower.

Service the camshaft and bearings as follows:

1 Check the riveting of the timing gear to the camshaft. Check the cams and bearing surfaces for excessive wear. The cam faces must be smooth and square, but light scoring can be smoothed down with a very fine oilstone.
2 If the camshaft can be mounted between centres, check the runout of the centre journal, which should not exceed .0008 inch. When installed, the end float of the camshaft should lie between .0024 and .0045 inch with a wear limit of .0055 inch. Renewal of the rear bearing liner may effect a cure for excessive float providing the thrust faces of the camshaft are not worn. When installed, bearing running clearance should lie between .0008 and .002 inch with a wear limit of .005 inch. Remember that there is a 'crush' on the bearing liners when assembled in the crankcase and this affects running clearance by reducing it.
3 Examine the bearing shells for wear and scoring. It is a good plan when renewing the shells to lightly chamfer the edges of the crankcase bores at the crankcase mating surfaces to prevent pressure on the shells causing seizure. Be careful to fit the tag on the shells into the notches in the crankcase.
4 The backlash between the timing gears can only be checked while the crankshaft is installed, so refer to the reassembly operations. With the crankshaft serviced and fitted into one half of the crankcase, fit the camshaft and rock the timing gears back and forth with both hands, at all points during a complete revolution of the large gear. The minimum backlash is desirable, the clearance lying between .0004 and .002 inch. Excessive backlash due to wear can be cured by fitting a new camshaft with an oversize gear. The pitch radius of the teeth is increased from standard in steps of $\frac{1}{100}$ mm and the gear is marked on the camshaft side with +1, +2 and so on. There are also undersizes marked —1 and so on, with a standard gear marked 'O'. Do not confuse the 'O' to indicate size, with the timing mark which is stamped near a tooth on the rear face of the gear.

Servicing camshaft followers:

Cam followers should be checked for wear on the face. Deep scores and breakdown of the surface will also probably be accompanied by excessive clearance in the crankcase bores, so that renewal is indicated. When new the clearance is between .001 and .002 inch. If it exceeds .005 inch the cam followers may be worn, but there is also the possibility that the crankcase halves will need renewal too. While checking the followers, examine the pushrod ends for signs of undue wear.

1:14 Reassembling the engine

Assuming that all servicing of the individual parts has been done according to the instructions in the preceding sections, it is now possible to proceed with the assembling. Do the following, observing absolute cleanliness and lubricating all working surfaces liberally:

1 Insert the cam followers in the lefthand case. Insert the bearing shell dowel pins for the main bearings, if they were removed. **FIG 1:25** shows the dowels and the drilled bearing at the front end.

2 Assemble the connecting rods to the crankshaft as instructed in **Section 1:12** and lower the shaft into place. Make quite sure that the shells are properly seated in the main bearing housings. The oil thrower at the fan pulley end must have its concave face to the rear.

3 Install the camshaft with the timing gears correctly meshed. The 'O' mark on the large wheel should mesh between the dots on the two crankshaft gear teeth as shown in **FIG 1:26**. Fit the sealing plug at the flywheel end of the camshaft, coating it with jointing compound first. Fit the oil seal at the flywheel end of the crankshaft.

FIG 1:26 Setting the camshaft timing. Tooth marked 'O' on large gear meshes between two teeth on smaller gear marked with dots

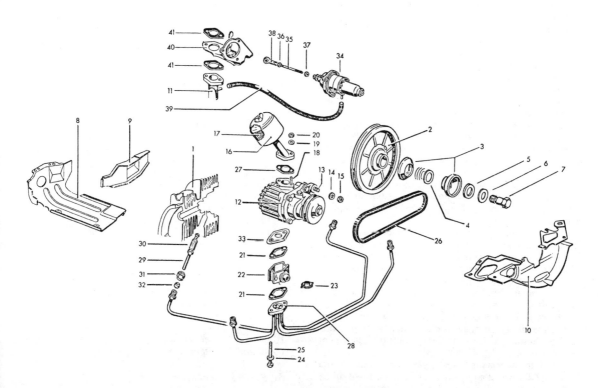

FIG 1:27 Components of exhaust port air injection system

Key to Fig 1:27 1 Cylinder head   2 Crankshaft pulley   3 Pulley for air pump drive   4 Distance piece 15 mm   5 Distance piece 3 mm   6 Spring washer   7 Bolt   8 Heater channel   9 Air deflector   10 Coverplate   11 Inlet manifold   12 Air pump   13 Mounting stud   14 Spring washer   15 Nut   16 Air filter   17 Paper element   18 Stud   19 Washer   20 Nut   21 Gasket   22 Safety valve   23 Check valve   24 Washer   25 Bolt   26 Belt   27 Gasket   28 Pipe union   29 Pipe   30 Union nut   31 Union nut   32 Seal   33 Plate   34 Throttle positioner   35 Connecting rod   36 Locknut   37 Nut   38 Ball joint   39 Vacuum hose   40 Throttle positioner mounting   41 Carburetter flange gasket

4 Prepare the righthand half of the crankcase by fitting the cam followers. These will need holding in place with the spring clips mentioned during dismantling.

5 Check that the mating surfaces of the crankcase halves are perfectly clean and free from burrs. Smear a thin and even film of jointing compound on the faces, being careful to keep it well away from the oil passages in the main and camshaft bearings. Join the halves together and fit the nuts. If, with moderate tightening, the crankshaft cannot be turned, split the case again and determine what is wrong. Start to tighten the securing nuts in the correct sequence. First do the 8 mm nut adjacent to the 12 mm nut for No. 1 main bearing at the flywheel end of the case. Tighten this nut to 14 lb ft and then do the remaining nuts part of a turn at a time until they are all tight. The torque figure for the 12 mm nuts is 24 to 26 lb ft.

6 Fit the oil relief valve and the oil pressure switch. Remove the spring clips from the cam followers in the righthand half of the case.

Continue with reassembling in the reverse sequence to dismantling. Fit the oil pump and the coverplate under the fan pulley. Fit the pulley, tightening the bolt to a torque of 40 to 47 lb ft. Fit the oil strainer and coverplate. Fit the flywheel, tightening the retaining nut to a torque of 217 lb ft. A long steel bar or piece of angle iron bolted to the flywheel face by two bolts in widely-spaced clutch fixing holes will hold the assembly while the central nut is tightened. Assemble the pistons to the connecting rods and fit the cylinder barrels. Hold these down with some temporary clamps if the crankshaft is to be turned before the heads are put on. Fit the pushrods and tubes and replace the cylinder heads. The actual sealing between the head and barrel is made without a gasket. It will be found much easier to fit the cylinder heads if the crankcase is set so that each pair of cylinders is vertical and upright in turn. Remember to fit the air deflector plates. Also make quite sure that the pushrods are correctly located when reassembling the rocker gear. Adjust to the correct clearance.

It will probably be as well to wait until after the engine is refitted in the car before fitting the distributor and its drive and the fuel pump. Details of correct ignition timing are given in **Chapter 3.**

Take extreme care when fitting the clutch cover, using a mandrel to centre the driven plate. This is not necessary if the clutch was not removed from the flywheel. Refer to **Chapter 5** for details of centring the driven plate. Keep the engine square with the transmission shaft and proceed with the operation after referring to the instructions in **Section 1:3.**

Fill the sump with oil of the correct grade. In cases of difficulty with the silencing and aircooling arrangements, refer to **Chapter 4.** The instructions cover the adjustment of the fan belt.

Adjust the accelerator cable correctly according to the notes in **Chapter 2** and carry out final adjustment of the slow-running after the engine has reached normal running temperature.

1:15 Exhaust emission control system

This system of which the components can be seen in **FIG 1:27,** is designed to reduce pollution from exhaust gases by injecting fresh air into the exhaust port of each cylinder to mix with and dilute the exhaust gases as they enter the exhaust pipe and before escaping into the atmosphere.

The air is fed from an air pump driven from the crankshaft by a rubber belt, to each exhaust port by way of a safety valve which prevents any blow back from the high pressure exhaust gases.

The efficient operation of this system is dependent on the engine being correctly tuned and the carburetters are set to fine limits and should not be unnecessarily disturbed by unqualified personnel without specialist analysing equipment.

A further addition is the fitting of a throttle valve positioner which delays the closing of the throttle valve when the accelerator pedal is released. This maintains the correct air/fuel ratio for full combustion and avoids the over-rich mixtures which normally occur at these times, eg. on the overrun. In this way the quantity of unburnt gases escaping with the exhaust is reduced.

When this device is fitted it is installed in two parts. The control is at the rear of the engine compartment and the operating part on a bracket on the carburetter flange.

If the throttle positioning lever is pulled back against the adjusting screw, the engine speed should be between 1450 and 1650 rev/min and the screw reset if necessary.

Test the closing time by pulling the throttle lever back to obtain 3000 rev/min, release it and carefully time the period elapsed for the speed to drop to 900 rev/min. This should be between $2\frac{1}{2}$ and $4\frac{1}{2}$ seconds. If necessary, loosen the setscrew on the control and turn the adjuster as required to obtain the specified closing time. Turning the adjuster screw to the right (clockwise) increases the closing time and vice versa.

1:16 Fault diagnosis

(a) Engine will not start

1 Defective ignition coil, but check that carbon brush in distributor cap contacts rotor arm
2 Faulty distributor capacitor (condenser)
3 Dirty, pitted or incorrectly set contact breaker points
4 Ignition wires loose, insulation faulty
5 Water on sparking plug leads
6 Battery discharged, corrosion of terminals
7 Faulty or jammed starter
8 Sparking plug leads wrongly connected
9 Vapour lock in fuel pipes
10 Defective fuel pump
11 Overchoking or underchoking. Check automatic choke
12 Blocked pump filter or carburetter jets
13 Leaking valves
14 Sticking valves
15 Valve timing incorrect
16 Ignition timing incorrect

(b) Engine stalls after starting

1 Check 1, 2, 3, 4, 5, 10, 11, 12, 13 and 14 in (a)
2 Sparking plugs defective or gaps incorrect
3 Retarded ignition
4 Mixture too weak
5 Water in fuel system
6 Fuel tank breather pipe blocked
7 Incorrect valve clearances

(c) Engine idles badly

1 Check 2 and 7 in (b)
2 Air leaks at manifold joints
3 Carburetter idling adjustment wrong, pilot jet blocked
4 If fast-idle, automatic choke not switching off
5 Over-rich mixture
6 Worn piston rings
7 Worn valve stems or guides
8 Weak exhaust valve springs

(d) Engine misfires

1 Check 1, 2, 3, 4, 5, 8, 10, 12, 13, 14, 15 and 16 in (a);
  2, 3, 4 and 7 in (b)
2 Weak or broken valve springs

(e) Engine overheats

1 Weak mixture, ignition over-advanced
2 Fan belt slipping
3 Thermostat defective or wrongly set
4 Control flaps inoperative
5 Loss of cooling air through badly fitted fan housing,
  ducts and coverplates
6 Oil cooling system not working

(f) Compression low

1 Check 13 and 14 in (a); 6 and 7 in (c) and 2 in (d)
2 Worn piston ring grooves
3 Scored or worn cylinder bores

(g) Engine lacks power

1 Check 3, 10, 12, 13, 14, 15 and 16 in (a); 2, 3, 4 and 7
  in (b); 6 and 7 in (c); and 2 in (d). Also check (e)
  and (f)
2 Leaking joints and gaskets
3 Fouled sparking plugs
4 Automatic ignition advance not operating
5 Exhaust system blocked

(h) Burnt valves or seats

1 Check 13 and 14 in (a); 7 in (b); and 2 in (d).
  Also check (e)
2 Excessive carbon round valve seats and head

(j) Sticking valves

1 Check 2 in (d)
2 Bent valve stems
3 Scored valve stems or guides
4 Incorrect valve clearance

(k) Excessive cylinder wear

1 Check 11 in (a) and check (e)
2 Lack of oil
3 Dirty oil
4 Piston rings gummed up or broken
5 Badly fitting piston rings
6 Bent connecting rods
7 Dirt under cylinder mounting flanges

(l) Excessive oil consumption

1 Check 6 and 7 in (c); and check (k)
2 Ring gaps too wide
3 Oil return holes in pistons choked with carbon
4 Scored cylinders
5 Oil level too high
6 External oil leaks, check oil cooler
7 Incorrect grade of oil

(m) Crankshaft and connecting rod bearing failure

1 Check 2 in (k)
2 Restricted oilways
3 Worn journals or crankpins
4 Failure of oil pump, oil cooler, relief valve or strainer
5 Loose bearings, loose connecting rod caps
6 Bent connecting rods or crankshaft

(n) High fuel consumption

1 Vehicle in poor mechanical condition
2 Bad driving habits, excessive acceleration in low gears
3 Incorrectly adjusted ignition and carburation
4 Flooding of float chamber
5 Automatic choke not working properly
6 Fuel leakage
7 Incorrect jet sizes

(o) Engine vibration

1 Loose generator mounting
2 Fan out of balance
3 Clutch and flywheel out of balance
4 Misfiring due to mixture, ignition or mechanical faults

NOTES

CHAPTER 2

THE FUEL SYSTEM

2:1 Description

The fuel tank is fitted in the front compartment. The fuel gauge is electrically operated by a float in the tank.

Pipelines carry the fuel to a mechanical pump mounted on the engine and driven by an eccentric cam on the distributor drive shaft. **FIG 2:2** shows the fuel pump with the filter fitted in the side.

The pump delivers fuel to a downdraught carburetter fitted with an air cleaner, the carburetters have automatic choke control. Diaphragm-operated accelerator pumps are fitted to all models to give a richer mixture when sudden demands are made on the engine.

Models for some markets from 1975 are fitted with an electronic fuel injection system and this is detailed in **Section 2:12**.

2:2 Maintenance of tanks and gauges

Removing fuel tank:

1 Disconnect the battery earth lead. Lift out the spare wheel, jack and tools and remove the luggage compartment lining.

2 It is best to remove the fuel tank when empty or nearly empty, so siphon out any fuel into clean, sealable containers and avoid storing them or working near a naked flame, heaters or any sources of naked light or spark.

3 From under the front of the vehicle, use a pinch clamp to shut the flexible fuel hose between the bottom of the tank and the steel fuel pipe. With the clamp remaining on the flexible hose, detach the hose from the steel pipe.

4 Remove the wire from the fuel tank gauge unit. Detach the filler hose and the breather pipe from the tank. Note that on some emission controlled models, three breather (evaporative loss control) pipes are fitted, one to the front and two to the rear of the tank. All these pipes will have to be detached from inside the luggage compartment.

5 Unscrew the four tank mounting screws and lift out the tank.

Re-installing fuel tank:

The tank must be cleaned by blowing out with compressed air. Refit the tank in the reverse order to dismantling, and renew the anti-squeak packing if it is damaged. Always ensure that breather pipes are not twisted or crossed when refitted.

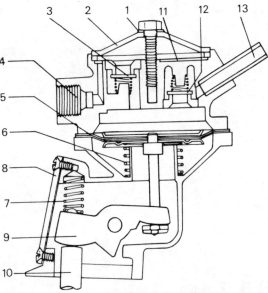

FIG 2:1   Cross-section of the fuel pump

Key to Fig 2:1
1 Gasket	2 Fuel pump cover
3 Suction valve	4 Fuel intake	5 Diaphragm
6 Diaphragm spring	7 Spring	8 Inspection cover
9 Rocker arm	10 Pushrod	11 Filter	12 Delivery valve
13 Fuel outlet	

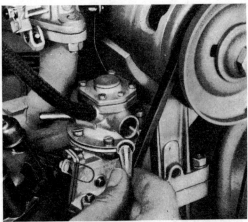

FIG 2:2   The fuel pump with tubular gauze filter removable after unscrewing a hexagon plug from the side.

Adjusting mechanical fuel gauge:

If the tank has been disturbed it will be necessary to reset the fuel gauge. This is best done with an empty tank. First remove the luggage compartment lining to reach the rear of the instrument panel and the sender unit in the top of the tank. Remove the unit cover. Examine the back of the gauge where a knurled screw will be found and an arrow marked on the case.

Enlist the aid of someone to watch the gauge needle inside the car. Press on the sender unit lever to which the cable is attached to ensure that the float inside the tank is at its lowest position. Turn the knurled screw on the back of the gauge in the direction of the arrow until the needle is at zero. In this position there is about one gallon of fuel left in the tank when the needle is on the 'R' mark. If the sender unit is removed from the tank at any time, renew the cork gasket under the flange on replacement, and adjust the gauge.

2:3 Fuel pump description

The principle of operation is the same for all types and **FIG 2:1** should be used for reference. This shows a section of the pump as fitted to earliest vehicles. Note, however, that later models are fitted with a tubular filter in the side of the pump. Under the top cover of this later pump there is a diaphragm-operated valve which stops the flow of fuel when the engine is not running. On starting up, pressure of fuel opens the valve.

Some cars may be found with a separate fuel cut-off valve adjacent to the pump.

Pushrod 10 in the sectioned illustration is driven to and fro by an eccentric on the distributor drive shaft. This operates lever 9 which flexes diaphragm 5 through a pull-rod. The diaphragm is pressed upwards by spring 6. Suction valve 3 takes fuel from the clean side of filter 11 and delivery valve 12 passes fuel to the carburetter.

When the diaphragm moves downwards the partial vacuum in the chamber above it causes valve 3 to open and fuel is drawn in. On the upward stroke of the diaphragm, aided by spring 6, the suction valve closes and delivery valve 12 lifts off its seat to allow fuel to be pumped through outlet 13 to the carburetter.

The latest type pump is a Pierburg with a spun-over casing which precludes dismantling except for filter cleaning. Any defects in this type necessitates renewal of the pump.

2:4 Fuel pump servicing

Routine maintenance is confined to filter cleaning. Do this every 6000 miles. Shut off the fuel supply by fitting a clamp to the flexible hose. Remove cover 2 and lift out the disc-type filter 11. Remove the hexagon-headed plug as shown in **FIG 2:2** to reach the tubular filter, or on the latest type remove the centre screw and remove the metal cap and lift out the filter. Clean filter gauzes with fuel and a brush, never a fluffy rag. When refitting the filter, renew the gasket if it is hard or damaged.

After completing this operation, run the engine and check that there is no fuel leakage from the cover or hexagon plug.

Removing and dismantling fuel pump:

Disconnect the pipes from the pump, unscrew the two flange nuts and lift off the pump. **It is important to remove the pushrod next,** followed by the intermediate flange and gaskets. These parts are all shown in **FIG 2:3.**

The latest pump is a sealed unit. Beyond removing the top cover to clean the filter, no further dismantling or servicing is possible. Earlier pumps, however, can be dismantled in the following manner.

Remove the filter. Remove the pump cover (six screws), press down on the diaphragm and disconnect it from the rocker arm. Remove the rocker fulcrum pin by driving it out after removing a spring ring, if fitted. Remove the inspection cover (two screws), and use a screwdriver to remove the rocker return spring. The six flange screws can now be removed, the diaphragm pressed down and the rocker arm removed.

Check the operation of the valves by sucking and blowing at the inlet and outlet ports. Sucking should not be possible at the inlet port, only blowing. Conversely, blowing should not be possible at the outlet port, only sucking. If faults are evident, the valves are worn or are not seating effectively and corrosion of the seats is suspected. In such cases, renew the top half of the pump.

Inspect the diaphragm and reject it if it is cracked or has hardened. Excessive wear of the rocker arm and fulcrum pin will also call for renewal.

Reassembling the fuel pump:

Reassemble in the reverse order to dismantling. Replace the diaphragm with the spring underneath and engage the pullrod with the rocker arm. Nip the pump flange in a vice and press the rocker arm 14 mm inwards measured from the flange joint face. Fit the pump cover and tighten the screws evenly and diagonally, making sure the diaphragm is not creased. Note that the inlet and outlet pipes should be above the side coverplate, and the diaphragm should be flat while the screws are tightened. Fill the lower pump chamber containing the rocker arm with universal grease.

Adjusting fuel pump stroke:

Pumping pressure is determined by correct adjustment of the pushrod stroke and also by the strength of the spring 6 under the diaphragm as shown in **FIG 2:1**. If stroke adjustment is correct and there is carburetter flooding the spring must be weakened or renewed. If the spring is already weak, giving fuel starvation, it can be stretched or renewed.

To adjust the pushrod stroke, fit the intermediate flange and gaskets over the pump fixing studs. **Always install the intermediate flange before inserting the pushrod as there might be a chance that the rod could slide through into the crankcase.** The rounded end of the rod should contact the eccentric on the distributor drive shaft.

The stroke of the rod is .16 inch. Turn the engine over and measure the amount the rod protrudes from the intermediate pump mounting flange with gaskets in place underneath the flange. When right in, the measurement should be .3 inch and when the rod is at full stroke the measurement should be .5 inch. To adjust the stroke fit the appropriate gaskets under the intermediate flange. Never use fewer gaskets than are actually required or damage to the diaphragm may result.

The Pierburg pump used on engines fitted with alternators is angled at 15 deg. The pushrod for this pump is 8 mm ($\frac{5}{16}$ inch) shorter than the standard pushrod.

Re-installing fuel pump:

Fit the pump so that the coverplate faces left. Retighten the flange nuts when the engine has reached running temperature but do not overtighten. Check that the rubber grommet carrying the fuel pipe is correctly fitted in the engine front coverplate.

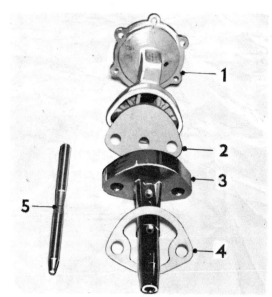

FIG 2:3   Components of the pushrod drive to the fuel pump

Key to Fig 2:3   1 Pump body   2 Gasket—pump to flange   3 Moulded plastic intermediate flange   4 Gasket—flange to crankcase   5 Pushrod

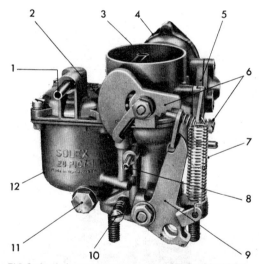

FIG 2:4   Solex carburetter, types 28 and 30 PICT-1

Key to Fig 2:4   1 Fuel inlet   2 Float chamber cover   3 Float chamber vent tube   4 Automatic choke (strangler)   5 Vacuum control for automatic choke   6 Stepped cam on choke valve shaft with idling adjustment screw   7 Throttle valve lever return spring   8 Vacuum connection to distributor   9 Throttle valve lever   10 Volume control screw   11 Main jet plug   12 Float chamber

2:5 The carburetters

A number of different carburetters in the Solex PICT range have been used on the cars covered in this manual, from the 28 PICT-2 to the 34 PICT-3. The general construction and operating principles remain the same, but steady development and refinement has taken place and a

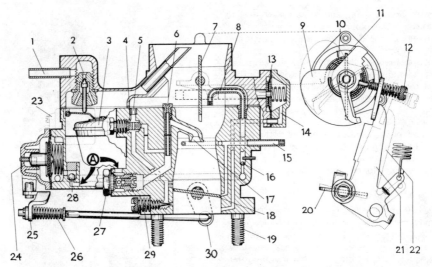

FIG 2:5   Section through early type Solex carburetter

Key to Fig 2:5   1 Fuel inlet   2 Float needle valve   3 Float   4 Pilot jet   5 Pilot jet air inlet   6 Air correction jet with emulsion tube   7 Choke valve (strangler)   8 Accelerator pump discharge tube   9 Fast-idle cam   10 Bi-metal spring   11 Ceramic plate   12 Idling adjustment screw   13 Vacuum diaphragm—choke control   14 Vacuum passage   15 Vacuum connection for distributor   16 Accelerator pump check valve   17 Emulsion discharge arm   18 Throttle valve   19 Mounting stud   20 Throttle valve   21 Throttle lever   22 Throttle lever in fast-idle position   23 Electromagnetic pilot jet   24 Diaphragm accelerator pump   25 Accelerator pump operating lever   26 Spring on accelerator pump rod   27 Main jet plug   28 Check valve for accelerator pump   29 Volume control screw   30 Intermediate lever for accelerator pump   **A** Fuel entry

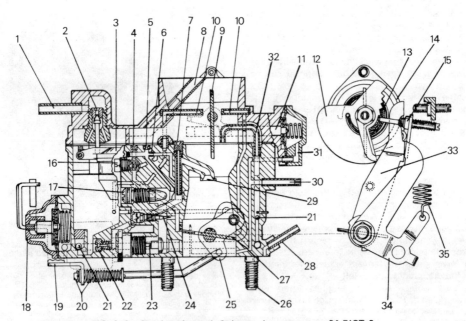

FIG 2:6   Section through Solex carburetter type 34 PICT-3

Key to Fig 2:6   1 Fuel inlet   2 Needle valve   3 Float   4 Idle air bleed   5 Supplementary bypass air bleed   6 Bypass fuel jet   7 Air corrector jet and emulsion tube   8 Float chamber vent   9 Automatic choke plate   10 Enrichment injector tube   11 Choke diaphragm and spindle   12 Fast idle cam   13 Bi-metal spring   14 Automatic choke   15 Fast-idle adjustment   16 Idle jet   17 Bypass adjustment screw   18 Accelerator pump   19 Accelerator pump lever   20 Accelerator pump operating rod and spring   21 Non-return ball valve   22 Main jet   23 Bypass cut off valve   24 Volume control screw   25 Accelerator pump intermediate lever   26 Stud   27 Throttle butterfly   28 Connection for ignition retard capsule   29 Discharge nozzle   30 Connection for ignition advance capsule   31 Depression take-off for automatic choke control   32 Accelerator pump injector tube   33 Throttle damping lever   34 Throttle lever   35 Spring

description of the basic instrument should enable the owner to understand how his carburetter works. Then, with an exploded diagram of his own particular type, he should have no difficulty in carrying out the few simple adjustments or in dismantling and reassembling the carburetter if ever this should become necessary.

It should be noted here that the prefixes 28, 30, 31 and 34 have no relation to the operation of the carburetter, but refer merely to the internal diameter of the flange.

Operation:

An early carburetter is shown in **FIG 2 : 4** and a sectional diagram in **FIG 2 : 5**. These illustrations are typical of the whole range and will help to follow a brief description of the method of operation.

To assist in cold starting an automatic choking device is incorporated which employs a temperature conscious bi-metal spring 10 and a vacuum operated diaphragm 13 to ensure the correct degree of choke plate opening at any time.

Before starting from cold, the accelerator pedal should be depressed briefly in order that the bi-metal spring can shut the choke plate through its operating lever. The idle adjustment screw 12 will then rest on one of the steps of the cam and so open the throttle butterfly a little to prevent over-choking.

Refer to **FIG 2 : 7**. When the starter is operated, the resultant depression in the manifold draws fuel from the float chamber 4, through the jet 5, emulsion tube and air correction jet 1 and out of the discharge nozzle 6. At the same time the choke plate is opened slightly by the vacuum diaphragm 13 against the tension of the spring, being acted on by the depression below the throttle butterfly.

As the bi-metal spring warms up, the choke plate will gradually open, being fully open after about 2 or 3 minutes. At the same time the idle adjustment screw will be closing the throttle to its normal idling position.

For additional fuel at high speeds an extra fuel enrichment tube is pressed into the carburetter bore and connected by way of a drilling and ball valve to the float chamber. At low or medium speeds the vacuum is not high enough to lift the ball valve and so no extra fuel is passed but as maximum depression is approached the vacuum lifts the ball off its seat and draws the additional fuel required for maximum power into the venturi through the orifice at 10 in **FIG 2 : 6**.

Electromagnetic cut-off valve:

This device, which may be seen at 23 in **FIGS 2 : 5** and **2 : 6** is incorporated in order to prevent running on when the ignition is switched off. It consists very simply of a needle which seals off the jet orifice until the ignition is switched on when it is raised by means of a solenoid connected in the ignition circuit.

To check the operation of this shut off valve, disconnect the electric cable from the jet body while the engine is idling and the engine should stop immediately. Still with the ignition switched on, touch the terminal with the cable end and a tick should be heard each time contact is made or broken as the needle moves in or out. Make sure that the grubscrew on the jet head is screwed fully in.

If the valve does not operate in this manner, unscrew it and blow through to ensure that there is no blockage. If the engine still tends to run on, the valve must be renewed.

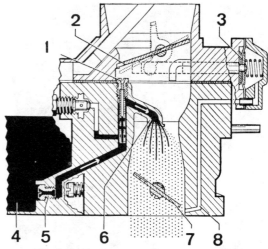

FIG 2 : 7   Early type cold start arrangement

Key to Fig 2 : 7
1 Air correction jet 2 Choke plate
3 Vacuum diaphragm 4 Float chamber 5 Main jet
6 Discharge nozzle 7 Throttle butterfly 8 Vacuum passage

Should a replacement part not be immediately available, the grubscrew in the jet head should be fully turned in an anticlockwise direction to open the jet for engine operation in the meantime.

2 : 6 Idle adjustment

Before commencing any adjustment it is essential that the engine should be at normal working temperature and that all engine systems, especially ignition, are in good order and correctly set, otherwise it will be impossible to obtain a satisfactory idle.

Make sure that the choke plate is fully open and that the idle adjustment screw is not resting on one of the steps of the fast-idle cam.

Connect a reliable tachometer according to the manufacturers instructions and use the idle adjustment screw to obtain an engine speed of 850 ± 50 rev/min. The location of this screw is shown in **FIG 2 : 8**.

FIG 2 : 8   Idle speed adjustment screw

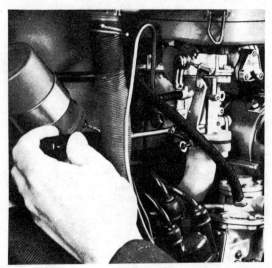

FIG 2:9   Idle mixture control screw

FIG 2:11   Idle adjustment on PICT-3 carburetter

Key to Fig 2:11   1 Balance or bypass screw   2 Mixture control screw   3 Throttle adjusting screw

Now turn the idle mixture or volume control screw (see **FIG 2:9**) in a clockwise direction until the engine speed just starts to drop off. From this point turn it back a quarter or half a turn until the engine is running smoothly. If necessary the engine can be brought back to its specified speed by means of the idle control screw and also further adjustment of the volume control screw if required.

The correctness of the setting thus obtained can be checked by opening the throttle wide and then snapping it shut with the clutch pedal fully depressed. If the engine stalls with this treatment, the mixture setting is too weak and the volume control screw should be opened by about a sixth of a turn.

Later models:

On later model carburetters, 31 PICT-3 and 34 PICT-3, the idling system has been completely redesigned as will be seen from the schematic diagram in **FIG 2:10**.

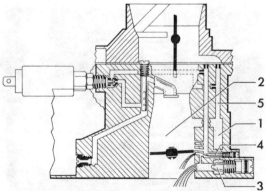

FIG 2:10   Later type idle circuit

Key to Fig 2:10   1 Bypass air chamber   2 Inlet duct   3 Balance or bypass screw   4 Mixture control screw   5 Air passage

At idling speeds the throttle butterfly is completely closed and the fuel/air mixture required for idling is formed in the bypass air chamber 1 and its entry into the intake duct regulated by the balance or bypass screw 3, by which all slow-running adjustments must be made with this kind of installation. The volume control screw 4 just above the bypass screw which regulates the ratio of the air/fuel mixture, is preset at the factory and must not be disturbed. This is particularly important in those areas where regulations with regard to exhaust emissions are in force (see **FIG 2:11**). However, in an emergency and until the carburetter is checked for correct adjustment by a fully equipped garage, the three screws may be set initially as follows:

Refer to **FIG 2:11**. Turn the throttle adjusting screw 3 until it is clear of the cam. Turn the screw in until it just contacts the cam and then add one more turn (inwards). Run the engine and adjust the idle by using the balance screw 1. If idling or running continue to be rough, switch off and turn the mixture control screw 2 fully in. From this position, turn the screw back about two and a half complete turns. Run the engine and once more adjust the idling speed using the balance screw.

It must be emphasised that on emission controlled vehicles, the maximum amount of carbon monoxide (CO) present in the exhaust gases must be checked using an exhaust gas analyser following the adjustment just detailed. The CO content must not exceed 3% ± 1% for all models. This is checked with the engine idling at the normal speed of 750 to 900 rev/min (800 to 1000 rev/min for automatic models) and normal operating temperature.

It is claimed that, with the closed throttle and the idle air supply directed as shown and detailed in the preceding paragraphs, a more accurate distribution of the inlet depression to the distributor capsules and the bypass channels is obtained, resulting in improved acceleration and reduced exhaust emissions.

Any alteration in the quality of the idling mixture by reason of a change in the quantity of air admitted is

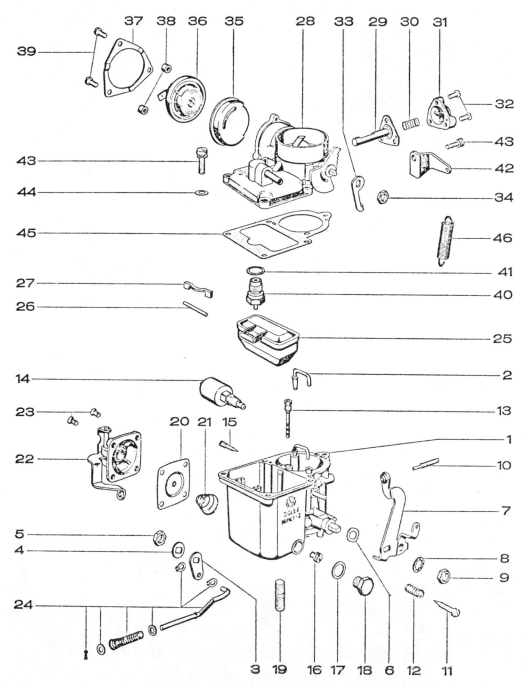

FIG 2:12 Components of Solex carburetter 30 PICT-2

Key to Fig 2:12   1 Carburetter body   2 Pump discharge nozzle   3 Pump lever   4 Washer   5 Nut   6 Spring washer
7 Throttle lever   8 Lockwasher   9 Nut   10 Threaded pin   11 Idle mixture screw   12 Spring   13 Emulsion tube
14 Electromagnetic idle valve   15 Pin   16 Main jet   17 Washer   18 Screw plug   19 Stud   20 Diaphragm   21 Spring
22 Pump lever   23 Screw   24 Pump rod assembly   25 Float   26 Float pivot   27 Clamp   28 Top cover   29 Diaphragm
30 Spring   31 Cover   32 Screw   33 Engaging lever   34 Nut   35 Cover   36 Automatic choke   37 Retainer   38 Spacers
39 Screw   40 Needle valve   41 Washer   42 Bracket   43 Screw   44 Washer   45 Gasket   46 Spring

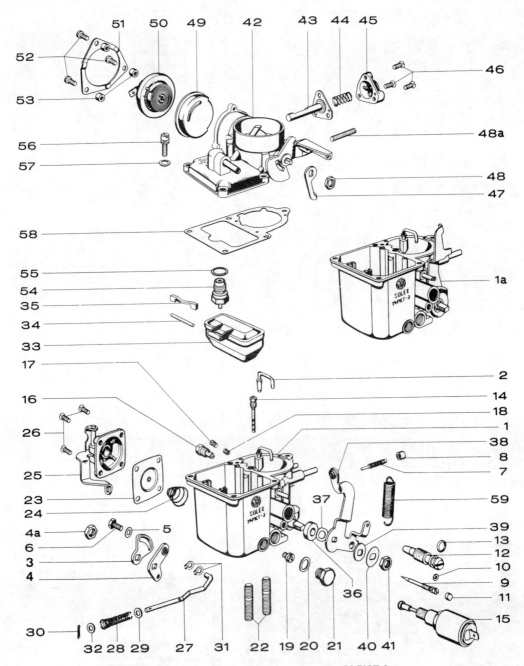

FIG 2:13 Components of Solex carburetter 34 PICT-3

Key to Fig 2:13 1 Body 1a Damping lever 2 Accelerator pump discharge tube 3 Pump lever 4 Pump lever 4a Nut 5 Washer 6 Screw 7 Threaded pin 8 Cover 9 Mixture control screw 10 O-ring 11 Cover 12 Idle air bypass control screw 13 O-ring 14 Emulsion tube 15 Bypass cutoff valve 16 Idle jet 17 Grubscrew 18 Jet 19 Main jet 20 Washer 21 Screw cover 22 Stud 23 Diaphragm 24 Spring 25 Pump lever 26 Screw 27 Pump rod 28 Screw 29 Washer 30 Splitpin 31 Circlips 32 Washer 33 Float 34 Float pivot 35 Clamp 36 Washer 37 Washer 38 Throttle lever 39 Washer 40 Washer 41 Nut 42 Upper body 43 Diaphragm and spindle 44 Spring 45 Cover 46 Screws 47 Engaging lever 48 Nut 48a Damping lever stop 49 Cover 50 Starter cover 51 Retaining ring 52 Screws 53 Distance pieces 54 Needle valve 55 Washer 56 Screw 57 Washer 58 Gasket 59 Spring

avoided by the addition of fuel through the passage 5 (see **FIG 2:10**), this supply being dependent upon the pressure ratios existing in the mixing chamber 1. In this way alterations in the flow past the balance screw 3 do not influence the overall composition of the air/fuel mixture which should remain constant at all times.

2:7 Dismantling the carburetters

Removal:

Detach the preheater pipe, and the crankcase breather pipe when fitted, from the connection on the air cleaner, loosen the clamp screw at the base of the air cleaner and lift it off.

Disconnect the fuel and vacuum pipes from the carburetter, also the electrical leads for the automatic choke and the electromagnetic fuel shutoff valve.

Disconnect the throttle cable from its lever and remove the spring, washer and swivel pin.

Remove two securing nuts and lift off the carburetter.

Dismantling:

Refer to **FIGS 2:12** and **2:13**. Remove the five retaining screws and washers, lift off the cover and from inside it unscrew the float needle valve.

Remove the three screws securing the flange for the automatic choke and take off the flange, spacers, ceramic plate and heater element, bi-metal spring and cover.

Lift out the float assembly. Unscrew the air correction jet and emulsion tube, the main jet and carrier. Unscrew the complete electromagnetic pilot jet and, using a second spanner, unscrew the jet from the valve carrier. Do not use a vice for this purpose or the body may become distorted with consequent erratic operation.

Unscrew the idle mixture volume control screw. Pull out the splitpin from the pump operating rod. Undo the four securing screws and remove the pump cover, diaphragm and spring.

Clean all the parts in fuel, with the exception of the internal components of the automatic choke, and dry with compressed air.

Inspection:

After cleaning, examine all the parts for damage or wear and renew any which are at all doubtful. Do not attempt to remove any blockage in the jets or passages with a wire, pin or similar instrument as the soft metal is easily scratched and the accurate calibrations may be upset.

The needle valve must be checked for leakage and if any signs of wear or corrosion are present, new parts must be obtained. Always use new sealing joints and gaskets. If there have been signs of flooding, the float may be tested by shaking it to see if any fuel is inside. Immersion in hot water will show up a leak if air bubbles are seen.

Check the heater and the bi-metal spring, noting that if either of these parts is damaged the complete cover must be renewed.

Check the pump diaphragm for any damage or deterioration which might cause leaks or impaired operation. Hesitation or spitting back on sudden acceleration are often indications of a faulty pump.

Make sure that the throttle and choke valve spindles are a close fit. Excessive slackness here, particularly in the throttle spindle, can lead to air leaks which will make

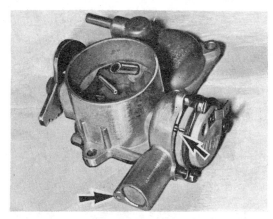

FIG 2:14 Showing location of automatic choke. Bottom arrow shows the vacuum control. Righthand arrow indicates cover alignment marks

accurate tuning impossible. If wear has developed to this stage, the most practical solution is to obtain a new carburetter.

Examine carefully the condition of the various adjustment screws, particularly the idle mixture control. Make sure that the tip is not distorted as a result of overtightening at any time.

Reassembly:

Always use new joint gaskets when assembling to ensure sound joints, but do not overtighten any screws otherwise the threads may be stripped.

When tightening the screws of the pump cover, the pump operating lever should be pushed away from the float chamber so that the diaphragm is secured in the pressure stroke position.

When reassembling the automatic choke make sure that the lug on the plastic insert engages the notch in the choke housing. Ensure also that the ceramic rod between the heater element and the bi-metal spring is correctly located and that the operating lever in the housing engages with the hooked end of the spring.

Fit the cap and turn it until the mark on the ceramic cover is inline with the centre mark on the housing before tightening the three screws (see **FIG 2:14**).

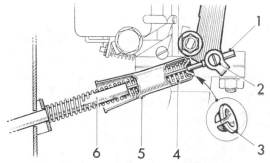

FIG 2:15 Throttle cable attachment

Key to Fig 2:15   1 Cable   2 Clamp screw   3 Spring seat   4 Spring   5 Sleeve   6 Cable guide tube

FIG 2:16 Air cleaner with weighted flap to control air intake

Fit the accelerator pump discharge tube, making sure that when the throttle is opened the fuel jet must spray straight down past the butterfly.

The specified jet sizes are given in **Technical Data** and it is always advisable to check that these are correct when making the final assembly.

When the assembly is complete, install the carburetter on to the manifold and connect the controls, making sure that there is no binding or unnecessary slackness. The throttle cable should be so connected that in the full throttle position these is a clearance of .04 inch (1 mm) between the throttle lever and the stop on the carburetter body.

2:8 Throttle valve positioner

This is a device fitted to certain carburetters whose function is to delay the actual closing of the throttle plate when the accelerator pedal is released. The purpose of this is to admit extra air at this time and so prevent the overrich mixture and associated exhaust pollution which would otherwise occur.

The throttle valve positioner (see **FIG 2:17**) consists of two parts connected by a vacuum pipe. The control element is mounted on the rear lefthand side of the engine compartment, the operating part is mounted on a bracket attached to the carburetter flange.

First make sure that the engine is at its normal working temperature and that the idle speed is set correctly, then connect a tachometer as advised by the maker.

Pull the throttle valve positioner lever back and hold it against the adjusting screw. The engine speed should be between 1450 and 1650 rev/min and the adjusting screw should be reset to obtain this speed if necessary. If the reading is in excess of 1700 rev/min the throttle valve positioner must be readjusted.

Now open the throttle to give an engine speed of 3000 rev/min, release the throttle and, using a stop watch or other suitable timer, count the time it takes for the speed to fall to 800 to 900 rev/min.

This closing time must be between $2\frac{1}{2}$ and $4\frac{1}{2}$ seconds. If it is not, loosen the setscrew on the control and turn the screw as appropriate. Turning the screw to the left (anti-clockwise) will decrease the closing time and vice versa.

Check the closing time again and tighten the setscrew. If satisfactory operation cannot be obtained, do not attempt to repair the device but fit a replacement.

On carburetters fitted with a throttle dash pot the clearance between the dash pot plunger in the fully in position and the throttle arm in the warm running position of the fast-idle cam should be 1 mm (.040 inch).

Adjust by loosening the two nuts and repositioning the dash pot in its mounting bracket.

2:9 The accelerator cable

Refer to **FIG 2:15** which shows how the cable is secured to the throttle lever on the carburetter and how the return spring is assembled. The cable passes inside guide tubes through the fan housing and under the body. At the front end it is hooked over a rod connected to the accelerator pedal.

To remove the cable, disconnect it from the throttle lever on the carburetter. Press on the outer sleeve to compress the spring and remove the spring seat shown in the inset to the illustration. Take off the sleeve and spring. Detach the rod from the accelerator pedal and disconnect the cable from the rod. It will be easier to pull the cable out if the rear of the vehicle is lifted. From underneath, pull the cable out of the fan housing guide tube. Pull the plastic hose off the cable and take off the rubber boot at the end of the guide tubes in the frame. Pull the cable towards the front out of the guide tube.

When installing the cable, grease it with universal grease. Take care that it is laid straight between the guide tubes, with rubber boot and plastic hose carefully seated to prevent ingress of water. Also make sure that the run of the cable is quite free from kinks. To attach it to the throttle lever, reassemble the spring, sleeve and spring seat and thread the cable into the swivel pin in the throttle lever. With the front end hooked to the accelerator pedal rod, open the carburetter throttle valve by the lever until there is about .04 inch clearance between the lever and the stop on the carburetter body. With an assistant to fully depress the accelerator pedal, connect the cable to the throttle lever. This will ensure that there is no excessive tension on the cable which might lead to breakage.

2:10 The air cleaner

Oil bath type:

This type collects dust in an oil-filled reservoir. There must always be at least $\frac{3}{16}$ inch of oil above the top of the sludge which collects in the lower part of the cleaner casing. If the oil level is lower than this, the cleaner must be removed, cleaned and filled with fresh oil. In wet climates on good roads it may be sufficient to check the air cleaner every 3000 miles, while a daily check may be necessary in very dusty conditions.

Remove the air cleaner as follows:

All models: Pull crankcase breather hose off air cleaner. Disconnect preheater hose from air cleaner intake elbow.

Karmann Ghia, '1500' Beetle and 1970 '1200' and '1300' Beetles: Slacken hexagon nut on screw for warm air control flap cable or remove retaining clip and unhook cable eye. Slacken outer cable retainer screw and

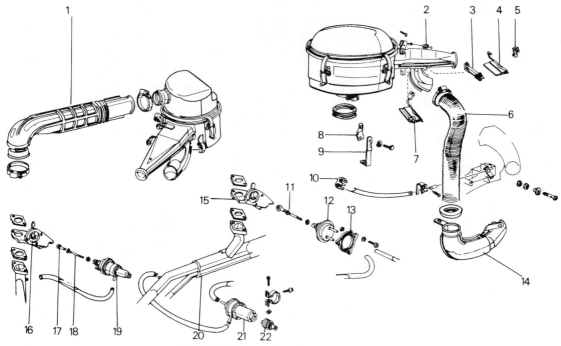

FIG 2:17 Alternative air cleaner systems

Key to Fig 2:17   1 Elbow   2 Carburetter preheating cable   3 Air cleaner flap bearing   4 Outer valve flap   5 Cable clamp
6 Warm air adaptor hose   7 Inner valve flap   8 Upper air cleaner bracket   9 Lower air cleaner bracket   10 Accelerator cable
clamp   11 Ball joint   12 Throttle positioner (later type)   13 Retainer (later type)   14 Righthand warm air adaptor   15 Throttle
positioner retainer   16 Throttle positioner retainer   17 Ball joint   18 Throttle positioner connecting rod   19 Throttle positioner
(early type)   20 Inlet manifold and preheating pipe   21 Throttle positioner control valve   22 Altitude corrector

pull out cable. Slacken screw in air cleaner support
bracket.

Karmann Ghia: Loosen clips holding cleaner on the
bracket and remove cleaner.

All models: Release clips and remove upper part of
cleaner and lay it down so that the filter element is
downwards. Clean the sludge out of the lower casing and
fill to the mark with fresh SAE.30 engine oil. If the
element is very dirty, clean it in paraffin or petrol and
allow to dry before refitting. Ensure that the gasket is in
good condition. Do not overtighten the cleaner clamping
screw when refitting. Check that the control flap moves
freely. The flap is thermostatically controlled on all '1500'
Beetles and the other models for 1970. On early '1200'
and '1300' Beetles the control flap is balanced by a weight
as shown in **FIG 2:16**. This keeps the intake closed
against cold air at low speeds and warm air from the preheater hose prevents carburetter icing. When the speed
of the vehicle increases the flap is opened by air pressure.
At temperatures above 50°F the flap on these models
must be fixed open by pushing the lever under the ridge
on the intake pipe.

Early '1500' Beetles had two flaps, the lefthand flap
is free to move but the righthand flap is thermostatically
controlled.

When refitting the cleaner, ensure that there is a uniform gap between the recess in the bottom of the cleaner
and the housing of the automatic choke.

Paper element type:

This type air cleaner was introduced on some models in
1973.

To remove the filter element pry off the four clips, and
lift the top cover. Remove the element and shake out any
accumulation of dirt.

Renew the element every 18,000 miles (30,000 km).

2:11 Fuel evaporative control

In order to conform with certain American regulations
a control system has been added to later models whereby
fumes from the fuel in the storage tank are absorbed in a
charcoal filter instead of venting directly to the atmosphere.

A hose fitted to the top of the fuel tank is connected
to an expansion tank and also a canister filled with
activated charcoal. While the engine is at rest, any fumes
will pass into this filter and be absorbed by the charcoal.

When the engine is started an air flow from the engine
cooling fan is forced through the filter canister and
thence to the carburetter air cleaner and so into the
engine in the normal induction procedure. This stream
of air draws off the hydrocarbon fumes from the charcoal,
which is thereby regenerated, and also absorbs any
further fumes from the fuel tank until the engine is stopped
again.

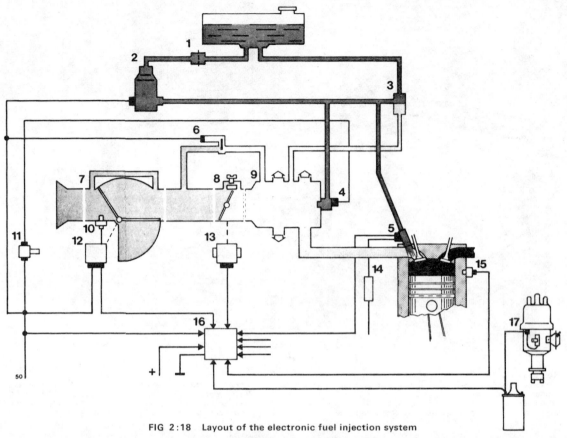

FIG 2:18   Layout of the electronic fuel injection system

Key to Fig 2:18   1 Fuel filter   2 Electric fuel pump   3 Pressure regulator   4 Cold start valve   5 Injector   6 Auxiliary air regulator   7 Intake air sensor   8 Throttle valve housing   9 Intake air distributor   10 Temperature sensor (1976 models)   11 Thermotime switch   12 Potentiometer (incorporating fuel pump switch)   13 Throttle valve switch   14 Resistor   15 Temperature sensor 2   16 Control unit   17 Ignition distributor

If the hoses which are included in the evaporative system are disconnected at any time, great care must be taken to ensure that they are refitted in their proper positions.

The complete unit must be changed at intervals of 30,000 miles (48,000 km).

2:12 The fuel injection system

The Bosch AFC (air flow controlled) system, fitted to some USA models from 1975 onwards, is a combination of an air metering system, fuel circuit and electronic control as shown in **FIG 2:18**. Several sensors are fitted and these monitor all prevailing conditions, such as air temperature (10), engine temperature (15) and position of throttle valve (13), to supply the information needed by the control unit 16. The control unit then computes and generates a pulse, upon which depends the length of time for opening the injector valve 5 to admit fuel into the combustion chamber. In this way, precise amounts of fuel are injected into the path of incoming air, also metered by the air sensor 7, to give the best fuel mixture suitable for the varying engine requirements such as part-throttle, idling or full load operations. This arrangement results in excellent engine performance plus greatly reduced exhaust emissions.

The cold start valve 4 is in effect a fifth injector which supplies an additional amount of fuel to enrich the mixture when the temperature is low during cranking operations. Once the engine starts, the thermotime switch 11 automatically cuts off the cold start valve. The thermotime switch also cuts off the cold start valve if cranking takes longer than the predetermined period, to prevent flooding.

Several emission control systems, such as the EGR (exhaust gas recirculation) and PCV (positive crankcase ventilation) are integrated into the fuel injection system. The EEC (evaporative emission control) system fitted to prevent fuel vapour from escaping to the atmosphere is the same as that described in **Section 2:11**. Additionally, some fuel injection models may be fitted with a catalytic converter (afterburner) in the exhaust system and these are identifiable by the smaller fuel tank filler neck that will only accept the small pump nozzle used to supply lead-free gasoline. In any case, the fuel injection system itself functions as a highly efficient emission

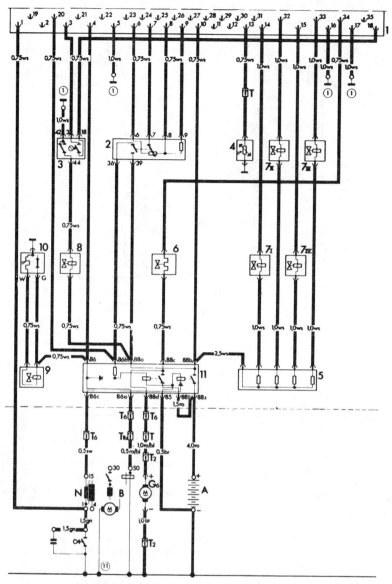

FIG 2:19 Fuel injection system wiring diagram

Key to Fig 2:19   1 Control unit multi-pin connector   2 Intake air sensor   3 Throttle valve switch   4 Temperature sensor 2
5 Series resistance block   6 Auxiliary air regulator   7 Injectors   8 EGR valve   9 Cold start valve   10 Thermotime switch
11 Double relay   N Ignition coil   G6 Fuel pump   A Battery   B Starter   T Wire connector   (I) and (II) Ground
connector

Colour code: ws White   **sw** Black   **br** Brown   **ro** Red   **gn** Green   **ro/bl** Red/blue

control system, referred to by VW as the CCS (controlled combustion system).

Fuel injection troubleshooting:

Testing the system components requires no complex equipment, only an ohmmeter and a circuit tester (or test lamp), but a basic knowledge of electronics and meter reading interpretations, together with the ability to follow circuit diagrams must be possessed.

Use the system circuit diagram shown in **FIG 2:19** and the control unit multi-pin connector. The relevant pin numbers are shown at the top of the illustration and the tests must be carried out at the connector, not the unit itself (see 'Control unit' at the end of this section).

Before suspecting the fuel injection system, ensure that the ignition system, especially the contact points gap and dwell, are correctly set. Ensure also that the mechanical condition of the engine is good so that good

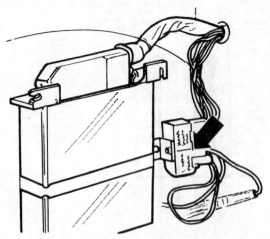

FIG 2:20 The control unit and double relay location in the rear luggage compartment

compression is provided and valve clearances are correct.

When adjustments are to be made, an accurate tachometer and infra red exhaust gas analyser must be available so that the CO (carbon monoxide) percentage of the exhaust gases can be correctly measured.

The relay:

A double relay is located under the cover in the rear luggage compartment, next to the control unit as shown in **FIG 2:20**. The relay controls the current supply to all parts of the injection system including the control unit. When the engine is not running, the relay cuts off all current from the system. Carry out the tests detailed next.

Checking the relay current supply:

Use a test lamp as shown in **FIG 2:21**. Connect one probe to terminal 85 of the relay. With the other probe, contact first terminal 88Y and then terminal 88Z. The

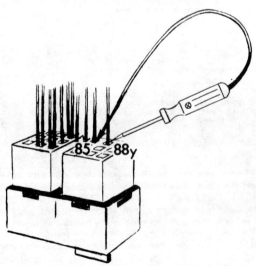

FIG 2:21 Checking the relay current supply

test lamp should light up in both cases to indicate that positive battery current is reaching these terminals.

Switch on the ignition and, leaving the first probe connected to terminal 85, connect the second probe to terminal 86C. Repeat this test, but this time crank the engine with the starter (using the ignition switch). The test lamp should light up in both cases, to indicate that current is reaching this terminal.

Crank the engine with the starter once more, this time using the second probe to contact terminal 86a. The test lamp should light up. Return the ignition key to the 'ON' position and the test lamp should not light up as there should be no current to terminal 86a except when the starter is being operated. If the lamp lights up during this test, the wires to terminals 30 and 50 of the starter motor solenoid have been accidentally cross-connected and this must be rectified by reversing these connections. Repeat the test once the solenoid wires are correctly connected to ensure that current does not reach terminal 86a except while the starter is being operated.

If any of the preceding checks does not produce the result mentioned, refer to **FIG 2:19** and trace the relevant wiring to check for a break in the circuit.

Testing the relay function:

With one test lamp probe connected to terminal 85 as shown in **FIG 2:21**, connect the second probe to terminal 88d of the relay and operate the starter. If the lamp fails to light up during cranking, the fuel pump relay is not closing and the complete double relay must be replaced by a new one.

Switch the ignition to the 'ON' position and connect the second probe to terminal 88b. If the lamp fails to light up, positive battery current is not reaching terminal 88b and the power relay is not closing. Again the complete double relay must be renewed to rectify this condition.

Removing and refitting the relay:

To remove the relay, disconnect the battery ground strap, remove the screw that secures the relay to the body of the car **(FIG 2:20)**, disconnect the multi-pin plugs and remove the relay. Fitting the new relay is the exact reversal of removal.

On completion use the circuit diagram in **FIG 2:19** and the double relay terminals **(FIG 2:21)** to check for any other wiring faults in the system. The components are all shown in **FIG 2:19** and if any is not being supplied with current at the appropriate time, the wiring may be broken or disconnected.

The cold start valve:

The cold start valve is located on top of the intake air distributor as shown arrowed in **FIG 2:22**. During cranking operation, and only when the engine and surroundings are cold, the cold start valve sprays additional fuel into the path of incoming air at the manifold. The operation of the valve is controlled by the thermotime switch which limits the period to 11 seconds, after which cranking continues with the valve remaining closed to prevent flooding. The current supply to the valve comes from terminal 50 of the starter solenoid, by way of the double relay and thermotime switch (see **FIGS 2:18** and **2:19**).

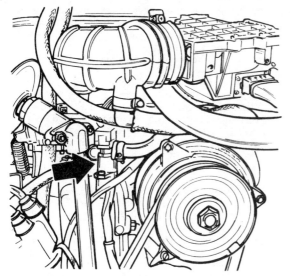

FIG 2:22   Location of the cold start valve

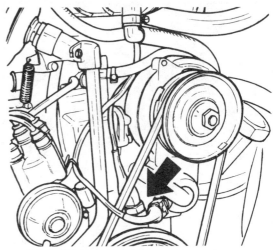

FIG 2:23   Location of the thermotime switch

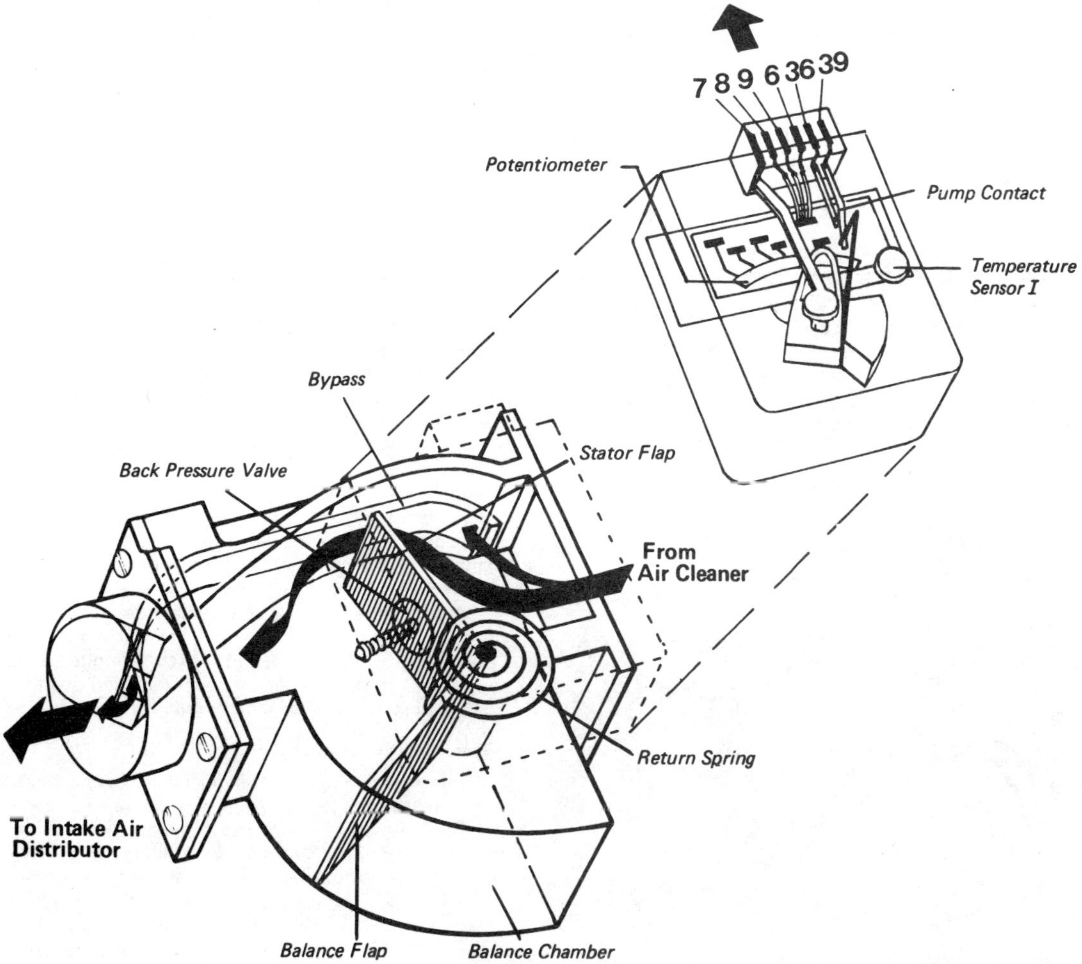

Voltage Signal

7 8 9 6 36 39

Potentiometer

Pump Contact

Temperature Sensor I

Bypass

Stator Flap

Back Pressure Valve

From Air Cleaner

Return Spring

To Intake Air Distributor

Balance Flap   Balance Chamber

FIG 2:24   Cut-away view of the intake air sensor

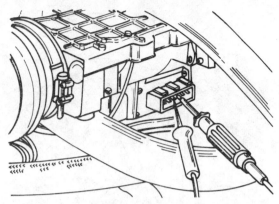

FIG 2:25 Checking intake air sensor potentiometer terminals for continuity and resistance

In cold weather, if the cold start valve fails to operate, it will be difficult or even impossible to start the engine. Conversely, if the valve is leaky, stuck in a slightly open position, flooding will occur during starting, especially when the engine is hot. Protracted flooding will result in engine oil dilution, starting troubles and high fuel consumption.

Testing the cold start valve:

1 Refer to **FIG 2:22** and disconnect the wire connector from the cold start valve. Tape the connector terminals to prevent accidental short circuiting which would cause dangerous sparking.
2 Remove the two screws which secure the cold start valve to the intake air distributor. Invert the cold start valve so that its nozzle points upwards, but leave the fuel hose connected to it.
3 Disconnect the ignition coil primary lead to prevent the engine from starting. Place a clean rag near the cold start valve nozzle to prevent fuel from spraying over a wide area.
4 Have a second operator crank the engine in the normal starting manner using the ignition switch.

FIG 2:26 The auxiliary air regulator. The arrow indicates one of two mounting screws

With the cold start valve wires disconnected, the valve should remain closed and no fuel should be sprayed from the nozzle unless the valve is leaking. If the valve leaks, it must be renewed, no repairs being possible.

If the valve does not leak, proceed to check that the closed, as follows:

5 Reconnect the wire connector of the cold start valve. valve operates when the thermotime switch contacts are
6 Refer to **FIG 2:23**, which shows the location of the thermotime switch, and disconnect the plug from the switch. Use a jumper wire to bridge the two terminals of the disconnected thermotime switch plug.
7 Hold the cold start valve as in the previous test and, have a second operator crank the engine with the starter for a few seconds.

Fuel should be sprayed from the valve nozzle to indicate that the cold start valve is operating correctly. If the valve fails to operate during this test, check the cold start valve wiring as detailed later.

When the valve operates correctly during this test but is suspected of not operating when fitted to the intake air distributor and the wires reconnected, suspect the thermotime switch, which should be tested as instructed later in this section.

Checking the cold start valve wiring:

Check the wiring when the valve fails to operate during the preceding test. Disconnect the cold start valve wire connector. Connect one lead of a 12-volt test lamp to the connector terminal which receives current from terminal 86 of the double relay (see **FIG 2:19**). Connect the other test lamp lead to a clean part of the engine so as to earth the circuit. Operate the starter and the lamp should light up if the wiring is sound. If the lamp does not light up, the wiring or the double relay itself is faulty or has poor connections. Additionally, the wire between terminal 50 of the starter solenoid and terminal 86a of the relay may be faulty or disconnected. Ensure during this test that the correct cold start valve wire connector terminal is being used, otherwise false results will be obtained.

Leave the test lamp connected as just described and return the ignition switch to the 'ON' position. The test lamp should not light up, and if it does, the wires of the starter solenoid terminals 50 and 30 are cross-connected causing the cold start valve to operate all the time the ignition switch is in the 'ON' position. Rectify this fault by reversing the connections on the starter solenoid.

When all the wiring is checked and found to be sound, correctly connected and battery current is reaching the cold start valve as detailed in the preceding tests, but the valve fails to operate either when removed or fitted, the valve must be renewed as no repairs are possible.

The thermotime switch:

This switch controls the operation of the cold start valve by limiting its operation or open-valve period to 11 seconds during cold weather cranking. When the temperature of the engine and surroundings is below 50°F (10°C), the switch permits operation of the valve, but when the temperature is above 50°F, the switch breaks the circuit to the valve. Additionally, a heating element receives current every time the starter is operated. After 11 seconds of steady starter operation, the element is hot enough to raise the temperature of the thermotime switch above 50°F, and the switch then cuts off the current to the cold start valve. In this way, flooding is avoided by closing the cold start valve if the engine does not start within the prescribed period.

Testing the thermotime switch:

1 Disconnect the ignition coil primary lead to prevent the engine from starting.
2 Ensure the temperature of the thermotime switch is below 50°C (10°C), cooling the switch with ice if necessary.
3 Disconnect the wire connector from the cold start valve (see FIG 2 : 22). Connect the leads of a test lamp to the terminals of the connector.
4 Operate the starter without interruption for at least 12 seconds. The test lamp should light up brightly and then become noticeably dimmer, or go out altogether, within 11 seconds, to indicate that the switch is operating satisfactorily. If not, renew the thermotime switch. The switch is screwed to the engine in the location shown in FIG 2 : 23.
5 If the lamp does not light up, check the cold start valve wiring as previously instructed.

The air intake sensor:

The sensor, shown in FIG 2 : 24 consists of a metal casing containing a stator flap, potentiometer and fuel pump switch. Air flow data is transmitted to the control unit by the potentiometer. The signals transmitted by the potentiometer vary according to the position of the stator flap whose position also varies according to the amount of air being drawn into the engine. The flap is spring-loaded and will return to the closed position when the engine is not running.

Testing the air intake sensor:

Before carrying out electrical checks, ensure that the stator flap is operating smoothly and fully for the complete range of its movement. Release the four spring clips that hold the air cleaner, separate the two halves of the air cleaner and remove the filter element. Insert a wooden bar into the air intake opening in the body of the air cleaner. With the wooden bar, move the stator flap throughout its entire range. The flap should operate smoothly without binding, jerking or excessive resistance. If faults are found in the operation of the flap, dismantle the intake air sensor by taking out the screws and carefully detaching the upper housing from the main body. Clean the flap and its pivoting points and recheck for smooth operation, but do not use any solvents. If the flap cannot be made to operate smoothly, renew the complete intake air sensor. When refitting the upper housing, use sealing compound on the periphery to ensure that the joint becomes air-tight.

Checking the intake air sensor potentiometer:

The intake air sensor electrical checks consist of checking for resistance and continuity between the terminals of the potentiometer as follows:
1 Remove the connector plug from the potentiometer.
2 Connect an ohmmeter between terminals 36 and 39 to test the fuel pump contact-switch as shown in FIG

2 : 25, the terminal numbers are marked on the sensor. With the sensor flap closed, no continuity must be detected between these terminals. When the flap is opened slightly, continuity should exist to indicate that the fuel pump switch contacts are operating. If no continuity is detected with the flap open, renew the air intake sensor.
3 Connect the ohmmeter probes to terminals 6 and 9. resistance between these terminals should be between 200 and 400 ohms on 1975 cars, and 100 to 300 ohms on cars from 1976 onwards.
Repeat the test, this time using terminals 7 and 8. The resistance should be 120 to 200 ohms (1975 cars), and 80 to 200 ohms (cars from 1976). If the resistance for either test is outside these limits, renew the intake air sensor.

Removing and refitting the sensor:

To remove the air sensor, remove the air cleaner cover and filter as detailed earlier. Disconnect the potentiometer connector, pulling the connector, not the wires. Loosen the clamp and disconnect the rubber air duct from the sensor, remove the two nuts which secure the sensor body to the car and remove the sensor and air cleaner together. Refitting is the reversal of removal, after separating the air cleaner from the old sensor and fitting it to the new one. The air cleaner is secured to the sensor by four bolts.

On completion, check and if necessary carry out the adjustments detailed under Fuel injection adjustment at the end of this section.

The fuel pressure regulator:

This regulator, located on the engine front cover plate, on the righthand side forward of the fan housing, controls the pressure of the fuel supplied by the pump. It limits the pressure to 2.5 kg/sq cm (35 lb/sq inch) and returns excess fuel to the tank. A spring loaded diaphragm is deflected to expose a fuel return (outlet) port when this pressure is exceeded, and excess fuel is returned to the tank

Additionally, engine vacuum is fed to the regulator, via the intake air distributor. When engine vacuum is high, it aids the fuel pressure to overcome the diaphragm spring resistance and return more fuel to the tank. In this way the fuel pressure is limited to approximately 2 kg/sq cm (28 lb/sq inch) when engine vacuum is high, such as during idling (throttle valve closed).

Test the regulator as detailed next. The regulator is not adjustable and must be renewed complete when faults are found.

Testing the pressure regulator:

Carry out this test with the engine at normal operating temperature.
1 Switch off the engine. Connect a fuel pressure gauge to the cold start valve fuel hose. The hose is shown in FIG 2 : 22, and care should be taken when disconnecting the hose and fitting it to the pressure gauge as a little fuel will escape while doing so.
2 Disconnect the vacuum hose from the regulator and plug the end of the hose.
3 Start the engine and observe the pressure gauge. If the pressure is between 2.35 and 2.65 kg/sq cm (33 to 37 lb/sq inch), the regulator is operating satisfactorily.

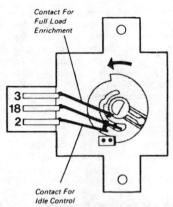

Contact For
Full Load
Enrichment

3
18
2

Contact For
Idle Control

FIG 2:27 The throttle valve switch. Terminal 2 is referred to as 42 in the wiring diagram (FIG 2:19). This switch also controls the operation of the EGR valve

4 Reconnect the vacuum hose to the regulator, and with the engine still idling, the pressure should drop to between 1.85 and 2.15 kg/sq cm (26 to 30 lb/sq inch) to indicate that the regulator is operating satisfactorily when engine vacuum is applied to it.

5 If the pressure during both tests seems correct but the engine lacks power when the car is driven, observe the pressure gauge when the throttle is opened fully, for a few seconds. Pressure must not drop considerably below 2.35 kg/sq cm (33 lb/sq inch), otherwise look for a kinked or restricted fuel line, a blocked fuel filter, dirt in the fuel tank or low fuel pump output and rectify this condition as necessary.

If the pressure, observed in the tests detailed in the preceding steps 3 and 4, varies from the limits specified, the regulator must be renewed, provided that the cause is not one detailed in step 5.

On completion remove the pressure gauge and refit the cold start valve fuel hose.

Removing and refitting the fuel pressure regulator:

1 Disconnect the battery ground strap and avoid working near naked flames or heaters.

2 Disconnect the vacuum hose from the regulator. Disconnect (and quickly plug) the two fuel hoses from the regulator.

3 Working under the car, remove the ring nut which secures the regulator to the engine front cover plate, taking care not to damage the regulator fuel outlet tube onto which the ring nut is threaded.

4 Detach the regulator from the engine front plate.

Refitting is the reversal of removal, reconnecting the two fuel hoses so that the pressure hose from the fuel pump connects to the side pipe of the regulator. Reconnect the battery ground strap and recheck the regulator pressure as previously detailed. The fuel pressure of the new regulator must be correct, as this affects exhaust emissions, otherwise recheck the items detailed in step 5 of the preceding tests.

The auxiliary air regulator:

This regulator (see FIG 2:18) provides additional air, and consequently additional fuel, during engine warm-up

operations. It is located at the rear of the engine between the crankshaft pulley and the alternator pulley as shown in FIG 2:26.

Battery current is supplied by the double relay to warm up a bimetallic strip (heating element) in the regulator while the engine is running. When the engine and surroundings are warm or when current has passed through the heating element for a predetermined period, the bimetallic strip deflects and gradually closes a rotary valve in the regulator, thus cutting off the additional supply of air and allowing the engine to operate only on the normal supply of air and fuel.

Testing the air regulator:

Carry out the air regulator tests with the engine cold, preferably after an overnight stop.

1 From the intake air sensor air duct (see FIG 2:22), disconnect the air regulator fabric covered intake hose.

2 Start the engine (from cold) and place a thumb over the end of the disconnected hose. Suction (vacuum) should be felt under the thumb and the engine should slow down noticeably. After several minutes of running, the suction should gradually diminish and, eventually disappear altogether to indicate correct regulator operation. In cold weather the time taken may be considerably longer but the suction must cease when the engine is hot.

If the regulator operation is not satisfactory, stop the engine and check the regulator resistance and current supply as detailed next.

Disconnect the wire connector from the air regulator and use an ohmmeter to measure the resistance between the two terminals of the regulator itself. Resistance should be 30 ohms if the regulator is satisfactory. If resistance is either infinite or considerably less than 30 ohms, renew the regulator.

If resistance is found to be correct, use a 12-volt test lamp to check for current in the regulator wire connector. Apply the test lamp probes to the two terminals of the connector. Start the engine and the test lamp should light up indicating that current is being supplied for the heating element. If not, refer to FIG 2:19 to check for wiring faults at the double relay. Check especially to ensure that the two leads which connect from the double relay to the starter solenoid terminals 30 and 50 have not been accidentally cross-connected.

Rectify any wiring faults and recheck the current supply (at the regulator connector). If this is now in order, refit the connector and recheck the regulator operation as detailed earlier. If regulator operation does not improve, renew the regulator.

Removing and refitting the pressure regulator:

To remove the regulator, refer to FIG 2:26 and detach both regulator air hoses. Disconnect the wire connector, remove the two screws which secure the regulator to the mounting bracket and remove the regulator.

Refitting is the reversal of removal, rechecking the regulator operation on completion.

The throttle valve switch:

This switch, fitted to the side of the throttle valve housing, has two functions. It signals the control unit to provide full load enrichment when the throttle valve is at or near the fully open position. The second function is to control the operation of the EGR (exhaust gas recirculation) valve and the mode of switch operation is shown in **FIG 2:27**. At closed throttle position the control terminal 18 is connected to terminal 2 (this is referred to as terminal 42 in the wiring diagram shown in **FIG 2:19**). In this position, the EGR valve is held closed to prevent recirculation. When the throttle valve is at or near the fully open position, the control terminal 18 is connected to terminal 3 which signals the control unit to provide full-load enrichment and again cuts off the recirculation of exhaust gases. EGR therefore occurs only in the mid-range of throttle valve operation.

Testing the throttle valve switch:

The switch, rectangular in shape and black in colour, is fitted to the righthand side of the throttle valve housing just to the left of the top of the alternator. To gain access to the switch it is best to remove the rubber air duct between the intake air sensor and throttle valve housing (see **FIG 2:22**). Remove the air duct, and with the engine stopped, test as follows:

1 Disconnect the wire connector from the throttle valve switch.
2 With the throttle valve closed, that is without touching the accelerator pedal or cable, take an ohmmeter reading between the switch terminals 18 and 2 (see **FIG 2:27**).
3 If no continuity is detected, adjust the switch by loosening the mounting screws and turning the switch body in the direction of open throttle until a little resistance is felt. Retighten the switch mounting screws in this position and recheck for continuity. If continuity is not detected this time, renew the switch.
4 If continuity is detected between terminals 18 and 2 at throttle valve closed position, gradually open the throttle while observing the ohmmeter. Continuity should be broken or interrupted at about 11 deg of throttle valve rotation. If continuity does not break, renew the switch.
5 If the preceding tests are satisfactory, check for continuity between terminals 18 and 3. At closed throttle position, there should be no continuity but when the throttle valve is opened by 75 deg or more, continuity must exist, otherwise renew the switch.

Removing and refitting the throttle valve switch:

To remove the switch, use an offset screwdriver to loosen and remove the two mounting screws. Carefully pull the switch towards the alternator until it is clear of the throttle valve shaft.

When refitting the switch, loosely install it taking care not to damage it against the throttle valve housing. Ensure that the throttle valve shaft is correctly engaged, it may be necessary to rotate the switch slightly to engage the cam on the shaft. Refit the mounting screws hand-tight and then adjust the switch as detailed in step 3 of the preceding tests, before finally tightening the screws. Reconnect the wire connector and air sensor duct on completion.

The temperature sensors:

One or two sensors may be fitted according to the year model (see **FIG 2:18**). Temperature sensor 1 is

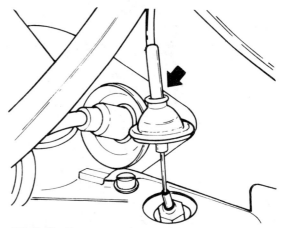

FIG 2:28 Temperature sensor 2 exposed by pulling up the rubber cover

fitted to 1976 models, while sensor 2 is fitted to all models and both are shown at 10 and 15 respectively. Sensor 1 is built into the intake air sensor, while sensor 2 is screwed into the rear of the lefthand cylinder head as shown in **FIG 2:28** and concealed by the rubber seal shown arrowed in the illustration.

The sensors provide the control unit with data of air and engine temperatures necessary for correct starting and warm-up enrichment. The air temperature sensor 1 is tested as part of the potentiometer tests detailed earlier under 'Checking the intake air sensor potentiometer', and any faults found in the potentiometer will entail renewal of the complete intake air sensor, part of which is the air temperature sensor.

To test the engine temperature sensor 2, proceed as detailed next.

Testing the temperature sensor 2:

1 Allow the engine to cool down to room temperature, 20 deg C (58 deg F).
2 Disconnect the sensor wire and use an ohmmeter to measure the sensor resistance by connecting the meter probes between the sensor and ground. At this temperature the resistance should be 2500 ohms. If the resistance is considerably higher or lower, renew the sensor.

To remove the sensor, remove the lefthand air duct between the heat exchanger and engine fan housing. Disconnect the sensor wire and slide the rubber seal (**FIG 2:28**) off the wire. Using a deep socket, unscrew and remove the sensor. Refitting is the reversal of removal, tightening the sensor to 1.5 kg m (11 lb/ft) and making sure the rubber seal fits tightly into the cylinder cover.

The injectors:

An injector is fitted to each cylinder intake manifold and retained by a plate which is screwed to the manifold by a small bolt.

A constant supply of battery positive current is delivered to the four injectors from terminal 88b of the double relay (see **FIG 2:19**). The control unit supplies negative (ground) current to the four injectors simultaneously at every other opening of the ignition distributor

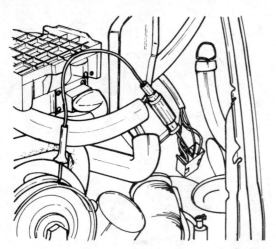

FIG 2:29   Checking the series resistance block

breaker points. In this way, the injector circuit is completed (closed) and the solenoids (of the injectors) open the injector needle valves, allowing fuel to be sprayed into the intake ports. A resistance block (see **FIG 2:19**) consists of four individual resistors, one connected in series with each injector circuit. The purpose of each resistor is to stabilise the voltage being supplied to the injector.

Before testing the injectors, and if running faults are detected, ensure that the fault does not lie with the ignition system. Once the fault is diagnosed as being a fuel injection one, proceed to test the injectors as detailed next, noting that vaporised fuel will be expelled during some tests, so care must be taken to avoid causing a fire by working away from flames, sparks or heaters. Also, before testing the injectors, check that the fuel pump is functioning correctly as detailed later in this section.

Checking injector operation:

Checking fuel discharge:

1 Disconnect the ignition coil primary wire to prevent the engine from starting. Tape the end of the wire to prevent accidental sparking.

2 Remove the injector(s) in question, leaving the wire connector and fuel hose connected to it. Details of injector removal are given later.

3 Crank the engine for a few seconds while observing the injector(s). Fuel should be discharged from the injector if it is operating satisfactorily, provided that the fuel pump and double relay are functioning correctly. If no fuel is discharged proceed with the next step.

Checking injector solenoid:

4 If one or more injectors fail to discharge fuel, disconnect the wire connector from the injector in question and use an ohmmeter to check for continuity between the terminals of the injector. If no continuity is detected, the injector solenoid windings are faulty (open-circuited) and the complete injector must be renewed.

Checking the resistance block:

5 If continuity exists in the preceding test, the injector solenoid is satisfactory. In this case, check that battery current is reaching the injector. Connect a test lamp between the injector wire connector terminals. Crank the engine with the starter and the lamp should flicker intermittently to indicate that current is reaching the connector, and hence the injector.

6 Next, if no current is detected in the preceding step, check that current is reaching the series resistance block from terminal 88b of the double relay when the ignition is switched on. This can be done using the test lamp and connecting it between the terminals of the resistance block and ground as shown in **FIG 2:29**. When the ignition is switched on the test lamp should light up. If current is reaching the resistance block, continue testing to determine whether any resistor is faulty. If no current is reaching the resistance block, check the wiring that connects the block to terminal 88b of the double relay. Check also the double relay itself as detailed at the beginning of this section.

7 When a resistance block is found to be faulty, renew it by disconnecting its connector plugs from the wiring harness, removing the two screws which hold the resistance block cover to the car body and then removing the block. Refitting is the reversal of removal, rechecking the resistance block as detailed earlier when installation is complete.

Checking the injector for leakage:

8 In addition to failing completely, the injectors may leak intermittently. To check for leakage, wipe clean the end of the removed injector(s) and with the wires and fuel hoses connected, turn the ignition switch on (do not operate the starter). A leaking injector will lose several drops of fuel every minute. If only one or two drops of fuel escape, or the injector nozzle becomes wet with fuel without dripping, check the fuel pressure regulator as detailed earlier. The regulator may be causing excessive fuel pressure, otherwise renew the leaking injector. A simple way of diagnosing leaking injectors is to observe the exhaust pipes while the engine is running. White exhaust smoke indicates a leaking injector or cold start valve (see also under the description of the cold start valve given earlier).

Removing and refitting the injectors:

1 Remove the large air duct hoses between the fan housing and exhaust system heat exchangers.

2 Disconnect the wire connector from the relevant injector.

3 Use a 10 mm socket to remove the injector retaining plate securing bolt from the intake manifold.

4 Without allowing the tip of the injector to contact the cylinder cover, withdraw the injector from the manifold. The tips are delicate and can easily be damaged.

5 Remove the injector seals and retaining plate. The inner seals may sometimes become stuck inside the injector seat in the manifold.

6 Loosen the fuel hose clamp and detach the injector from the hose.

Refitting is the reversal of removal, using new seals and prying off the old inner seal if it is stuck to the injector seat in the manifold. The smaller seal should fit around the injector tip and the larger seal around the barrel of the injector. Do not overtighten the retaining plate bolt as only 60 kg cm (52 lb/inch) of torque is needed.

The fuel pump:

An electric fuel pump is used with the fuel injection system. It is fitted beneath the front righthand side of the car near the righthand front wheel (see **FIG 2:30**).

The operation of the pump is controlled by the pump relay which is part of the double relay described earlier. During starting, current for the pump relay is supplied by the starter solenoid, but when the engine is running current is supplied by the intake air sensor.

Testing the fuel pump:

Pressure test:

1 Carry out the fuel pressure test as detailed earlier under 'Testing the fuel pressure regulator'. If fuel pressure is within the limits specified, the fuel pump is operating satisfactorily. If no pressure is indicated, check that current is reaching the pump as detailed next:

Current test:

2 Jack up the front of the car and firmly support on stands. Carefully detach the two wire connectors from the fuel pump. Label the connectors for correct refitting. Connect a test lamp between the two connectors and operate the starter for a few seconds. If the lamp lights up, current is reaching the connectors and hence the fuel pump. In this case the pump is at fault and must be renewed.

3 If the test lamp does not light up, check the relay wiring as detailed at the beginning of this section.

4 Whenever the pump is renewed, recheck the fuel pressure and if this is still unsatisfactory, check for a blocked fuel filter or hoses, a defective pressure regulator, or dirt in the fuel tank. Check also for cross-connected fuel pump wires or pressure regulator hoses and pump hoses.

Removing and refitting the pump:

1 Jack up the front of the car and firmly support on stands. Remove the front righthand wheel for ease of access.

2 Disconnect the battery ground strap and the fuel pump wire connectors. Label the connectors for correct refitting.

3 Loosen the pump hose clamps, remove and quickly plug the ends of the hoses. Small bolts of a suitable size will make excellent plugs for this purpose.

4 Take out the securing screws and detach the pump. Refitting is the reversal of removal noting the following:

1 The supply fuel hose (from the tank) which has the filter connected to it, must be fitted to the rounded end of the pump.

2 The discharge hose (from pump to pressure regulator) must be connected to the flat side of the pump (the side to which the wire connectors are attached).

3 Use new hose clamps and make sure that the hoses are in good condition and fit tightly.

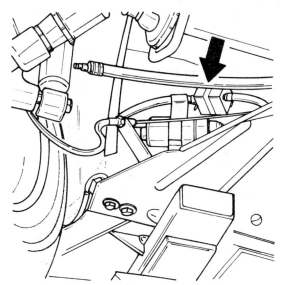

FIG 2:30 Location of fuel pump and filter under the front of the car

The fuel filter:

An in-line filter is connected to the supply fuel hose between the tank and pump as shown in **FIG 2:30**. Access to the filter is gained in exactly the same manner described for the fuel pump removal.

When removing the filter, pinch the hose between tank and filter to prevent leakage. Pinch clamps are available from most accessory shops.

Fit a new filter so that the arrow stamped on it, which indicates the direction of fuel flow, is pointing towards the fuel pump. Use new hose clamps and ensure tight and leakage-free fitting.

The control unit:

The function of the control unit is detailed at the beginning of this section. The unit is located on the righthand side of the rear luggage compartment as shown in **FIG 2:20**.

Before carrying out any tests on the control unit, refer to the beginning of this section and ensure that all other systems, such as ignition, are correctly set. Additionally, and before suspecting the control unit, ensure that all other components of the fuel injection system have been checked and any faulty items rectified or renewed as necessary. If no other fuel injection system faults are found and the engine still does not run right, renew the control unit.

Refer to **FIG 2:31**. Detach the multi-pin connector from the control unit and carry out the necessary wiring checks using an ohmmeter as shown and referring to **FIG 2:19** for the wiring diagram of the system. **Do not test at the control unit itself, only at the multi-pin connector.** Continuity or current supply tests for any component can be carried out in this manner using the details given in most of the preceding tests regarding checking the wiring of the components.

To detach the multi-pin connector, carefully raise the rear of the connector. Raise the other end and disengage

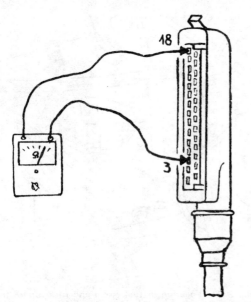

FIG 2:31 Method of using an ohmmeter to check the injection system wiring using the control unit multi-pin connector. Terminals shown being tested are throttle valve switch terminals

the hook from the lug on the control unit. Ensure that the ignition is switched off when detaching or refitting the connector.

The control unit can be removed after detaching the connector and removing the mounting strap fitted around the unit.

Fuel injection adjustments:

During routine maintenance, the only adjustment that may become necessary is the idle speed adjustment. Do not attempt to adjust the idle mixture without a good quality infra red exhaust gas analyser. An accurate

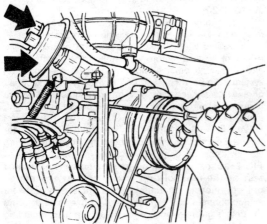

FIG 2:32 Adjusting the idle speed by turning the bypass screw. Also shown is the EGR valve and wiring connector

tachometer, connected in accordance with the manufacturer's instructions, must be used for either adjustment.

Adjusting the idle speed:

Before carrying out this adjustment, check and if necessary, adjust the valve clearances (see **Chapter 1**) and the ignition breaker gap, dwell and timing (see **Chapter 3**).

1 Run the engine until it attains normal operating temperature, preferably after a drive of several miles.
2 Stop the engine and connect a tachometer in accordance with the manufacturer's instructions.
3 Run the engine at idle and adjust the idle speed as shown in **FIG 2:32**. Keeping the hands and tools clear of the moving pulleys and drive belt, use a long screwdriver to turn the bypass screw in the throttle valve housing as shown. Turning the screw clockwise will decrease the idle speed and vice versa. Adjust the idle speed to 800 to 950 rev/min (manual transmission) or 850 to 1000 rev/min (automatic). Note that adjusting the idle speed does not alter exhaust emissions provided that the speed is set accurately.

If turning the bypass screw fully out fails to increase the idle speed, or if the speed was exceptionally low before adjustment, check for air leaks at the crankcase or around the intake manifold hoses. Check also that the oil filler cap is tight and that no hoses are disconnected from the intake air distributor. Check also the EGR valve as detailed later.

If the bypass screw has to be turned fully or nearly fully in to obtain the correct idle speed, or if the speed was exceptionally high prior to adjustment, check the auxiliary air regulator, fuel pressure regulator and the pressure regulator vacuum hose for leakage or other faults. If no faults are found in these items, check the deceleration air enrichment valve (decel valve) as detailed later.

Idle mixture adjustment:

This adjustment should not be carried out unless exhaust emissions are outside the range specified on the engine emissions decal fitted on top of the fan housing on the lefthand side. If the decal is missing, adjust the CO percentage at idle to between 0.2% and 2%. Adjust as follows:

1 Allow the engine to idle at normal operating temperature.
2 Insert the analyser probe into the exhaust tailpipe, or into the port provided ahead of the catalytic converter on cars equipped with this unit.
3 Compare the analyser readings with those given in the decal. Check also, where applicable, the hydrocarbon emissions and compare with the values in the decal.
4 If necessary, refer to **FIG 2:33**, remove the plastic blanking plug from the mixture adjusting screw, and turn the screw as shown until exhaust emissions are correct. Keep the hands and clothing clear of the moving pulleys and drive belt to avoid injury.
5 On completion, readjust the idle speed as previously instructed and recheck the analyser reading. Refit the blanking plug to seal off the screw and remove the analyser.

Emission controls:

The EGR valve:

The exhaust gas recirculation valve and inlet pipe are located as shown in **FIG 2:32**. The purpose of this valve is to divert a portion of the exhaust gases back into the intake manifold, modifying the density and content of the incoming air. The recirculated exhaust gases lower the flame peaks in the combustion process, thereby reducing the formation of oxides of nitrogen, a major air pollutant. The operation of the EGR valve is controlled by the throttle valve switch as detailed under the switch description given earlier. The EGR valve operates only in the mid-range of throttle valve operation.

Engine vacuum is applied to the EGR valve, holding it open and permitting the recirculation of exhaust gases. At closed throttle and full throttle positions, current is applied by the throttle valve switch to a solenoid in the EGR valve (see **Throttle valve switch**). This solenoid then interrupts the vacuum supply and stops the recirculation.

Checking the EGR valve:

1 With the engine idling (at normal operating temperature), refer to **FIG 2:32** and disconnect the EGR valve wire connector. The engine should slow down or stall, indicating that exhaust gases are being recirculated (which normally does not take place during idle).

2 If the engine speed does not alter, stop the engine and then switch on the ignition without restarting the engine. Connect a test lamp between the terminals of the disconnected EGR valve wire connector and then operate the throttle valve from its idle (closed) position to a point midway in its movement range. The test lamp should light up in the idle position, indicating that current is reaching the connector (and hence the EGR valve) during idle. Conversely the test lamp should not light up near the midway throttle position. Finally the lamp should light up again when the throttle valve is moved near or at the fully open position.

3 If the sequence of test lamp operation is as described in the preceding step, the throttle valve switch is supplying current at the appropriate times, and the fault lies with the EGR valve. In such cases, renew the EGR valve.

4 If the test lamp operation is not as described in the preceding step 2, the throttle valve switch is faulty. Check the throttle valve switch as detailed earlier in this section, under the appropriate heading.

Removing and refitting the EGR valve:

1 Remove the two nuts securing each end of the EGR valve inlet pipe. Collect the pipe and gaskets.

2 Disconnect the vacuum hose, wire connector and the throttle return spring from the valve.

3 Remove the two nuts that secure the EGR valve to the pipe on the throttle valve housing. Remove the EGR valve and gasket.

Refitting is the reversal of removal, using new gaskets and tightening the nuts to 1 kg m (7 lb/ft).

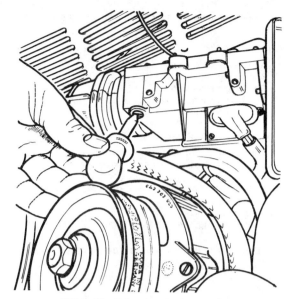

FIG 2:33 Adjusting the fuel mixture

Decel valve:

The deceleration air enrichment valve is located on the engine hood lefthand hinge mounting, forward of the fan housing. Two hoses are connected to the valve, a large inlet hose and a smaller vacuum hose. The purpose of this valve is to prevent the emission of unburned hydrocarbons during closed throttle deceleration.

A faulty decel valve will result in exceptionally high idling speeds. Test the valve as detailed next.

Checking the decel valve:

With the engine idling, open the hood and hold the decel valve large inlet fabric covered hose (not the smaller vacuum hose). Pinch-closed the hose and the engine speed will drop noticeably if the valve is faulty (failing to close). The only remedy is to renew the valve.

Removing and refitting the decel valve:

Stop the engine. Disconnect the hoses from the valve and then remove the screws which hold the valve to the car body. Remove the valve.

Refitting is the reversal of removal, the domed end of the valve is the side to which the smaller vacuum hose must be connected.

2:13 Fault diagnosis (carburetter models)

If there is no fuel at the carburetter check that there is plenty in the tank. If satisfactory, disconnect the fuel pipe at the carburetter and operate the starter. If fuel is delivered, check the carburetter float needle valve and jets for blockage.

If no fuel is delivered, disconnect the fuel feed to the pump. If fuel pours out, check the fuel pump filters, valves and diaphragm. If no fuel comes out of the fuel feed pipe it is blocked. Remove the tank and clean with compressed air. Blow through the fuel pipe with compressed air. Other faults covered are as follows:

(a) Leakage or insufficient fuel delivered

1 Air leaks at pipe connections
2 Pump diaphragm defective
3 Diaphragm screws loose
4 Diaphragm spring weak or gasket too thick
5 Pump valves sticking or leaking

(b) Excessive fuel consumption

1 Carburetter out of adjustment or worn
2 Wrong jets fitted, automatic choke defective
3 Float needle valve stuck open, float punctured
4 Excessive fuel pump pressure, diaphragm spring too strong, gasket too thin
5 Air cleaner choked
6 Brakes binding, tyres under-inflated

(c) Engine will not start with fuel supply

1 Automatic choke not working
2 Bi-metal spring in automatic choke unhooked or broken
3 Ceramic plate broken, heater element not working

4 Float needle stuck, carburetter flooding
5 Jets blocked

(d) Idling speed too high

1 Automatic choke not switched off
2 Heater element defective
3 Slow-running screws incorrectly adjusted
4 Worn throttle butterfly valve

(e) Engine 'runs-on' after ignition is switched off

1 Idling mixture too rich
2 Idling speed too fast
3 Electromagnetic pilot jet valve not working

(f) Engine runs unevenly

1 At idling speed, pilot jet blocked or wrongly adjusted
2 With black exhaust smoke, float chamber flooding through stuck needle valve or punctured float. Pressure from pump may be excessive
3 At full throttle, fuel starvation

(g) Banging in exhaust on overrun

1 Idling mixture on weak side
2 Ignition timing too far retarded

CHAPTER 3

THE IGNITION SYSTEM

3:1 Description

The distributor fitted to the VW Beetle and the associated Karmann Ghia incorporates a vacuum-controlled advance mechanism. However, 1300 cc engines fitted with automatic transmission have a distributor which also incorporates a centrifugal advance mechanism.

All the models with 1300, 1500 and 1600 engines covered in this manual have 12-volt electrical systems. 1200 models had a 6-volt system until 1969, a 12-volt system thereafter.

It is possible for '1200' Beetles with 6-volt systems to be fitted with a distributor manufactured either by Bosch or by VW. This, fortunately, will not seriously affect the servicing instructions, the chief difference being in the method of adjusting the contact breaker points. The VW distributor is recognisable because the capacitor (condenser) is mounted outside.

3:2 Operation

The function of the ignition coil is to transform the low voltage of the vehicle's electrical system into a high voltage capable of producing a spark at the plug points. The high voltage is induced by a current surge produced at the moment when the contact breaker points open. The points are part of the low-tension circuit and are opened by a four-lobed cam mounted on the distributor shaft. These parts can be seen in **FIGS 3:1** and **3:2**. At two revolutions of the engine and one of the distributor, the points open four times and four surges of high-tension electricity are sent out by the coil. These are fed to the respective sparking plugs in the correct firing order by a rotor arm which coincides with a segment and plug lead in the distributor cap at the precise moment when ignition is required. The current is passed to the rotor arm by way of a carbon brush connected to the coil lead. Note that there is a small gap between the rotor arm electrode and the segment in the cap, so that there is no mechanical contact. The high-tension current jumps this gap on its way to the sparking plug.

Automatic control of the moment of ignition is necessary, due to varying loads and speeds of the engine. On distributors fitted with the centrifugal control, rising speed of the engine causes weights to fly out under the restraint of springs, to advance the ignition. The weights 21, springs 24 and assembly with cams and rotor arm 15, 29 and 70, are shown in **FIG 3:1**. As this control has no effect on the ignition point when there was a varying load on the engine, a vacuum control is fitted.

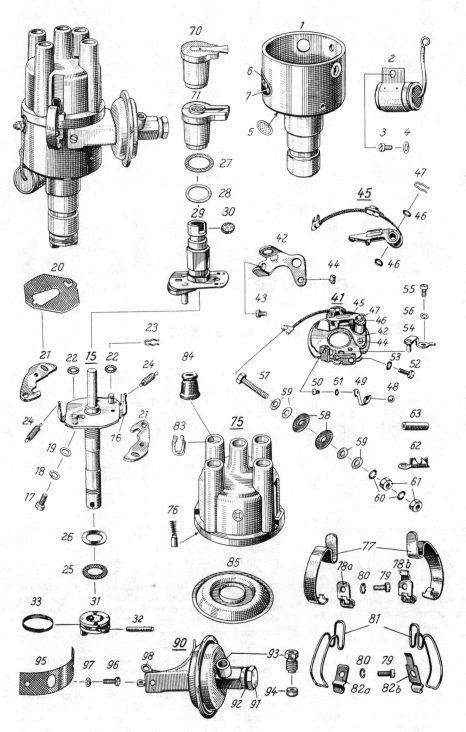

FIG 3:1   Components of typical distributor with centrifugal and vacuum controls

Key to Fig 3:1   1 Body with bush and lubricating felt   2 Capacitor   3 Screw   4 Lockwasher   5 Dust filter   6 Nameplate   7 Rivet
15 Shaft   16 Bracket for spring   17 Screw   18 Lockwasher   19 Washer   20 Centrifugal weight damper   21 Centrifugal weights   22 Washers under weights
23 Weight retainer   24 Springs   25 Fibre washer   26 Shim washer   27 Fibre washer on cam   28 Shim washer on cam   29 Camshaft
30 Lubricating felt   31 Driving dog   32 Pin for dog   33 Retaining clip   41 Contact plate and breaker assembly   42 Fixed contact bracket   43 Screw
44 Eccentric adjusting screw   45 Moving contact assembly   46 Washers   47 Retaining clip   48 Ball   49 Ball holder   50 Screw   51 Lockwasher
52 Screw   53 Lockwasher   54 Holding bracket   55 Bracket and earth cable screw   56 Lockwasher   57 Terminal 1   58 Insulating washers
59 Washers   60 Lockwashers   61 Nuts   62 Cable terminal   63 Sleeve for terminal   70 Rotor arm   71 Rotor arm with suppressor   75 Cap
76 Brush with spring   77 Retaining clip for cap   78 Shackle for clip   79 Screw   80 Lockwasher   81 Early-type clip   82 Shackle for early clip
83 Cable sleeve   84 Rubber ferrule for cable   85 Shield   90 Vacuum unit assembly   91 Locknut   92 Washer for nut   93 Threaded bush   94 Bush packing   95 Packing
strip   96 Screw   97 Lockwasher   98 Earthing cable

52

This is connected by small-bore pipe to a port adjacent to the closed position of the throttle valve in the carburetter. The vacuum control is shown as assembly 90 in **FIG 3:1,** and 60 in **FIG 3:2.** The casing contains a diaphragm, one side of which is subjected to atmospheric pressure when there is a depression on the other side due to the connection with the carburetter. Movement of the diaphragm is transmitted to the contact breaker plate by a rod which can be seen facing left. When the vehicle is cruising along with the throttle only partially opened, there is a strong depression in the bore of the carburetter, the diaphragm is deflected and this advances the ignition even more than the centrifugal weights have done. Wide opening of the throttle, particularly under conditions of heavy load and low engine speed means a considerable reduction in the degree of depression in the carburetter. The diaphragm will tend to return to its unflexed position under the influence of an internal spring and will retard the ignition accordingly. This method of controlling the point of ignition is used without the centrifugal weights on all models except those with 1300 cc engines fitted with automatic transmission. Note that on some later cars there are two vacuum capsules. In addition to the vacuum advance unit there is also one for retarding the ignition point under certain conditions. This is found chiefly with emission control systems and the retard unit is identified by the green vacuum pipe connected to it.

Red plug leads are fitted which incorporate radio suppressors. In **FIG 3:1,** item 71 is a rotor arm with suppressor, and item 45 in **FIG 3:2** is the same part as fitted to Bosch distributor ZV.PAU.R4.

3:3 Maintenance and adjustment
The coil:

Keep the insulating cap of the coil clean and dry to prevent current leakage. If the coil is removed during an overhaul, upon replacement the connections are— terminal 15 to ignition switch, terminal 1 to the distributor (contact breaker) and terminal 4 to the distributor cap.

To test whether a coil is defective or not, check the length of spark it will deliver. Before doing this, make certain that the battery and the distributor are in good order. Disconnect lead 4 from the centre socket in the distributor cap. Make sure the lead is not damp, and hold it with a piece of dry rag, keeping well away from the exposed metal end. Hold the end about $\frac{3}{8}$ inch away from the crankcase and crank the engine over. A spark should jump from the lead to the crankcase if the coil is working properly. If the coil is not satisfactory, first check that the capacitor in the distributor is not defective.

The distributor:

Release the spring clips and lift off the distributor cap complete with plug leads. Clean the inside and outside of the cap with a dry cloth and examine for cracks or 'tracking'. The latter will show up as a thin black line between adjacent metal parts and the cure for both defects is a new cap. The electrodes in the cap and on the rotor arm are subject to some erosion due to the sparking which takes place over the gap between them. This is not detrimental unless it is obviously excessive. The rotor arm

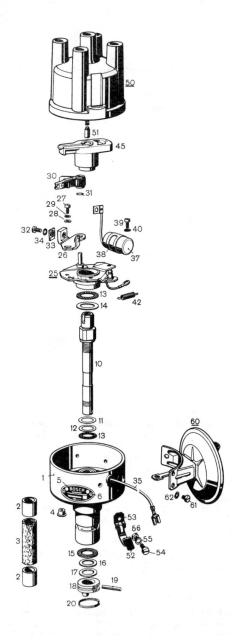

FIG 3:2 Bosch distributor in the range ZV.PAU.R.4. This type has a vacuum control unit only

Key to Fig 3:2   1 Body   2 Bearing bushes
3 Lubricating felt 4 Dust protector 5 Nameplate
6 Rivet 10 Camshaft 11 Shim washer 12 Washer
13 Fibre washer 14 Shim washer 15 Fibre washer
16 Washer 17 Shim washer 18 Driving dog
19 Pin for dog 20 Retaining clip 25 Contact breaker plate
26 Fixed contact bracket 27 Screw 28 Washer
29 Lockwasher 30 Moving contact 31 Washer
32 Terminal 1   33 Plate 34 Lockwasher
35 Connecting cable 37 Capacitor 38 Clip 39 Screw
40 Lockwasher 42 Return spring 45 Rotor arm 50 Cap
51 Brush   52 Clip for cap 53 Shackle for clip
54 Screw 55 Lockwasher 56 Nut 60 Vacuum unit
complete 61 Screw 62 Lockwasher

is readily pulled off. Observe the condition of the carbon brush in the centre of the cap. This bears on the metal part of the rotor arm. The face should be polished and the brush should be capable of being pressed in and should spring out again quite freely.

Lubrication of the distributor:

This varies in the different models, but one feature is common to them all. **It is essential to be sparing with lubricant and it must not reach the contact breaker points.** Add two or three drops of thin oil into the recess in the top of the shaft after the rotor is removed.

When the centrifugal advance mechanism is known to be fitted, squirt a few drops of thin oil downwards in the space between the contact mounting plate and the shaft. The effect of the centrifugal mechanism can be felt by turning the rotor clockwise until a stop is reached. The rotor should return to the stop in the opposite direction when released. If it does not, the springs are probably faulty.

Add a tiny smear of universal grease to the cam on the shaft below the rotor arm, and put one drop of oil on the top of the pivot for the moving contact breaker point. The drive shaft runs in a self-lubricating bush.

The contact breaker points:

Examine the condition of the points by opening them with a finger. They should both have a clean, frosted look. After several thousand miles, it is common for a 'pip' to form on one point and a corresponding hollow to appear in the opposite point. This will not necessarily affect the performance of the ignition system, but if there has been trouble, the points can be removed and finished to a smooth flat surface. This must be done with a measure of skill because the surfaces must be flat and square so that they meet perfectly. To remove the points proceed as follows:

1 Remove the cap and rotor arm.
2 Pull off the low-tension cable connection.
3 Remove the fixed contact securing screw just above the contacts.
4 Remove the circlip from the moving contact pivot pin.
5 Lift off both contacts. Note the breaker arm washers so that they will be replaced correctly.

Cleaning the points:

While in situ they can be cleaned with a cloth moistened in fuel. They may also be held together while a piece of cardboard is drawn between them. When the points have been removed they may have any serious roughness removed with a magneto file. If the tungsten tips to the points are badly worn it is hardly worth trying to restore them, as replacement points are not expensive. The points must be polished with a fine oilstone. This must be done with great care so that the faces are flat and meet squarely when they are re-installed.

Reassembling the contact breaker:

This is simply a reversal of the dismantling instructions, but it is important to ensure the correct replacement of the insulating washers used for the breaker arm. After reassembly the gap must be adjusted.

Adjusting the contact breaker gap:

The correct gap is .016 inch when the points are fully opened by one of the cam lobes. If there is evidently only a few thousandths of an inch difference between the actual and the recommended gap it is not worth making an alteration to it.

To set the gap, remove the sparking plugs and turn the engine over with a spanner on the crankshaft pulley nut. Stop when the gap between the points is at its maximum. Use feeler gauges to check the gap. If there is considerable variation from the recommended gap slacken the fixed contact locking screw adjacent to the contacts.

There are two methods of adjustment according to the model and year of manufacture of the distributor. The two methods are shown in simple form in **FIG 3:3**. The Bosch method of adjustment is to place a screwdriver blade between two pips and twist the blade where it engages in the slot in the fixed contact plate. On VW distributors with the type of adjustment shown in the righthand illustration the screwdriver is twisted while it engages the two slots in the plates at the opposite end to the contacts. After locking the fixed contact plate, check the gap again, and on well-used vehicles it is sensible to check the gap on all four cam lobes. Serious variation may be due to a worn shaft and bushes and renewal is necessary.

After making adjustment to contact breakers it is advisable to check the ignition timing. This must also be done if the distributor is removed and replaced.

3:4 Checking the ignition timing

This operation must be carried out when the engine is cold and it is important to check that the contact breaker points are adjusted to the correct gap of .016 inch as described in **Section 3:3**.

There will be one, two or three small notches on the inner edge of the crankshaft pulley. A single notch is the correct timing mark, and may represent 5 deg. ATDC, TDC, or $7\frac{1}{2}$ deg. or 10 deg. BTDC according to model and year. If there are two notches ($7\frac{1}{2}$ deg. and 10 deg. BTDC) the lefthand notch is correct for all models covered by this manual (1968 onwards). If there are three notches (TDC, $7\frac{1}{2}$ deg. and 10 deg. BTDC) the lefthand notch is used with one exception: 1500 engines with semi-automatic transmission from August 1969 (engine number H 1124670) should be timed on the middle notch.

In some cases there is also a semi-circular groove in the outside rim of the pulley, representing TDC.

Note that on models since August 1970 the mark provided is for stroboscopic timing, and static setting will give only an approximate result.

Rotate the engine in a clockwise direction until the appropriate notch on the rim of the crankshaft pulley is in line with the joint between the two halves of the crankcase, as shown in **FIG 3:4** and No. 1 piston at TDC on the compression stroke—this can be confirmed by both valves being closed. The rotor arm of the distributor must also be in line with the No. 1 cylinder notch on the rim of the distributor body.

Loosen the distributor clamp and connect a 6 or 12-

volt test bulb as applicable between terminal 1 on the coil and earth. Switch on the ignition.

Turn the distributor in a clockwise direction to ensure that the points are closed and then slowly anticlockwise until the test lamp illuminates. This indicates the moment at which the points open. Tighten the distributor clamping screw.

This setting may be checked by turning the engine through two revolutions and observing the test lamp light up again as the timing marks coincide.

Stroboscopic timing:

This method of ignition timing should be used on later cars with only one notch in the rim of the crankshaft pulley, at an idle speed of 850 ± 50 rev/min.

On single vacuum units, the vacuum pipe for the advance/retard mechanism should be disconnected when setting the timing. On units fitted with a double-acting vacuum unit (two hoses), the unit should be left undisturbed and both hoses connected.

Connect up a stroboscopic lamp in accordance with the makers instructions and also a reliable tachometer.

Bring the engine up to full working temperature and set it to idle at 850 ± 50 rev/min, then aim the timing lamp at the central split between the two halves of the crankcase. Loosen the distributor clamp bolt and rotate the body of the distributor carefully until the notch is shown to be in line with the split. Tighten up the clamp and remove the timing equipment.

Note that the idle speed on late models is to be adjusted if necessary by means of the bypass screw (see **Chapter 2, Section 2:6** and **FIG 2:11**). Do not use the throttle screw (where fitted) or the volume control screw as these are set during manufacture.

On units fitted with a double-acting vacuum unit, if the retard (green) vacuum pipe is disconnected when idling, the pulley notch should appear to move 15 to 18 mm (.5 to .7 inch) to the left on the pulley. If it does not do so the retard mechanism is not functioning correctly or the throttle valve is not closing fully. In such cases, refer to **Chapter 2, Section 2:6** and **FIG 2:11** for the method of correctly setting the throttle valve by carrying out the carburetter adjustments detailed.

3:5 Distributor removal and refitting

Remove the distributor as follows:

1 Remove the vacuum pipe(s) at the distributor and disconnect lead 1 from the coil.
2 Take off the distributor cap.
3 Remove the screw holding the distributor retaining bracket to the crankcase. Lift out the distributor.

Refit the distributor as follows:

1 Set the appropriate mark on the crankshaft pulley in line with the crankcase flange as shown in **FIG 3:4**. No. 1 piston will now be at TDC.
2 Look down into the distributor housing in the crankcase and observe the position of the slot in the distributor drive shaft. Note that it is offset. The largest offset must be to the front, away from the crankshaft pulley and the slot must be parallel to the pulley flanges, that is, at right angles to the crankcase joint line, as

FIG 3:3 Two types of contact breaker gap adjustment. **A** is the locking screw and **B** the adjusting device. A screwdriver is used in the notches indicated in the two illustrations.

FIG 3:4 Timing ignition showing distributor and pulley wheel alignment

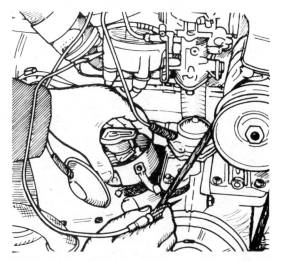

FIG 3:5 Using the electrical method for accurate ignition timing

shown in **FIG 3:4**. If the offset is reversed, rotate the pulley through one turn and again line up the timing mark. Details of the slotted drive shaft can be seen in **Chapter 1, FIG 1:19**. Make sure the distance spring is properly seated in the drive shaft head. If the drive shaft has been taken out for any reason, use the instructions in **Chapter 1, Section 1:9**, to replace it correctly.

3 Insert the distributor and turn the rotor arm until it points to the notch on the distributor body rim as indicated in **FIG 3:4**. Move the arm slightly backwards and forwards until the driving dogs engage and the distributor can be pressed right home. Fix the clamping plate and then check the ignition timing as instructed in **Section 3:4**. Always remember, when checking the timing, to turn the engine backwards about a quarter of a revolution to take up the play in the drive before turning it forwards to line up the pulley mark.

3:6 Dismantling and reassembling distributor

These instructions, together with **FIGS 3:1** and **3:2** will help in dismantling all types of distributor, bearing in mind the variations mentioned at the beginning of this Chapter. One important point must always be considered before attempting to dismantle the vacuum unit. **The adjustment of the threaded rod and the spring must not be altered.** The adjustment of the spring affects the advance curve of the distributor and if anything is done to upset this adjustment the distributor must be returned to a Service Station for correction.

To dismantle the distributor:

1 Remove the cap and rotor arm. Remove the nut from terminal 1 and take off the low-tension cable and washers. Pull out the connecting cable to the breaker plate.
2 Remove the capacitor 37 in **FIG 3:2**. Remove the contacts 26 and 30.
3 Disconnect the vacuum unit pullrod. Remove the vacuum unit or the two units on later cars.
4 Remove the retaining screw and bracket (if fitted) and lift out the breaker plate. Pull out the low-tension cable.
5 Knock out pin 19 after removing spring clip 20. Pull off driving dog 18 which will permit removal of the shaft 10, or in the case of a distributor with centrifugal timing device, assembly 15 in **FIG 3:1**. Note the position of fibre washers 13 and 15 in **FIG 3:2** and any washers and shims 16 and 17 or 11 and 12. If necessary remove the rubber ring and clamp from the body.

Clean all the parts with a solvent such as petrol but do not immerse the body 1 in it or get solvent on the bushes 2 or lubricating felt 3, or the self-lubricating qualities will be lost. Check the shaft for wear in the body bushes. If excessive renew the distributor. End play can be eliminated by shimming. Check the condition of the contact points, the breaker spring and the action of the vacuum unit pullrod. If the breaker spring is pitted with rust it must be renewed as breakage is very likely. Renew the rubber ring which forms an oil seal on the body spigot.

To reassemble the distributor:

1 Oil the shaft and fill the space between the bushes in the body with grease if there is no felt. Fit the washers correctly and insert the shaft. Turn the shaft so that the rotor arm slot is in-line with the notch in the rim of the body which denotes the position for No. 1 cylinder.
2 Assemble the fibre and steel washers on the bottom end of the shaft and fit the driving dog so that the driving lugs are offset towards the notch in the body rim. Insert the pin and peen over the edges of the hole on both sides to prevent the pin coming out accidentally.
3 When assembling the terminal screw, make sure the washers are correctly fitted, as shown in **FIG 3:1**. There is a large insulating washer inside and outside the body and there may be an insulating bush to prevent contact between the screw and the body.
4 Fit the breaker plate and connect up the return spring and the low-tension lead. Fit the vacuum unit. Install the capacitor and adjust the contact points to the correct gap.

3:7 Checking the capacitor (condenser)

A defective capacitor can lead to starting troubles, burned contact breaker points and even a complete failure of the ignition system. To test a suspected capacitor, remove the distributor cap. Turn the engine until the contact points are fully open. Disconnect cable 1 from the ignition coil. Make up a 6- or 12-volt test lamp according to the system fitted to the vehicle, and connect one lead to terminal 1 on the coil and the other lead to the low-tension distributor cable. Switch on the ignition. If the test lamp lights up, the capacitor is earthed and it must be renewed. To continue the test, remove the lamp and reconnect cable 1 to the coil. Remove the central high-tension cable from the distributor cap and hold it carefully by the insulation so that the metal end is about $\frac{1}{4}$ inch from a good earth. Switch on the ignition and open and close the contact points quickly, using a small screwdriver. A spark should jump the gap. If there is no spark try a new capacitor. Substitution is always the easiest way to check for a defective capacitor. It is most important to obtain the correct value of capacitor from the manufacturer or Service Station as an incorrect type will adversely affect the life of the contact points.

3:8 Sparking plugs and leads

The sparking plugs should be removed, cleaned and tested every 3000 miles, and more frequently if there is known to be excessive oil consumption or trouble with starting and misfiring. The preliminary examination of the plugs will be most helpful in assessing the working conditions. A plug which has been fitted to a worn engine which uses oil will be fouled by a wet black deposit or the plug itself may be faulty. If the deposit is black and soft the fuel mixture is too rich. A light grey or brown deposit, if almost white, is a sign of a weak mixture, but if of a darker colour it can be taken as a sign that the plug is firing properly and the mixture strength is correct.

The best way to clean and test plugs is to have them shot-blasted on an official machine and tested under pressure. A sparking plug may spark quite well in the open and yet fail under cylinder pressures. If the plug must be cleaned by hand, go over the threads and the electrodes with a wire brush. Clean the plug interior with a pointed piece of wood, not a sharp metal object. File the electrodes to a bright metallic surface and set them to the correct gap **by bending the outer electrode only. FIG 3:6** shows the method of checking the gap, which should lie between .024 and .028 inch.

It is always advisable to renew the sealing washers when replacing the plugs in the engine. Do not over-tighten.

Running an engine in the dark will often show where leakage is occurring, particularly in proximity to earthed metal objects. Renew all faulty leads and thus avoid constant trouble from difficult starting and erratic running.

Plug leads which are coloured orange-red have a graphited synthetic core which might result in a very high resistance if broken. Misfiring would then be troublesome. A break in the core will eventually damage the outer insulation, particularly at a bend. If an ohmmeter is available, all the leads or cables can be tested for resistance to prove whether a break is present. Remove them complete with connectors and join to the ohmmeter, ensuring good contact with the ends. Move the cable about and stretch it slightly during the test.

At approximately 20°C (68°F) the following readings should not be exceeded:
Ignition coil cable 6000 ohms. Cables to cylinders 1 and 2, 25,000 ohms and cables to cylinders 3 and 4, 15,000 ohms.

If the reading is not steady and the needle flicks to higher readings the core is defective.

Interference on radio and television is eliminated by the use of these synthetic core cables, but fitting them demands the use of the gland-type connectors instead of the standard internal-screw-type. If, for example, a VHF radio is to be installed it is necessary to fit a suppressed distributor rotor arm and four suppressor adaptors in the sparking plug connectors. To fit the connectors to the cables, care is needed to ensure perfect contact. The method is as follows:

It is possible for the synthetic core to be pushed out of the cable by the gland screw. Therefore, squeeze the cable with a pair of pliers at the place where the connector fits. Incorrect assembly will lead to faulty contact and the cable may be burned through.

The gland-type connectors are only suitable for cables with synthetic cores, that is, those which are coloured red or orange-red. Do not use them on cables with a copper wire core.

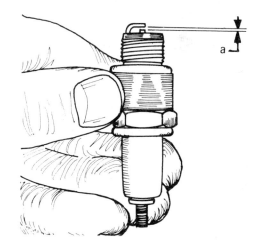

FIG 3:6 Gauge thickness (a) should be .024 to .028 inch when setting the sparking plug gap

3:9 Fault diagnosis

(a) Engine will not fire

1 Battery discharged
2 Contact breaker points dirty, pitted or out of adjustment
3 Distributor cap dirty, cracked or 'tracking'
4 Carbon brush inside distributor cap not in contact with rotor arm
5 Faulty cables or loose connections in the low-tension circuit
6 Distributor rotor arm cracked
7 Faulty coil or coil lead to distributor
8 Broken contact breaker spring
9 Contact points stuck open
10 Faulty capacitor
11 Faulty ignition switch

(b) Engine misfires

1 Check 2, 3, 5 and 7 in (a)
2 Weak contact breaker spring
3 Plug and coil high-tension leads cracked or perished
4 Loose sparking plugs
5 Sparking plug insulation cracked
6 Sparking plug gap incorrect
7 Ignition timing too far advanced or retarded

NOTES

CHAPTER 4

COOLING AND HEATING SYSTEM

4:1 Description

The cooling and heating system is illustrated in FIG 1:1. The curved blades of the fan 12 can be seen behind the filler cap 13. The fan is mounted on the front end of the generator shaft, the rear end of the shaft carrying a pulley. This is belt-driven from a pulley on the end of the crankshaft and turns at approximately twice engine speed.

The fan revolves in the top semi-circular half of the sheet metal housing on top of the engine, drawing its air from an intake in the front face of the housing. Large volumes of air for interior heating are available at all times. The engine cooling air is controlled by flaps connected to a thermostat 18. This ensures a rapid warm-up from cold.

To prevent the possibility of contamination of the air in the heater system by oil and exhaust fumes, the air heating arrangement consists of finned heat exchangers 21 in FIG 1:1. The exhaust gases passing through the inner bore of these devices transmit heat to a large surface area of finning. Some of the cooling air from the fan is diverted to the outside of these heat exchangers, where it is heated and ducted to the car interior if required.

4:2 Removing fan and housing

This can be done with the engine in the car as follows:
1 Remove the fan belt. **Do not try to prise the belt over the pulley flanges.** Hold the inner pulley flange by inserting a screwdriver in the hole provided, as shown in FIG 4:1. Undo the pulley nut, remove the outer flange, the spacing washers, and the belt.
2 Disconnect the battery and remove the rear hood and hinge brackets.
3 Remove the two large heater hoses, one from each side of the fan housing.
4 According to model, remove the generator cables and those for the carburetter choke and oil pressure switch. Remove the cables from the coil. Remove the vacuum pipe and the fuel hose.
5 Disconnect the accelerator cable and pull it out through the front. Remove the carburetter. Take off the distributor cap and pull off the sparking plug connectors. Also remove the righthand rear part of the lower hot air duct and the thermostat securing screw. Unscrew the thermostat from its rod.
6 Remove the generator securing strap and the two screws, one from each side of fan housing. Lift off the fan housing together with the generator and fan.

FIG 4:1 Locking the back flange of the fan pulley to enable the nut to be unscrewed

It is possible to check the flaps by removing eight screws from the lower edges of the fan housing. The flaps will come away, complete with a connecting link, after the link return spring has been unhooked. Note that there is a rubber stop in the righthand flap housing.

Removing the fan:

FIG 4:2 shows the fan mounting in section. If the fan housing has not been removed, disconnect the generator cables, remove the driving belt and then unscrew the four setscrews which secure the fan cover to the fan housing. Release the generator strap and lift away the generator complete with fan and cover.

Hold the rim of the fan and unscrew the shaft nut 4. Pull off lockwasher 6, fan 8, spacing washers 7, thrust washer 1, and hub 2. Note Woodruff key 3 in the shaft.

Replacing the fan:

Press the hub right home on the shaft, taking care to ensure that the key is properly seated. Fit the spacing washers, followed by the fan. Tighten the securing nut to a torque of 40 to 47 lb ft. Now check the clearance between the fan and the cover at point **A** in the illustration. The dimension should be .06 to .07 inch and it can be adjusted by means of the spacing washers. If only one washer is needed, place it between the hub and thrust washer 1, putting the other two between the lockwasher 6 and the fan. Spacing washers can only be effective if placed between the hub and the thrust washer. Finally, fit the generator and fan, tighten the cover screws, then the generator strap and reconnect the cables. Fit and adjust the belt as described in **Section 4:6**.

4:3 Removing silencer and heat exchangers:

To remove the silencer, first remove the rear coverplate (see operation 1 in **Section 4:4**). Remove the heat exchanger clamps at the outer ends of the silencer (two bolts each). Remove the clips from the rising rear ends of the heat exchangers where they connect to the warm air channels on the silencer. Remove the nuts from the silencer-to-cylinder-head flange. Take off the preheater adaptor pipe by removing the screw from the left exhaust flange and withdrawing the pipe to the rear. Remove the four screws securing the manifold preheater pipe flanges just outboard of the exhaust flanges. Take off the silencer and remove the old gaskets.

When replacing the silencer, fit new gaskets and check that the flanges are meeting squarely. Check all connections to ensure that they will be leaktight.

To remove the heat exchangers, remove the rear cover as described in operation 1 of **Section 4:4**. Remove the exhaust flange nuts at the front ends of the cylinder heads. Remove the clips connecting the rising rear ends of the heat exchangers to the warm air channels on the silencer ends. From underneath, detach the two brackets on each exchanger from the coverplate (two screws). Remove the exhaust pipe clamps at the extreme outer ends of the silencer and take the exchangers off in a forward direction.

Check the outer shell and exhaust pipes for signs of damage or leaks. If the heat exchangers leak, it is possible for poisonous fumes to enter the car. Make sure all flanges meet squarely and fit new gaskets.

4:4 Removing and replacing coverplates

1 Remove the front and rear coverplates as shown in **FIG 1:17**. The rear cover is removed by detaching the two large hoses and the carburetter preheater hose.

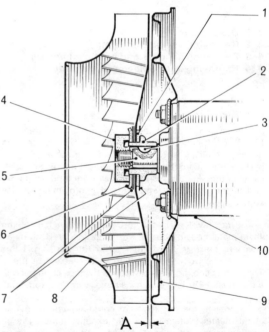

FIG 4:2 Mounting of fan on generator shaft. **A** is the required clearance

Key to Fig 4:2
1 Thrust washer	2 Fan hub
3 Woodruff key	4 Fan securing nut	5 Generator shaft
6 Lockwasher	7 Spacing washers	8 Fan
9 Fan cover	10 Generator	

The fan pulley cover is then removed. Outboard of the large hoses are the small-diameter manifold pre-heater pipes. Remove the three screws from the sealing plate behind each pipe, noting the asbestos seals. Remove the cover.

2 Remove the exhaust system and then lower heating channels (see the end of the preceding **Section 4 : 3**). Remove both cylinder coverplates after removing the sparking plug connectors. Remove the crankshaft pulley and then the pulley coverplate. Take off the pushrod tubes and remove the cylinder deflector plates.

3 Remove the generator and fan housing complete with control flaps. Remove the carburetter and inlet manifold with preheater pipe. Remove the rear air deflector plate and the lower part of the warm air duct. Remove the adaptor pipe for the carburetter preheater pipe from the lefthand side. Take off the fan pulley and remove the pulley cover.

Replacing the coverplates:

Reverse the removal sequence. Check the fit of the cylinder coverplates. They must make complete contact with the fan housing to prevent loss of cooling air. Also check the sealing caps round the sparking plug

FIG 4 : 4 Outer flange of fan pulley removed to show spacing washers used for adjusting belt tension

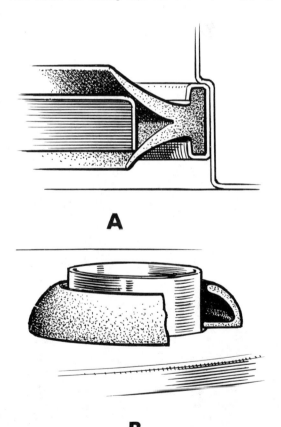

FIG 4 : 3 Correct fitting of weatherstrip on edge of coverplate at **A**. Correct fitting of rubber grommets round large air hoses to heat exchangers at **B**.

connectors. When fitting the coverplates make sure that the two lips of the weatherstrip embrace the edges of the plates so that both are sealed as shown at **A** in **FIG 4 : 3**.

Check the asbestos seals round the manifold preheater pipe. The coverplate must not touch the heat exchanger pipe connections and the two rubber grommets for the large hoses must be fitted with their flat faces in contact with the coverplate, as shown at **B** in **FIG 4 : 3**.

4 : 5 Air control adjustment
Adjusting the air control flaps:

It is assumed that the cylinder coverplates and fan housing have been installed with the control flaps in position in the bottom righthand and lefthand corners of the housing. Screw the thermostat on to its connecting rod from below but do not secure to the bracket. It can be seen as item 18 in **FIG 1 : 1**. Loosen the nut securing the thermostat bracket, press the control flaps into the open position and move the bracket until the top of the thermostat is touching the upper part of the bracket. Tighten the bracket nut and check the operation of the flaps by moving the thermostat up and down. Tighten the thermostat securing screw after checking that the trapped boss fits snugly in the bracket.

4 : 6 Adjusting the fanbelt

As the belt has to drive both generator and fan it must transmit considerable power at high speeds. It is therefore essential to keep it free from oil and consequent deterioration, and to make sure that it is tensioned correctly. A belt which is too slack will slip and cause engine overheating and undercharging of the battery. A belt which is too tight will be liable to break and may cause damage to the generator bearings.

The method of tensioning the belt can be seen on **FIGS 4 : 1** and **4 : 4**. First remove the outer generator flange as shown in the first illustration. The screwdriver is inserted in a hole in the inner flange and supported against the upper generator housing bolt. When the nut is unscrewed the assembly will come apart as in the second illustration. The packing washers are used to alter the distance between the two pulley flanges and thus tension the belt. Any spacing washers which are not actually used between the two flanges must be fitted on the outside, under the nut.

If the belt has been running slack, remove a packing washer, reassemble the parts and check the belt tension. Press one section of the belt midway between the pulleys. The belt should yield about $\frac{1}{2}$ inch under firm pressure. If the belt is too slack, remove washers, if it is too tight add washers. On 1971 and later models a stouter type of belt is used, and on these the correct belt movement has been reduced to $\frac{1}{4}$ inch.

Renew the belt if it has stretched so far that no washers remain between the flanges when the tension is right. Also renew it if it has evidently been running on the spacing washers, or if it has become oily. Be particularly careful when adding oil to the engine to keep it away from the belt. **Do not try to lever the belt over the pulley flanges, or the belt will be ruined and the pulley may be damaged.** Always slacken off the shaft nut.

4:7 Fault diagnosis

(a) Engine overheats

1 Fanbelt slipping
2 Control flaps not opening
3 Cooling air leaks out through cover joints and sparking plug covers
4 Sump, oil cooler and cylinder fins caked with dirt
5 Carburetter out of tune, ignition wrongly timed
6 Exhaust system blocked

(b) Heating system ineffective

1 Control cables broken or out of adjustment
2 Heater box valves and flaps not operating
3 Heater pipes disconnected or leaking
4 Engine not warming up properly

(c) Heating system will not shut off

1 Check 1 in (b)
2 Heater control valves not closing, gaskets faulty

CHAPTER 5

THE CLUTCH

5:1 Description

The VW single-plate clutch is bolted to the front face of the flywheel as shown in the sectioned view in FIG 5:1. Flywheel 12 is secured to the crankshaft by a hollow gland nut which carries a needle roller bearing 10. This bearing supports the rear end of the transmission drive shaft 3 which is the connection between the engine and the gearbox when the clutch is engaged. Loosely splined to this shaft is the driven plate 11 which carries a friction lining 13 on each face. The plate is sandwiched between the front face of the flywheel and pressure plate 14. When the clutch is engaged the friction linings are firmly gripped between the flywheel and the pressure plate by the action of compression springs 8. In this position power is transmitted from the engine through the driven plate to the transmission shaft.

When the clutch pedal is depressed, shaft 1 is partially rotated and a fork mounted on the shaft moves release bearing 2 towards the flywheel until it contacts release plate 4 and moves the plate to the right. The release plate then presses on the inner ends of three levers 6 which pivot on fulcrum points. The outer ends of the levers draw the pressure plate away from the driven plate against the pressure of the springs through the agency of bolts and nuts 7. Now released from pressure, the driven plate slows to a stop and the engine is no longer connected to the gearbox.

5:2 Routine maintenance

The clutch linings wear slowly and this affects the clearances in the operating mechanism. Every 6000 miles check the amount of free play at the clutch pedal pad as shown in FIG 5:2. The distance A should be not less than $\frac{7}{16}$ inch nor more than $\frac{13}{16}$ inch.

To adjust for correct clearance it is necessary to locate the cable end at the clutch operating lever just above and behind the rear axle on the lefthand side, as shown by the top arrow in FIG 5:3. Adjustment is made by unlocking and turning a wing nut. While making the adjustment hold the unthreaded part of the cable end with a pair of pliers. Check the adjustment by depressing the clutch pedal several times and then measure the free movement at the top of the pad as before. It is important to ensure that the stops on the wingnut engage in the recesses in the operating lever. After making the adjustment, smear the nut and thread with grease.

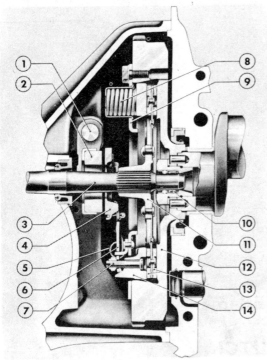

FIG 5:1 Section through typical clutch assembly. Carbon thrust ring **2** may be a ballbearing on some models. Bolt and special nut **7** differ on recent models

Key to Fig 5:1   1 Operating shaft   2 Carbon thrust ring
3 Main drive shaft   4 Release plate   5 Release lever spring
6 Release lever   7 Bolt and special nut   8 Thrust or
pressure spring   9 Cover   10 Needle bearing in gland nut
11 Driven plate   12 Flywheel   13 Clutch friction lining
14 Pressure plate

5:3 Removing and inspecting the clutch

The first operation is to remove the engine as instructed in **Chapter 1**. If it is likely that the same clutch assembly will be replaced, mark the relative positions of the clutch cover and the flywheel to ensure correct balance on reassembly. To prevent distortion of the clutch cover, release the securing bolts a turn or two at a time, working diagonally to avoid tilting. Lift away the clutch assembly and the driven plate.

Examine the contact surfaces of the flywheel and pressure plate. If they are scored or cracked it is possible for them to be reconditioned by grinding and a VW agent should be consulted. Scrap the driven plate if the linings have worn thin, or if they are oily or have a very dark glazed deposit on them. It must be remembered however that a glaze is quite normal providing the lining material is not obscured by a deposit. In any case, if the clutch has been in use for a long mileage it is advisable to replace the driven plate. The minimum permissible thickness is approximately $\frac{9}{32}$ inch. If it is decided to retain the original plate, check the fit of the splined hub on the transmission shaft. The splines should slide freely yet without excessive play. Tight splines will affect clutch operation and gear changing. Maximum permissible lateral runout of the linings is .003 inch.

Check the condition of release bearing 2 in **FIG 5:1**. The illustration shows the earlier type using a carbon ring in a cup. Later assemblies use a ballbearing. If the carbon ring has worn thin so that there is a danger of the cup contacting the release plate, renew the assembly. It is not possible to fit a new carbon ring into an old cup. **If the assembly uses a ballbearing do not try to degrease it or clean it in solvents because it is packed with grease and sealed.** If the bearing feels rough it must be renewed. To release the bearing, lever out the wire clips from each side. These have hooked ends which engage behind the operating fork arms as shown in **FIG 5:7**.

Check the fit of the operating shaft in the transmission casing bushes. The bushes can be renewed if necessary.

5:4 Dismantling the clutch

The procedure detailed next applies only to the type of clutch shown in **FIG 5:4**. Some later models use the diaphragm type clutch cover plate which is not adjustable and cannot be dismantled (see **Section 5:10**).

It must be understood that this is an operation which the inexperienced should not attempt. A press is needed to dismantle and reassemble the clutch and very careful setting of the release plate and levers is needed if there is to be no trouble with a fierce or juddering clutch.

If the owner feels competent to carry out the work, the following instructions will enable him to do so. He must, however be prepared to renew the three bolts and special nuts 7 in **FIG 5:1** as they are inevitably damaged during the unlocking process.

1 The first operation is to mark the relative positions of the cover and the pressure plate and the release levers with respect to the cover. In this way the original components can be reassembled so that the balance is correct. If major components need renewal it is recommended that a VW service station be consulted, as balance will certainly be affected.

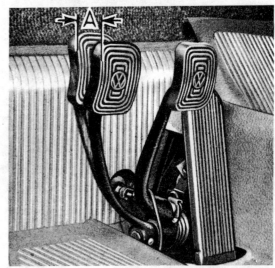

FIG 5:2 Clutch pedal free play is measured at **A**. It should be not less than $\frac{7}{16}$ inch or more than $\frac{13}{16}$ inch

2 Place the clutch in the flywheel and put the two assemblies under a press. Using three distance-pieces, press down on the cover flange until it contacts the flywheel. Proceed to unlock the three nuts from bolts 7 and unscrew them. Remove the springs from the release plate and levers, release the plate and finish dismantling.

3 Checking of all the parts then continues. A warped or grooved pressure plate 14 in **FIG 5:1** must be reground or renewed. Maximum permissible runout is .004 inch. Also check the fit of the pressure plate lugs where they pass through the coverplate as slackness here will cause faulty clutch operation. Check the tightness of the pins in the plate. Check the thrust springs 8 against the information given in **Technical Data**. Never renew one or two springs but always a complete set. Check the cover for cracks or warping. Renew it if cracked and straighten it if warped. Check the release levers 6 and release plate 4, renewing any parts which are cracked, worn or distorted. Renew the release lever springs 5 if they have weakened. It will be understood that the contact face of the flywheel is also part of the clutch and its condition must also be checked.

5:5 Reassembling the clutch

There are a few points to be noted before reassembling and refitting the clutch. **An important one is that a new driven plate must be used in order to adjust the release mechanism correctly.** The bolt and nut 7 which carries the outer end of each release lever has been superseded by an eyebolt carried on a split tubular pin and provided with locking flats for the nut. It is extremely difficult to unlock the nuts without ruining them and replacements are always necessary.

Reassemble the clutch as follows:

1 Insert the release lever bolts into the pressure plate. On the latest type using the tubular pivot pins and eyebolts, fit the pins so that the slots face away from the pressure plate. Always fit new parts.

2 Place the flywheel on the bed of the press and refit the new driven plate and the pressure plate. Fit the spring caps into the cover 9 in **FIG 5:1**, then assemble the springs 8 with spring seats. Fit the cover over the pressure plate so that the three lugs line up and the marks made before dismantling line up too. Check that the spring seats are correctly located in the plate. Take a 2 inch bolt and screw it into one of the cover fixing holes in the flywheel. This will ensure that the cover lines up with the flywheel holes.

3 Compress the cover on to the flywheel, taking care that the pressure plate lugs enter the square holes in the cover correctly. Bolt the cover in place and remove the guide bolt. Release the press.

4 Put a touch of lithium grease on the release lever pivot points and fit them, taking care to check the marks made before dismantling so that balance will not be affected. Install the nuts, or the washers and nuts on later models, always using new parts. Adjust the levers to the same height provisionally. Use a little lithium grease on the contact points of the release plate 4. Install the plate and the sets of springs.

FIG 5:3 Clutch cable adjustment on lefthand side of transmission casing. Top arrow shows adjusting wing-nut. Lower arrow shows bolt which locates shaft bush

FIG 5:4 Checking the squareness of the clutch release plate using a steel straightedge. Measure at several points on the clutch periphery

5 Refer to **FIG 5:4** which shows the method of checking the alignment of the release plate when the clutch is fitted to the vehicle. This method is also used when the clutch has reached the point of assembly in Operation 4. Adjust the release lever nuts until the release plate working face is $1\frac{1}{16} \pm .008$ inch away from the flywheel. Check the runout of the plate at several points It must not exceed .012 inch. Now press down on the release plate several times to operate the clutch and recheck the adjustment. When satisfied, lock the adjusting nuts by peening.

6 Remove the clutch from the flywheel by undoing the nuts a little at a time, working diagonally to prevent tilting and distortion. At the same time block the release levers or press down on the release lever plate.

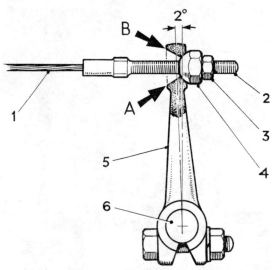

FIG 5:5 Correct setting of clutch withdrawal lever. With release bearing contacting release plate, lever **5** must incline forward not more than 2 deg. See text for setting at **A** and **B**

Key to Fig 5:5	1 Clutch cable	2 Adjusting thread
3 Locknut	4 Adjusting nut	5 Withdrawal lever
6 Operating shaft		

5:6 The release mechanism

While the transmission casing and the engine are apart it will be a good opportunity to check the condition of the release mechanism. The removal and examination of the release bearing has been covered in **Section 5:3**. To remove the clutch operating shaft 1 in **FIG 5:1**, first remove the outside lever to which the cable is connected. The lever is located on the shaft by a circlip. Remove the circlip and pull off the lever, followed by the return spring and the spring seat.

The shaft runs in bushes in the transmission casing. Remove bolt indicated by lower arrow in **FIG 5:3**. This secures the lefthand bush. Slide the shaft to the left and remove the bush, the washer and the spacer sleeve. Note that the bush in a plastic one with a rubber seal on each side. The removal of the bush gives the clearance required to slide the shaft to the right inside the casing so that it can be removed. Check both shaft and bushes for wear. Renew the return spring if it is weak.

Reassemble in the reverse sequence, lubricating the shaft with lithium grease. Refit the operating lever and check it against **FIG 5:5** after the engine and clutch have been refitted. This operation is covered in **Section 5:8**.

5:7 Refitting the clutch

Before bolting the clutch into place, clean the transmission shaft splines and then coat them with some molybdenum-disulphide powder applied with a piece of clean cloth or a brush and the surplus blown away.

The next step is to provide a mandrel to centre the driven plate while the clutch cover is bolted to the flywheel. As shown in **FIG 5:1** it is essential for the driven plate hub 11 to be in-line with needle bearing 10

before the transmission drive shaft can be pushed into place while the engine is being fitted. If available, a spare drive shaft can be used or a stepped mandrel fashioned on the lines of the one shown in **FIG 5:6**. For one application only, it would be enough to turn up a wooden mandrel from a piece of dowel rod. One diameter must enter the needle bearing and the other would be a neat fit in the driven plate hub splines.

Having centralized the driven plate, fit the clutch cover and tighten the securing bolts evenly and diagonally a little at a time to avoid tilting the cover. While the mandrel is still in place, operated the release mechanism a few times and check the alignment of the release plate. This operation can also be performed if the engine has just been removed and the owner wishes to check the condition of the driven plate. The mandrel must be in place and the release plate pressed a few times. Measurements are then taken as in **FIG 5:4**, working in three or four positions round the periphery. If the dimension is down to 1.45 inches then the linings are worn and the plate must be renewed. Remove the mandrel.

Refit the engine, taking the greatest care to ensure that the weight of the engine does not hang on the main drive shaft. If everything is kept square there should be no chance of damage to the release bearing.

5:8 The operating cable

When the cable is reconnected to the operating lever it will be possible to check the angles according to **FIG 5:5**. On the type illustrated, it will be seen that the adjusting nut has a spherical face in contact with the lever. On this type the lever will be correctly positioned if the cable thread just lightly touches the edge of the hole in the lever at **A**, with the clutch engaged. When the release bearing can just be felt to be in contact with the release plate the lever must incline not more than 2 deg. When the pedal is depressed and the clutch withdrawn, the upper edge of the hole at **B** must not touch the cable thread. Any trouble at these points will lead to buckling

FIG 5:6 Using a mandrel to centre the clutch driven plate

and failure of the cable. Often the fault lies with a worn release bearing. Apply a little grease to the face of the adjusting nut.

Renewing a clutch cable:

Raise the rear end and take off the lefthand rear wheel. Disconnect the cable from the operating lever and withdraw the rubber boot from the guide tube. Pull the cable through the boot. Disconnect the piston pushrod of the brake master cylinder. Disconnect the accelerator cable and then remove the pedal cluster from the frame tunnel. Pull the cable through the hole thus exposed.

Grease the new cable with universal grease and insert it in the hole in the tunnel. To feed it into the guide tube, put two fingers behind the tube so that they form a trough and push the cable along the trough until it enters the tube. Push the cable right through and fit the rubber boot. Apply universal grease to the eye at the front end of the cable and attach it to the pedal shaft hook. With an assistant to keep the cable under tension and holding the pedal vertically, attach the pedal cluster to the tunnel. Make sure the pedal stops are correctly placed and that the master cylinder pushrod has a clearance of .04 inch in the piston. Grease the cable adjusting nut at the rear end and finish the installation by adjusting the pedal free play as instructed in **Section 5:2**.

Setting the clutch cable guide tube:

This adjustment applies to all models and is carried out if the cable proves to be stiff in operation. Refer to **FIG 5:8** which shows the rear end of the guide tube and cable. If the guide tube is bent down too much the cable will be stiff to operate and may also be liable to break. A small bow is deliberate and gives a slight degree of friction to the cable to prevent chatter and also makes the cable smooth in operation.

FIG 5:7 The clutch release bearing. Inset shows one of the two clips securing the bearing to the operating fork

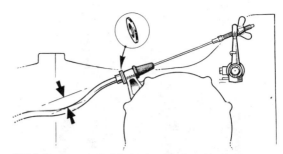

FIG 5:8 Amount of bow in clutch cable guide tube indicated by lefthand arrows. Correct figures are given in Section 5:8. Adjustment is made by fitting or removing washers as shown

If the bow is too much the guide can be shortened slightly by removing the tube and cable. To increase the amount of bow, insert washers at the point indicated. These must go between the guide tube and the bracket which is part of the transmission cover. The bow should be between 1 and $1\frac{3}{4}$ inch.

5:9 The automatic clutch

A section through the automatic clutch is given in **FIG 5:9**. The device is a combination of a starting clutch, parts 12, 13, 14, 23 and 24 and a gearshift clutch, parts 11, 15 and 22, both operating independently. There is no normal clutch pedal. When moving off, the engine is speeded up and centrifugal rollers 12 tend to fly outwards. This action, against inclined faces, forces pressure plate 14 against driven plate 24 and the latter is pressed hard against the face of flywheel 23, so taking up the drive. When coming to a stop, with the engine ticking over, the weights move inwards and release the driven plate so that the drive is disconnected.

For gear shifting there is a separate clutch. This is similar to the standard car clutch but the release mechanism, by way of shaft 5 and a vacuum servo unit can disengage this clutch for gearshifting. When the gearlever is moved to initiate a gearchange, a switch in the lever passes current to a solenoid which operates a valve in the control valve box. This connects the vacuum servo unit to the depression in the engine intake manifold. The diaphragm in the unit is deflected by atmospheric pressure and this movement is transmitted to the operating lever to disengage the gearshift clutch. A vacuum tank is inserted in the system to ensure that there is a reserve of vacuum available in all conditions.

As soon as the gearlever is released the clutch starts to re-engage in two carefully-regulated stages. At first the degree of vacuum falls rapidly and the clutch starts to grip. The second stage is then a more gradual engagement depending on engine speed and the depression in the intake manifold. Valves in the control box are vacuum-operated so that fast opening of the engine throttle after gear changing leads to rapid engagement of the clutch and vice-versa.

There is a freewheel 20 between the two clutches. The gearshift clutch is engaged on starting off. When coming to rest the starting clutch starts to disengage at approximately 1000 rev/min. The freewheel now starts to function and transmits the engine braking effort through the gearshift clutch. The freewheel also connects the

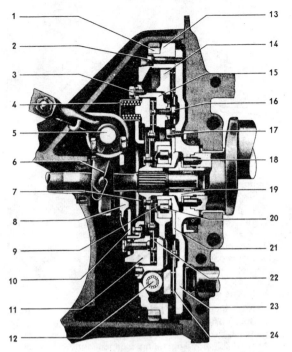

FIG 5:9 A section through the automatic clutch. Plate 22 is for the gear shift clutch and plate 24 for the starting clutch

Key to Fig 5:9   1 Starter ring   2 Socket head screw
3 Hexagon head screw   4 Inner and outer clutch springs
5 Clutch operating shaft with lever, spring and clamping bolt
6 Clutch release bearing   7 Coverplate   8 Release plate
9 Oil seal   10 Release lever   11 Pressure plate
12 Centrifugal rollers 13 Roller housing 14 Pressure plate
15 Drive housing 16 Socket head screw 17 Socket head screw
18 Dowel pin 19 Gland nut with inner serrations 20 Free wheel
21 Bearing flange 22 Clutch plate (gear shift) 23 Flywheel
24 Starting clutch plate

engine and road wheels when the vehicle is parked on a gradient and the gear is engaged, or when tow-starting.

Automatic clutch removal:

Remove the cable from the ignition coil to the control valve. The valve will be found on the extreme lefthand side of the engine compartment. Remove the pipes from the intake manifold to the control valve box, the one from the valve to the servo unit and the one to the carburetter.

Remove the engine, mark the position of the clutch and release screws 3 in **FIG 5:9** a little at a time, working diagonally to avoid distorting the clutch cover 7. Further dismantling to examine the starting clutch will be virtually impossible for the normal owner because a special serrated wrench is required to unscrew the gland nut 19 which secures the flywheel.

Check the gear shifting clutch in the manner described for the ordinary transmission clutch in **Sections 5:3, 5:4** and **5:5. Note that the carbon ring release bearing must never be replaced by the ballbearing type.** Check the release mechanism and refit the clutch according to **Sections 5:6** and **5:7.**

Control valve box removal:

Lift the rear of the vehicle on blocks and remove the lefthand rear wheel. Detach the cable and pipes from the control. Release the control from the side panel. If the control has been faulty in action, only the solenoid can be renewed. The valves are set during manufacture and need no maintenance. The filter must be cleaned every 15,000 miles, but more frequently in very dusty conditions. Remove the filter, wash it in solvent and blow dry with compressed air. Do not wet it with oil.

Clutch servo removal:

Lift the rear of the vehicle on blocks and remove the lefthand rear wheel. Note the position of the adjusting nut on the servo rod and the location of the bracket. Remove the cotter pin and unscrew the adjusting nut, pressing down on the clutch lever to relieve pressure. Remove the connecting pipe and remove the nuts to release the servo unit bracket.

To replace the unit, check that the rubber boot between the unit and the bracket is properly seated. Restore the adjusting nut to its correct position. The measurement should be .9 inch and the distance between the clutch lever and the servo unit bracket should be 1.418 inch. This must be measured with the clutch lever pulled down until the resistance of the release plate can be felt. If adjustment is required, loosen the lever clamp bolt. If necessary, renew the aluminium washer between the two levers. When satisfied, tighten the clamp bolt to 43 lb ft. Take up all play in the operating mechanism while the clamp bolt is being tightened.

Cleaning and adjusting gearlever contacts:

On the gearlever, bend up the sleeve lockplate, hold the sleeve with a spanner and loosen the locknut. Unscrew the sleeve and remove the upper part of the lever with the spring. Polish the contact surfaces and remove rough edges with a fine file. If the contacts are badly worn, renew them. This is done by disconnecting the cable at the valve control box and pulling it through the gearlever. Lift the gearlever boot and push the rubber ring off the cable. Pull out the contact and cable. Reverse the removal sequence to install the new parts, placing a new lockplate over the locknut on the gearlever. The small raised part must be uppermost. Refit the upper lever, with sleeve and spring, and screw on tightly. Adjust the contact gap by screwing the sleeve on until the contacts are closed. Turn the locknut until it touches the sleeve with the raised part of the lockplate engaging properly in the sleeve. Turn the sleeve back one-third of a turn to give the required clearance of .010 inch. Hold the sleeve with a spanner and tighten the locknut, finally turning the lockplate down over the nut.

5:10 Diaphragm clutch

Some later models including 1600 cc versions have a diaphragm spring clutch made either by Luk or Fichtel and Sachs. The clutch can be removed from the flywheel in the same way as the coil spring unit, but any further dismantling of the cover and pressure plate assembly is not recommended as special equipment is required. If any parts of the assembly are damaged or excessively worn the complete unit should be renewed.

5:11 Fault diagnosis

On standard clutch:

(a) Noisy clutch

1 Drive shaft bearing in gland nut worn
2 Driven plate fouling pressure plate
3 Weak or unequal release lever springs
4 Defective release bearing

(b) Chatter or grabbing

1 Transmission case mountings loose
2 Bow in cable guide tube incorrect
3 Uneven pressure plate
4 Release plate running out of true
5 Unequal strength of pressure springs
6 Distorted cushioning segments in driven plate centre
7 Grease or oil on friction surfaces

(c) Dragging or incomplete release

1 Excessive clutch pedal free play
2 Bow in cable guide tube too great
3 Driven plate or main drive shaft running out of true
4 Uneven setting of driven plate cushioning segments
5 Driven plate friction linings broken
6 Needle bearing in gland nut defective or not greased
7 Tightness of drive shaft and driven plate splines
8 Sticky friction linings
9 Felt sealing ring in gland nut tight on main drive shaft
10 Stiffness in operation of clutch pedal, cable and release mechanism

(d) Slipping

1 Lack of free play of clutch pedal
2 Grease or oil on clutch linings

On automatic clutch:

(e) Noisy clutch

1 Check (a)

(f) Grabbing of gearshift clutch

1 Check 3 to 7 in (b)

(g) Grabbing of starting clutch

1 Check 7 in (b)
2 Friction faces of pressure plate and flywheel uneven

(h) Vehicle 'creeps'

1 Check 1 in (a) and 3, 5 and 7 in (c)
2 Idling speed too high
3 Starting clutch release springs weak
4 Centrifugal rollers sticking
5 Driven plate too thick, segments unevenly set
6 Excessive clearance in clutch operation

(i) Slipping

1 Check 1 and 2 in (d)
2 Faulty gearshift clutch
3 Sintered coating on starting clutch plate worn

(j) Clutch will not disengage when changing gear

1 Electrical circuit of solenoid faulty
2 Gearlever contacts dirty or worn
3 Defective solenoid
4 Connecting pipes leaking or disconnected
5 Servo unit diaphragm defective

(k) Vehicle jerks when lever is released after changing gear, with engine idling

1 Starting clutch not freeing, centrifugal rollers sticking
2 Starting clutch plate release springs weak

(l) Gearshift clutch will not engage even when accelerator is depressed

1 Gearlever contacts sticking or bridged by burrs
2 Shortcircuit in cable between contact and solenoid
3 Control valve solenoid sticking

(m) Gearshift clutch slips too long after gear has been selected

1 Pipe between carburetter and control valve diaphragm leaking or disconnected
2 Control valve diaphragm defective

(n) Clutch may fail to engage after gear selection but grips hard when accelerator is depressed

1 Defective freewheel

NOTES

CHAPTER 6

THE TRANSMISSION

6:1 Description

The 4-synchromesh transmission is illustrated in **FIG 6:1**. The casing is a tunnel type with the gears and shafts fed in from the front and the assembly completed by fitting a cover as shown In **FIG 6:1**. It will be seen that first, second, third and fourth gears are helical and are in constant mesh to ensure silent operation.

The reverse gears are shown in **FIG 6:1**. A gear 18 meshes with reverse gear 32 to drive shaft 31 in the opposite direction to the main drive shaft. Splined gear 30 can be engaged with first-speed gear 11 to give reverse.

The all-synchromesh gearbox operates as follows. The front main drive shaft 12 in **FIG 6:1** carries fixed first and second gears and also drives the hub of synchromesh selector 7. The third and fourth gears run freely on needle roller bearings. The shaft of drive pinion 17 carries a similar arrangement, but the lower gears of pairs 4 and 8 are keyed to the shaft together with the hub of synchromesh selector 11. Forks slide the outer members of the synchromesh assemblies 7 and 11 to right or left to select each of the four forward gears, the driving dogs meshing when the synchromesh cone clutches have matched the speeds of both members. The gear teeth on the outer ring of synchromesh assembly 11 are meshed with sliding gear 30 to provide reverse gear.

The final drive pinion and the crownwheel are made in matched pairs and their correct relative positions are most important if silent running is to be ensured. Sideways adjustment of the crownwheel and differential assembly is made by shims 37 in **FIG 6:1**. Fore and aft adjustment of the drive pinion is made by shims 15 in the same illustration. As the rear bearings are not positively located endwise in the casing it can be appreciated that the shims behind the front bearing of the pinion shaft will adjust the fore and aft position of the pinion, positive location being assured by the clamping of the front bearing under the front cover.

For 1302 and 1303 cars, fitted with double-jointed drive shafts, the differential side gears and side covers are modified. The side gears are carried in taper roller bearings instead of the ball races in the swing-axle type unit.

Before proceeding with instructions for servicing the transmission we must stress that official VW Service Stations use many precision devices to set the pinions and crownwheel positions correctly. It will also be understood that when the gears and shafts are assembled in the tunnel type of casing shown in **FIG 6:1** it is not possible to check the assembly, nor the correct functioning of the selector forks. Official VW methods employ a fixture in which the shafts and selectors are assembled and checked before they are fitted into the casing. As these fixtures and

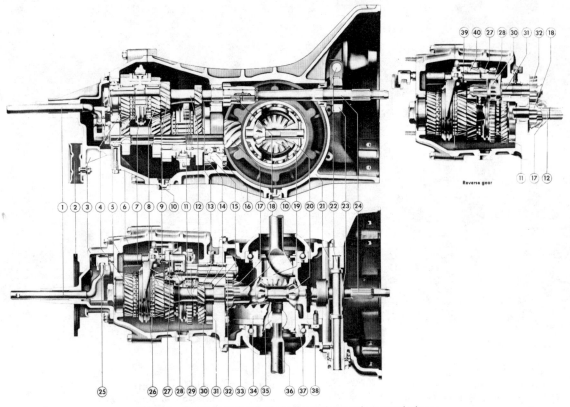

FIG 6 : 1 Sectioned views of the 4-synchromesh transmission

Key to Fig 6 : 1   1 Gearshift lever   2 Front rubber mounting   3 Gearshift housing   4 4th gear train
5 Synchronizer stop ring for 4th gear   6 Gear housing or carrier   7 Synchronizer sleeve and hub for 3rd and 4th gear
8 3rd gear train   9 2nd gear train   10 Magnetic drain plug   11 Synchronizer sleeve and hub for 1st and 2nd gear (also
used in reverse gear train)   12 Main drive shaft (front)   13 1st gear train   14 Bearing retainer   15 Shims for drive
pinion meshing   16 Bearing (ball or taper roller)   17 Drive pinion   18 Reverse gear   19 Differential side gear
20 Differential pinion   21 Transmission casing   22 Clutch operating shaft   23 Clutch release bearing   24 Main drive
shaft (rear)   25 Selector rod (3rd and 4th gear)   26 Selector fork (3rd and 4th gear)   27 Lever for reverse gear
28 Selector fork for reverse gear   29 Oil filler plug   30 Reverse sliding gear   31 Reverse gearshaft   32 Reverse drive gear
33 Final drive or side cover   34 Crownwheel   35 Fulcrum plate   36 Rear axle shaft   37 Shim   38 Differential housing
39 Reverse lever support   40 Reverse lever guide

devices are not available to the normal owner we advise him to entrust the assembling of a transmission which incorporates new parts to a VW Service Station. The alternative is to use the Exchange system. There is no reason why the transmission should not be dismantled providing every care is taken to record the position and thickness of shimming for correct reassembly. Those parts which do not affect the position of the selector forks or the drive pinion can be renewed. Renewal of the casing parts, the pinion and crownwheel, the differential cage and bearings and the pinion shaft bearings will all require the special techniques for accurate location just mentioned.

6 : 2 Transmission maintenance

This is confined to topping up or changing the lubricating oil, but there is an associated adjustment which has a great effect upon the satisfactory working of the gearchange mechanism inside the transmission casing.

This adjustment is to the clutch operation. Refer to **Chapter 5** and make sure that the clutch pedal clearance is maintained at the correct figure. Any tendency for the clutch to drag will have a bad effect on the synchromesh cones, causing them to wear rapidly.

Every 6000 miles check the oil level in the transmission by removing the level plug in the lefthand side of the casing just forward of the axle tubes, as shown in **FIG 6 : 2**. Top up with SAE.90 Hypoid oil until it starts to overflow. Too hurried a filling may give a false impression, so wait a few minutes and add more lubricant if the level inside has fallen. There is only one filler plug, as the gearbox and rear axle are lubricated from a common source.

Every 30,000 miles drain the oil completely while it is still warm. Remove both drain plugs as indicated in **FIG 6 : 3**. On all-synchromesh gearboxes the drain plugs are magnetic, so clean them of adhering particles of steel. Refill with Hypoid oil, using slightly less than $4\frac{1}{2}$ pints. Sudden overflowing from the filler hole may be due to rapid filling, so pause now and then to allow the oil to settle inside the casing. The oil level should be up to the bottom edge of the filler hole. A newly-assembled transmission will take almost $5\frac{1}{4}$ pints.

If the drained oil is contaminated with many metallic particles and these also adhere in quantity to the magnetic drain plugs it is advisable to remove and dismantle the transmission to find the cause of excessive wear.

6:3 Removing transmission assembly

With swing-axle rear suspension, any dismantling of the transmission entails the removal of the gearbox and rear axle as a unit, as described in **Chapter 7, Section 7:4**. With the double-jointed layout (1302 and 1303), the drive shafts can be disconnected from the transmission (see **Section 7:11**) and then the transmission unit removed as for the earlier type but without disturbing the rear suspension.

6:4 Servicing 4-synchromesh transmission

Refer to the three views of this transmission system in **FIG 6:1**. It will be noted that the casing is of the tunnel type with a deep front gear housing 6 and gearshift housing 3. The main drive shaft is in two parts 12 and 24, joined by a coupling 18 which incorporates a pinion used in the reverse gearing assembly shown by the view on the right. The large bearings for the differential housing 38 make it possible to remove the axle shafts 36 and side gears 19 without dismantling the complete unit. It can also be seen that the first- and second-speed synchromesh unit 11 is mounted on the pinion shaft 17, the synchromesh unit 7 for the third- and fourth-speeds being located on the front drive shaft. It must be appreciated that the renewal of any parts which call for readjustment of the selector fork positions must be entrusted to a VW Service Station because the adjustment cannot be made with the transmission assembled in the casing. The Service Station uses a special jig which holds the assembly in the relative position it will occupy in the casing and permits the adjustment to be carried out.

The differential side bearings are preloaded by .004 to .007 inch by selecting suitable shims 37. These shims together with those at the other end of the differential housing also control the sideways position of the ring gear or crownwheel 34 relative to the drive pinion 17. When double-jointed drive shafts are fitted, the adjusting shims are located outside the outer races of the taper roller side bearings. Endwise location of the pinion with respect to the crownwheel is determined by the thickness of shims 15. If either the pinion and crownwheel, the casing, the bearing 16, or the differential housing 38 is renewed, the meshing of the drive gears must be checked and reset by a VW Service Station equipped with the necessary precision gauges and assembly jigs. Renewal of the sideplates carrying the differential bearings, or the bearings themselves, may call for crownwheel readjustment only. **Note that the pinion and crownwheel are produced in matched pairs and must be renewed together.** Worn changespeed gears must also be renewed in pairs and never singly. Any adjustment of the pinion position will affect the selector forks and these will also need readjustment.

From the preceding remarks it will be realised that servicing this type of transmission should not

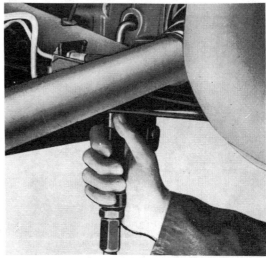
FIG 6:2 Location of filling and level plug for lubricant

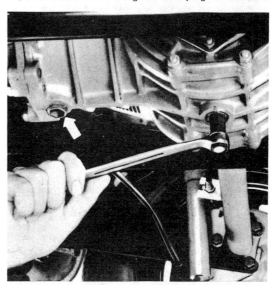
FIG 6:3 Location of transmission drain plugs

be lightly undertaken, particularly if it is thought that the renewal of many worn parts might be needed. If the parts to be renewed do not affect the adjustment of the pinion and crownwheel or the selector forks then the following instructions can be used. **During dismantling it is most important to record the position and number of shims so that they can be replaced in their original positions on reassembly.**

Dismantling transmission:

This can proceed after the axle shafts and side gears have been removed as instructed in **Chapter 7**. Then do the following:

1 Remove the front mounting 2 and the housing 3 together with the gearshift lever 1. Move the reverse

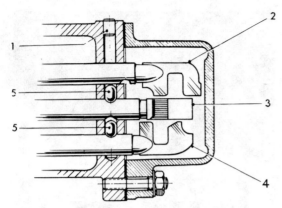

FIG 6:4   Selector rods and interlocking plungers

Key to Fig 6:4   1 Plug   2 Selector rod for reverse
3 Selector rod for 1st and 2nd gears   4 Selector rod for 3rd
and 4th gears   5 Interlocking plungers

selector rod and the third and fourth selector rod 25 so that the simultaneous engagement of reverse and one of the forward gears will lock the shafts. Flatten the lockwashers and remove the nuts from both shafts. These washers must be renewed upon reassembly. On later boxes the two nuts are dispensed with, and the shaft assemblies are held together instead by circlips which can be left in place at this stage.

2 Remove the nuts securing the gear carrier or housing 6, noting the positions of the earthing strap and throttle cable guide. Turn the transmission so that the lefthand side plate is on top.

3 With great care, remove the side plate, keeping it square all the way. Use a soft-faced hammer if force is needed. Use a wooden block to drive out the differential assembly and housing 38 from the opposite side. **Keep the bearing shims 37 together in sets so that they can be replaced correctly upon reassembly.** On the 1302/3 type unit, remove the sealing cap from the drive flange centre by prising it out with a screwdriver: discard the cap and fit a new one on reassembly. Remove the circlip round the splines and lever the flange off. Take out the spacer ring behind the flange. Then remove the side cover, keeping any shims together for correct replacement. Note that on some of the latest units only the left side cover is removeable, the other side being integral with the casing.

4 Remove the circlip to the rear of the reverse gear coupling 18, pull the gear back and unscrew the rear drive shaft 24. Withdraw the shaft to the rear, taking care that the splines do not damage the oil seal just in front of release bearing 23. Remove the remaining side plate.

5 Round pinion 17 will be seen four bolts which retain the pinion bearing 16. Prise up the locking tabs and unscrew these bolts. Later boxes have a castellated locking ring to retain the bearing. Mark its position for refitting, loosen it by careful use of a hammer and drift (or special spanner if available) and unscrew it from the casing. Using a lever and wooden blocks, press the pinion to the front so that the transmission

is pushed out of the casing. **Make a very careful note of the shims under bearing retainer 14.**

6 Remove the circlip and reverse drive gear 32 from shaft 31. Prise out the key and tap the shaft out from the rear. The shaft runs in needle roller bearings and these can be drifted out after removing a setscrew which locates the spacer between them. Remove the setscrew retaining the needle roller bearing for the main drive shaft 12 and drift out the bearing. Remove the clutch release bearing 23 and shaft 22.

7 Remove reverse shifter fork 28 and gear 30. Use soft jaws to clamp housing 6 in a vice. Loosen the clamp screws of the selector forks **after marking or taking measurements** to ensure that they can be replaced in their original positions. Remove first- and second-speed selector fork from gear 11. Withdraw the selector shaft 25 for third- and fourth-speed gears out of the selector fork.

8 Fit a strong rubber band round the first-speed gears 13 to keep the shafts together and press out the shafts from the front end. This must be done simultaneously so that the drive pinion cannot tilt and damage the needle roller bearing at the front end of the pinion shaft. This bearing can be pressed out after removing the long setscrew shown in the illustration. The main drive shaft ballbearing can be pressed out from the rear.

9 Remove the screw from the reverse lever guide 40, withdraw the reverse selector shaft and remove the lever guide. Withdraw the selector shaft for first- and second-speed gears and remove the reverse lever from its support. Remove the selector shaft for third- and fourth-speed gears. Take out the interlock plungers and balls and remove the plugs from the outside of the housing adjacent to the selector rod holes. Lift out the springs with a thin screwdriver. See **FIG 6:4** for a similar assembly.

The free length of new detent springs is 1 inch with a wear limit length of .9 inch. In cases of difficulty with gear changing, check the force required to move the selector rod shafts with the pinion and main drive shafts removed. It should need 33 to 44 lb effort to overcome the detent balls and springs.

Dismantling main drive shaft:

This is the assembly on shaft 12 in **FIG 6:1**. Proceed as follows:

1 In the case of a later box where no nut has been removed from the end of the shaft, the circlip must now be taken off. The circlip retains a concave spring thrust washer under pressure, so take care on removing it. If the shaft had a nut fitted, proceed with the next stage.

2 Remove the thrust washer and fourth-speed gear 4, the needle bearing and stop ring 5. Press the bearing race and assembly 7 off the shaft and remove the needle bearing and third-speed gear 8.

3 The synchromesh assembly can be dismantled by prising out the spring rings and removing the three small blockers, making note of the shape of the latter for correct reassembly.

After cleaning the parts, check for wear. Put the shaft between centres and check the runout of the bearing surface for the third-speed gear. It should not exceed .0006 inch. Check the front section of the shaft for wear and check the reverse gear splines. Check the needle bearings and surfaces. Clean the internal cones of the stop rings with a wire brush. Renew the gears if worn, but only in pairs with the mating gear on the pinion shaft. As the first- and second-speed gears are solid with the shaft, worn teeth imply renewal of the shaft. In this case it is not necessary to renew the mating gears on the pinion shaft as well.

Check the clearance between the stop ring face and the small teeth on each gear with a feeler gauge as shown at **A** in **FIG 6:5**. Normally it should be .043 inch with a wear limit of .024 inch. If worn near to the wear limit renew the stop rings. Abnormal wear of the stop rings may be due to a worn clutch or incorrect operation of the clutch. Wear of the stop ring slots causes misalignment of the stop ring teeth with the splines of the operating sleeve of assembly 7. This condition makes it difficult to engage a gear even though the clutch is fully depressed.

While checking the front shaft it is a good plan to check the rear shaft 24 as well, first trying the pilot at the extreme rear end for fit in the gland nut bearing in the flywheel. Check the splines for wear and the working surface for the rear oil seal for pitting and scoring. Check the reverse gear and renew if worn.

Reassembling main drive shaft:

1 Assemble the synchromesh unit, noting that the sleeve which engages the selector fork is paired with its hub and these must be renewed together. The 1 mm groove in the sleeve must face towards the fourth-speed gear on assembly and the hub has a chamfer on the third-speed gear side to help when pressing it onto the shaft. Note in **FIG 6:5** that there is an etched line to assist in the correct assembly of the sleeve and hub. The marks must be in-line.

2 Fit the three shifting or blocker plates in their slots and install the spring rings with ends offset to each other. Check that the rings engage properly behind the blocker plates.

3 Fit the Woodruff key in the shaft and put the stop ring for the third-speed gear into place. Press the synchronizing hub and sleeve into position on the shaft, lifting the third-speed gear slightly and turning it until the slots in the stop ring engage the three blocker plates. Some synchromesh assemblies are stamped with the numeral 4 which should face the fourth-speed gear. Press the inner race for the front needle bearing onto the shaft, then fit the bearing, the stop ring and the gear 4. Renew the thrust washer if it is worn or scored.

Dismantling pinion shaft:

Before starting work on the shaft, remember that renewal of the shaft or the double-row ballbearing (or taper roller bearing) will call for readjustment of the final drive gears by a VW Service Station. Proceed to dismantle as follows:

1 At the front end, remove the circlip if fitted, remembering that it is under pressure, then press the shaft out of the inner race of the needle bearing and the fourth-speed gear 4 (lower). Prise out the Woodruff key. Take off the spacer sleeve, the concave washer shims and the concave washer which precedes the third-speed gear 8 (lower). Remove the gear and second-speed

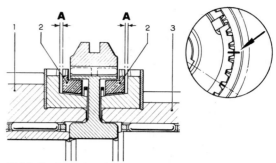

FIG 6:5 Stop ring clearance on synchronizing assembly is measured at **A**. Inset shows marks on sleeve and hub correctly aligned (main drive shaft)

Key to Fig 6:5   1 4th speed gear   2 Synchronizer stop rings 3 3rd speed gear   Clearance at **A** not less than .024 inch

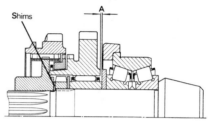

FIG 6:6 First gear end float is measured at **A**. Shims are used to obtain required end float of .004 to .010 inch

gear 9 (lower), the needle bearing cage and the synchronizer stop ring.

2 Remove the clutch gear assembly 11 complete with spring rings, shifting or blocker plates and sliding gear. Dismantle by prising out the spring rings, noting the correct way round for the shifting plates to ensure correct reassembly. Remove the stop ring, the first-speed gear 13 (lower) and the shims controlling first gear end float.

3 Hold the pinion by soft jaws in a vice and unscrew the round nut from the shaft, removing any burrs from the side faces of the nut afterwards. Remove the needle rollers, thrust washers and bearing inner race by pressing off the double-row ball or taper roller bearing. Note, in the case of the taper roller bearing that there are two types in use. One has a spacer ring between the two inner races. The other type has inner races which touch each other. See **FIG 6:6** for a typical assembly. Clean and inspect all the parts.

If the drive pinion is worn or damaged, a matched pair of pinion and crownwheel gears must be fitted and correctly meshed by a VW Service Station. This must also be done if the double-row bearing is renewed. Worn third- or fourth-speed gears must be renewed in pairs with the mating gear on the main drive shaft. First- and second-speed gears are renewed in pairs, but only if the teeth are damaged.

Refer to the preceding section on dismantling the main drive shaft for details of the manner of checking the clearance of the stop rings according to **FIG 6:5**. The same clearance is required and the same comments about premature wear also apply. Check all thrust washers and shims and renew if obviously worn.

Reassembling the pinion shaft:

If facilities do not exist for checking the torque required to turn the taper roller bearing type of pinion shaft when it is installed, the assembling must be entrusted to a VW Service Station. This torque must lie within a certain range and can only be corrected by renewal of the large bearing, the pinion or the housing.

1 Heat the inner races of the pinion bearing and the needle bearing in an oil bath to 100°C (212°F). Fit the first inner race, install the bearing and press the second inner race into position. When dealing with earlier ballbearing types, fit the inner races so that the numbers stamped on one face of a ring are in-line with those on the second ring.

2 Fit the thrust washer and inner race of the needle bearing. Cool the pinion to room temperature in paraffin and press the parts fully home in a powerful press. Fit the needle bearing and thrust washer and tighten the round nut to a torque of 90 lb ft for ballbearing types and to 108 to 144 lb ft for taper roller bearing types.

3 If the pinion shaft is fitted with taper roller bearings, install the pinion in the housing and tighten the bolts of retainer 14 to a torque of 36 lb ft. Turn the pinion 15 to 20 revolutions in each direction and then use a gauge to record the torque while turning steadily. With new bearings the torque should be 5 to 18 lb in. After vehicles have covered at least 300 miles the torque should be 1.7 to 6.1 lb in. **Never run the pinion if the gauge shows no torque or if there is end float in the bearing.**

4 Refer to **FIG 6 : 6** and fit the shims for first-speed gear. Fit the bearing retainer and the first-speed gear and the hub of synchromesh assembly 11. Check the end float between the first-speed gear and the thrust washer at **A**. It should lie between .004 and .010 inch. Correct by using suitable shims which are available in five thicknesses. Fit the first-speed stop ring. This differs from the second-speed stop ring by having smaller recesses for the shifting or blocker plates and a larger number of oil scraper grooves.

5 Assemble the synchromesh assembly 11. Slide the outer sleeve and gear over the hub so that the slots for the shifting plates are in-line. The longer boss of the hub must face away from the pinion as shown in the illustration. Fit the shifting plates and spring rings. The rings should be offset to each other so that their ends do not coincide and they must be properly engaged behind the steps on the shifting plates or blockers. Slide the assembly onto the shaft and turn the first-speed stop ring until the shifting plates engage in the slots.

6 Continue the assembling by fitting the second-speed gear, the needle roller bearing and the third-speed gear. The hubs of the synchromesh assembly and of the third-speed gear must not be tight on the shaft, so test by hand for backlash or free movement. This backlash of not less than .002 inch is controlled by a concave washer which is fitted in front of the third-speed gear and which exerts a pressure on the gear and hub to prevent vibration in the drive. It is fitted to newer pinion shafts and checking instructions are given in Operation 7. The pressure should be about 220 lb. If the hub and gear are tight on the shaft or the concave washer presses too heavily on them the transmission may be noisy. Conversely, if the washer is not tight enough, second gear may tend to jump out. Special devices are needed to find the thickness of shims required to give the desired result and this is part of the VW Service Station equipment. The principle is readily understood if it is realised that the fourth-speed gear 4 (lower) is pressed on to the pinion shaft against a shoulder and it also presses on the tubular spacer to the rear, between the fourth and third-speed gears. The spacer does not fill the gap because it must also accommodate the concave washer and the shims. The concave washer is always .041 inch thick and its action as a spring must be restricted to .007 inch. The length of the spacer is measured accurately and subtracted from the distance between the shoulder on the pinion shaft and the front face of the third-speed gear. If this difference is .08 inch and the combined thickness of the concave washer and its prescribed spring travel is .048 inch, the space to be filled by shims is .08—.048 inch= .032 inch. Nine thicknesses of shim are available and the nearest to the figure is selected.

7 The concave washer follows the third-speed gear, backed up by the shims and the spacer. Heat the fourth gear and the front needle roller bearing inner race to 90°C (194°F), and after fitting the key in the shaft the parts are pressed home. Follow the inner race with the circlip if the shaft has no thread for a nut at the end. The wider shoulder on the gear should abut the spacer. Older transmissions had a gear which was stamped or marked in black and the mark should face to the front. **Note that the concave washer can only be installed on newer pinion shafts.** Check by measuring the distance from the second shoulder on the pinion shaft (the one which locates the rear face of the fourth-speed gear) to the front face of the pinion. This distance is 164.5—1.0 mm for early shafts and 165.9—.4 mm for later shafts (or 6.476—.039 inch and 5.531—.016 inch).

Servicing the differential assembly:

Before tackling this operation, note that renewal of the differential cage or housing, or of the crownwheel, means that the meshing of the drive gears must be readjusted by a VW Service Station. The renewal of worn parts must therefore be confined to the differential gears and shaft. It can be seen in **FIG 6 : 1** that there is a locking pin through the shaft in the upper view of pinions 20. Remove any peening round this pin and drive it out. The shaft can then be drifted out and the differential pinions removed. Check the teeth and the spherical bearing surfaces at the back of the pinions, and inside the housing, for wear and renew the shaft if it is shouldered. The crownwheel can be removed, if necessary, bearing in mind that renewal will also mean renewal of a matched drive pinion and readjustment of the meshing. The wired bolts on later transmissions are also fitted with spring washers on some models. If spring washers are fitted to a housing without machined recesses to accommodate them, check that the bolt heads do not foul the casing. Before refitting the crownwheel remove all dirt and burrs from the mating surfaces. Tighten the bolts to a torque of 43 lb ft and wire the heads so that any tendency to unscrew will tighten the wire. Generally speaking it is preferable to replace the

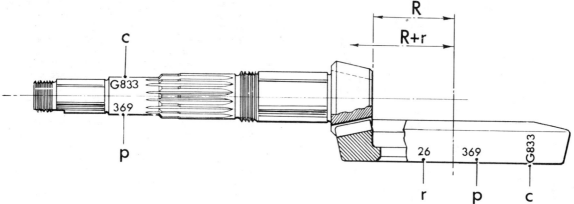

FIG 6:7 Pinion and crownwheel markings as guide to correct meshing

Key to Fig 6:7   **R** Standard dimension from crownwheel centre line to drive pinion face   **r** Deviation from **R** in hundredths of a millimetre   **p** Matching number of gear set   **c** Type of teeth (G Gleason, K Klingelnberg) and number of teeth 8 to 33

wired bolts with the later self-locking bolts with integral washer.

When reassembling the differential gears, peen round the hole after the locking pin for the shaft has been driven home.

Adjustment of drive pinion and crownwheel:

These are produced in matched pairs and cannot be renewed singly. To ensure silent running and correct tooth contact, the pinion must be adjusted endwise, and the crownwheel given a backlash of .0067 to .0098 inch. **FIG 6:7** shows the markings given on each pair of gears but note that markings have also been given on the face of the pinion instead of on the shaft. The gear sets are made either by Gleason or Klingelnberg and identified by **G** or **K**. The deviation from **R** is given as **r** and stamped on the pinion face as well as the crownwheel. The figure represents hundredths of a millimetre, and is added to **R** to give the correct endwise position of the pinion with respect to the centre line of the differential assembly.

Normally it is only necessary to readjust the meshing of the pinion and crownwheel if parts have been renewed which affect the position of the two gears. If the differential housing, side covers or differential bearings are renewed it is only necessary to reset the position of the crownwheel. Both gears must be reset if the transmission casing, the two gears or the rear bearing on the pinion shaft have been renewed.

Referring to **FIG 6:1** it can be seen that adjustment to the thickness of shims 15 will enable the dimension **R + r** to be determined. Then the ring gear is adjusted to give the required backlash by altering the thickness of shims 37. It must be remembered however, that the side covers 33 are fitted in such a way that they preload the side ball bearings by .0028 inch on each side, so that shims to that thickness must be added at each end of the differential housing.

VW Service Stations use a number of specialized jigs and precision measuring devices when carrying out the meshing of the gears and it is not an operation which can be lightly undertaken by the normal owner. It is therefore recommended that the adjustment is entrusted to them.

Renewing the main drive shaft oil seal:

This is the seal at the rear end of the drive shaft 24, just in front of the clutch release bearing. This can be renewed with the transmission installed in the vehicle. To remove the old seal, remove the engine and the clutch release bearing 23. Prise out the seal, taking care not to damage the transmission casing. To fit the new seal, lightly coat the fitting surface with sealing compound and oil the shaft and the sealing lip. Slide the seal into place, being careful not to damage the lip on the splines nor to displace the spring surrounding the lip. Keep the seal square and drive it home with a tubular drift.

Reassembling the transmission:

Being satisfied that all worn parts have been renewed and that the clearance between the selector forks and the operating sleeves does not exceed .004 to .012 inch, oil the parts well and proceed as follows:

1 Refer to **FIG 6:1** and fit the selector rod detent springs into the three outside holes in gear carrier or housing 6. Fit new plugs to close the holes. Fit a detent ball and insert the reverse selector rod complete with reverse lever 27 and guide 40. The ball can be pressed down as the rod is inserted.

2 Perform the same operation with the two remaining selector rods, remembering that there are two inter-lock plungers to be introduced into the drillings between the three selector rod holes. There will then be a plunger between each outside rod and the centre one. Engaging a gear by moving either of the outside rods should lock the centre one. Engaging a gear by moving the centre rod should lock both the outside rods. The principle can be understood by referring to **FIG 6:4**.

3 Fit the bearings for the two shafts, locking the needle bearing outer race with the long setscrew. Prepare to fit the two shafts by fitting a strong rubber band round the small gear 13 (upper) at the rear of the main drive shaft and the large gear 13 (lower). Press the gear carrier bearings on to the shafts after placing selector fork 26 into the sleeve for assembly 7. When pressing, lift the drive pinion slightly, make sure the selector fork 26 is fitted to the selector rod and

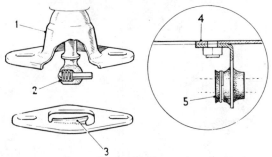

FIG 6:8 Details of gearlever mounting. Inset shows bush in tunnel for shift rod

Key to Fig 6:8   1 Gearlever cover   2 Peening to retain locating pin   3 Lever stop plate with turned-up edge   4 Tunnel   5 Shift rod bush

see that the fork does not jam on the shaft. On the late pattern assembly without nuts, fit the concave thrust washer and circlip to the end of the main shaft when the two shafts have been fitted into the carrier. Drive the circlip into place using a suitable piece of tube or a socket as a drift.

4 Install the selector fork to engage in assembly 11. Fit the reverse sliding gear 30 with fork 28 and attach to reverse lever 27. If no parts have been renewed which will affect the position of the selector forks, restore them to the marks or recorded measurements made during dismantling and tighten the clamping screws to a torque of 18 lb ft. Tighten the reverse lever guide screw to 14 lb ft. **If the selector forks**

must be reset, the adjustment can only be done in a special jig which simulates the assembly in the transmission casing. This is used in VW Service Stations and is the only satisfactory way of positioning the selector forks correctly. It is suggested that if an old transmission casing is available it is possible to cut holes to see what is happening when the gears are selected and to reach the fork clamping screws. It is important to adjust the forks only after the drive pinion has been correctly adjusted for mesh with the crownwheel and after tightening the shaft nuts at the front end to the correct torque values. Tighten first to 87 lb ft, slacken off and then retighten to 43 lb ft. Always fit new lockplates.

5 Before fitting the completed assembly into the main transmission casing, check the starter motor bush for wear. Also check the bushes and shaft for the clutch release mechanism. Note that reverse drive gear 18 must not be too loose on the splines or vibration of the main drive shaft may cause trouble with a worn oil seal, lost lubricant and a slipping clutch. If a new transmission casing is fitted it will be necessary to readjust the meshing of the crownwheel and pinion. A new side cover 33 means the resetting of the crownwheel only.

6 Insert the needle bearings and spacer for reverse shaft 31, locking the spacer with the shouldered setscrew. Fit the main drive shaft needle bearing and secure. Fit the reverse gear shaft 31, with the thrust washer. At the rear, fit the Woodruff key and reverse drive gear 32. Check that the circlip has not been strained and fit it.

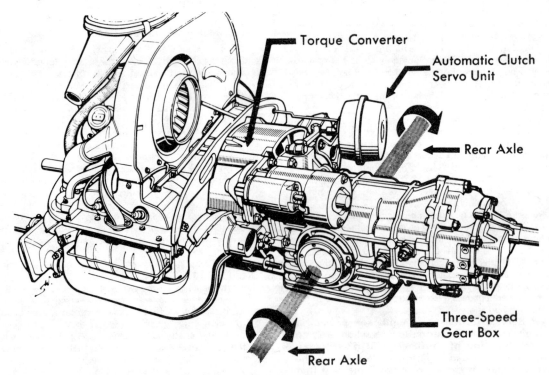

FIG 6:9 View of automatic transmission showing torque converter and gearbox

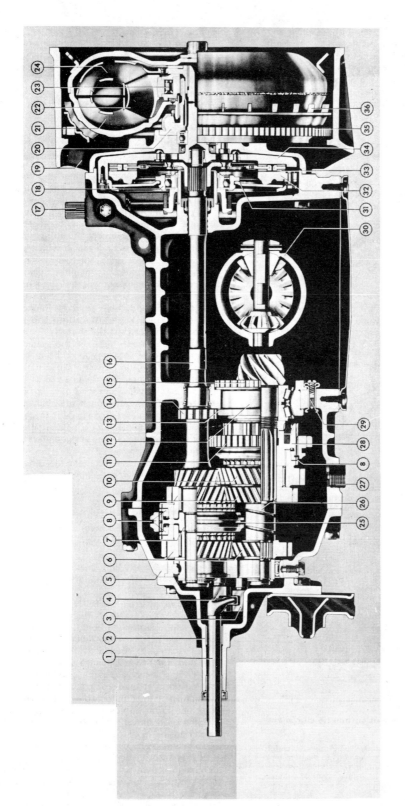

FIG 6:10 Sectional view showing main components of automatic transmission

Key to Fig 6:10 1 Inner shift lever   2 Gearshift housing   3 Shift rod for drive ranges **L** and **R**   4 Shift rod for drive ranges 1 and 2   5 Gear carrier   6 Gears for drive range 2   7 Synchronizer hub   8 Synchronizer ring   9 Gears for drive range 1   10 Gears for drive range **L**   11 Operating sleeve for drive ranges **L** and **R** with gear for drive range **F**   12 Double taper roller bearing   13 Shim for pinion   14 Gear for drive range **R**   15 Retaining ring   16 Drive shaft   17 Clutch release shaft   18 Release bearing   19 Converter housing   20 One-way clutch support   21 Impeller   22 Stator   23 One-way clutch   24 Turbine   25 Operating sleeve for drive ranges 1 and 2   26 Spacer spring   27 Magnetic drain plug   28 Synchronizer hub   29 Retaining ring   30 Differential   31 Diaphragm spring   32 Pressure plate   33 Clutch plate   34 Clutch plate carrier   35 Starter ring   36 Cooling air blades

7 Set the pinion shaft with the pinion uppermost and fit the shims 15. Fit two temporary studs about 4 inches long in opposite holes in the bearing retainer 14 to act as guides. Fit a new gasket to the gear carrier and insert the gear assembly into the transmission casing whilst engaging the reverse gear with its shaft. Use a rubber hammer to make sure that the drive

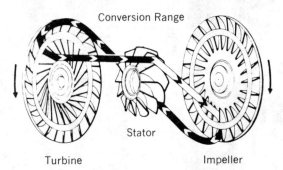

Conversion Range

Turbine   Stator   Impeller

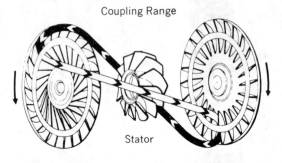

Coupling Range

Turbine   Stator   Impeller

FIG 6:11 The path of fluid in the torque converter is shown by arrows. The upper view illustrates the Conversion Range, during this stage the stator is locked to the shaft and engine torque is being multiplied. The lower view shows the Coupling Range, the stator freewheels and the torque converter acts as a fluid coupling

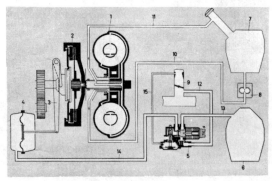

FIG 6:12 Diagrammatic view of automatic clutch and torque converter

Key to Fig 6:12   1 Torque converter   2 Automatic clutch   3 Clutch lever   4 Servo   5 Control valve   6 Vacuum tank   7 Oil tank   8 Oil pump   9 Carburetter   10 Converter pressure line   11 Return line   12 Intake manifold vacuum line   13 Vacuum reservoir vacuum line   14 Servo vacuum line   15 Air filter vacuum line

pinion is fully home, remove the two temporary studs and tighten the bearing retainer setscrews on new lockplates to a torque of 36 lb ft. Alternatively, screw in the castellated locking ring (fitted to later boxes) and tighten it until the marks made before dismantling line up. On later models there is an extended selector rod which may not move freely because of an adjacent retainer setscrew. Turn the screw until there is clearance but do not exceed the stipulated torque figure and check the rod for freedom. Use only setscrews of 10K grade.

8 Oil the rear seal and fit the rear half of the main drive shaft. Screw the shafts together and then back off until the splines are in-line. **The shafts must not be screwed tightly together.** Slide reverse gear 18 into place and fit the circlip, making sure that it is not strained as it must fit securely in its groove.

9 Fit the differential assembly, the righthand cover 33 is fitted first. The covers are sealed with a paper gasket on swing-axle type units. The thickness of this gasket will affect the preload on the differential bearings and the position of the crownwheel so use a genuine spare part. On the 1302/3 type the side cover has an O-ring seal and is fitted without a gasket. Renew the O-ring if it is damaged. **When installing the differential assembly make certain that the correct shims are fitted to each side.** Fit the second cover and tighten the nuts to a torque of 22 lb ft. Check the tightness after a run of 300 miles in case of settling. Tighten the gear carrier nuts to 14 lb ft.

10 Engage both reverse and third or fourth gears to lock the transmission and tighten the shaft nuts if fitted. Use new lockplates, tighten to 87 lb ft, slacken off and retighten to 43 lb ft. Turn up locking tabs.

11 Set the three selector rods in the neutral position and fit the gearshift housing 3.

12 On the 1302/3 type unit, refit the drive flanges by reversing the removal procedure. Fit new centre sealing caps.

6:5 Gearlever and control rod

Removing and refitting lever:

On all models except Karmann Ghia proceed as follows:

1 Remove the front floor mat and then the screws retaining the gearlever cover to the tunnel. Lift out the lever assembly.

2 Turn the spring to remove it clear of the pin. This spring-loaded pin can be seen in **FIG 6:8**.

3 Remove the stop plate from the tunnel and clean all components. Renew the rubber boot if deteriorated. Check the spring-loaded pin for free movement. The ball end of the lever is peened over to retain the pin.

To refit the gearlever, first grease all the working parts. Fit the diamond-shaped stop plate to the tunnel with the turned-up lip on the righthand side. Fit the lever assembly so that the pin at the lower end engages in the slot in the shifting rod socket inside the tunnel. The flanges of the ball housing must then fit over the stop plate. Fit the retaining screws and tighten when the lower part of the gearlever is vertical when in neutral. Difficulty in selecting gears may be cured by moving the ball housing slightly and it may be necessary to enlarge the slotted holes slightly.

Removing and refitting shift rod:

1 Remove gearlever. Remove rear seat and inspection cover on the tunnel over the rod coupling. Cut the locking wire and release the front screw in the coupling. Remove the bumper and cover.

2 Use a pair of pliers through the rear inspection hole to push the rod forward out of the coupling so that it can be withdrawn from the front. There is a plastic bush for the shift rod inside the tunnel behind the gearlever opening, as shown by the inset in **FIG 6:8**. If this is worn, turn it so that the long slot faces down. Pass a wire loop through the slot next to the long slot and pull out the bush. A later type of bush is fitted with a wire ring and this helps to eliminate shift rod noise. Fit this with the ring forward and press the bush home in its bracket. Lubricate with universal grease.

3 Check the shift rod for wear and misalignment. Coat it with grease and insert from the front, into the guide bush. Pass it back until it can be inserted in the coupling and the coupling screw tightened. Lock the screw with wire after gear selecting has been found satisfactory.

Gearlever on Karmann Ghias:

To dismantle the cover and remove the switch on later models, disconnect the battery earthing strap. Remove the foot-rest. Remove as much tunnel covering as required and disconnect the three cables from the lock at the front. At the rear, remove the securing screw and push the lock upper part forward and lift off. Remove the switch. When refitting the parts make sure the cables are correctly connected.

6:6 Automatic transmission

Description:

This was introduced in 1967 as an optional extra on all models, including the '1200' Beetle when fitted with the 1285 cc engine. The automatic transmission consists of three basic units, namely a torque converter, a servo operated clutch and a threespeed gearbox. **FIG 6:9** shows the general layout of the automatic transmission. When the vehicle moves off from rest, the converter multiplies the engine torque by 2:1 and as the speed differential between the impeller and turbine decreases, the torque multiplication also decreases until the turbine is transmitting the same torque as the engine.

The three element torque converter or fluid coupling, consists of an impeller, a stator and a turbine. The impeller blades 21 (see **FIG 6:10**) are fixed to the inside of the converter housing which is attached to the crankshaft. Rotation of the impeller causes fluid to flow into the turbine 24, this causes the turbine and the clutch carrier plate to which it is attached, to rotate. The fluid impinges off the turbine blades at such an angle as to pass through the stator 22, which is mounted on a one-way clutch. The blades of the stator are angled so as to assist rotation of the impeller. This stage is referred to as the Conversion Range and is shown diagramatically in the upper view of **FIG 6:11**. When the coupling point is reached, that is when the turbine is rotating at approximately 86 per cent of the impeller speed, the converter ceases to multiply engine torque and acts merely as a fluid coupling. At this stage the direction of fluid flow from the turbine to the impeller has changed, as shown by the black arrows in

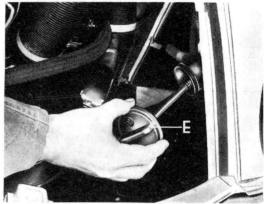

FIG 6:13 Filler cap and dipstick for automatic transmission fluid reservoir

FIG 6:14 Oil filler plug **A** and magnetic drain plug **C** in transmission housing. The lower cover is shown at **D**

the lower view of **FIG 6:11** and the stator freewheels on a one-way clutch 23 in **FIG 6:10**.

The torque converter has a separate oil supply reservoir 7 (see **FIG 6:12**) and oil pump 8 which circulates the automatic transmission fluid to the torque converter via pressure line 10. The oil then returns to the reservoir via pipeline 11.

A red warning light on the lefthand side of the speedometer indicates if the torque converter is overheating. There are two thermostats in the torque converter housing, one operates at 125°C and the other at 140°C. If the lamp lights up, a lower gear should be selected. This lessens the load on the torque converter and turns the converter housing faster, thus assisting cooling. If the lamp lights again it will be necessary to select low gear. External cooling fins are mounted on the outside of the converter housing to assist cooling of the automatic transmission fluid.

The clutch is similar to the automatic clutch described in **Chapter 5,** but without the centrifugal rollers. Movement of the gearshift lever closes a switch at the base of the lever. Current passes to a solenoid which actuates control valve 5 shown in **FIG 6:12**. This connects a vacuum servo unit to the engine intake manifold via vacuum line 12. A diaphragm in the servo unit deflects and disengages the clutch via a pushrod and lever 3. The transmission is thus disengaged from the converter and further movement of the gearshift lever enables the required gear to be selected.

Another vacuum pipe 15 connects the control valve to the carburetter air filter. The depression in the filter varies according to engine load, this variation modulates the speed of operation of control valve 5 causing the clutch to close quickly during rapid acceleration and more slowly for lighter engine loads. The initial movement of the clutch is rapid, regardless of engine load, until the clutch is about to re-engage.

A further vacuum pipe 13 connects the control valve to a vacuum reservoir 6 which provides vacuum for five to six gearchanges independent of the degree of vacuum in the inlet manifold.

Torque is transmitted to the gearbox from the clutch via drive shaft 16 (see **FIG 6 : 10**) and then through the selected gear train to the differential 30.

The gearbox is a completely new threespeed transmission but has a similar layout to that of the fourspeed synchromesh transmission. The three forward gears of the automatic transmission, low, first and second have the same ratios as second, third and top respectively for the 4-synchromesh transmission (see Technical Data).

An 8 amp fuse for the control valve is situated in the engine compartment on the fan housing near the coil.

Vehicles fitted with automatic transmission have semi-trailing arm rear suspensions with double-joint rear axles, this is described in **Chapter 7**.

Maintenance:

The automatic transmission fluid does not need to be changed, but the level should be checked at regular intervals and topped up if necessary using the recommended grade of automatic transmission fluid. The filler cap for the torque converter fluid reservoir is situated on the righthand side of the engine compartment. The filler cap **E** shown in **FIG 6 : 13** incorporates a dipstick. The fluid level should be between the two marks but must never be allowed to drop below the lower mark.

The transmission and final drive are lubricated with hypoid oil. Periodically the oil level should be checked. If necessary the gearbox should be topped up to the edge of the filler hole **A** shown in **FIG 6 : 14**. Every 30,000 miles the oil should be drained when warm by removing the magnetic drain plug **C**. The plug should be cleaned carefully. Remove the transmission bottom cover **D** after unscrewing fourteen screws. Clean the cover thoroughly

and refit using a new gasket. Tighten the screws uniformly with a torque of 7 lb ft. Fill the transmission with 5.3 pints of the recommended grade of hypoid oil.

The control valve filter should be removed and cleaned at intervals of 6000 miles. Clean the contacts at the base of the gearshift lever or renew if badly burnt or pitted.

6 : 7 Fault diagnosis

(a) Difficulty in changing gear

1 Bent or worn gearshift mechanism
2 Faulty synchronizing mechanism
3 Faulty clutch or release bearing
4 Clutch cable maladjusted

(b) Crashing of gears when changing down

1 Check 2, 3 and 4 in (a)
2 Wrongly placed or broken synchromesh spring rings
3 Transmission oil too thick

(c) Slipping out of first and second gears

1 Weak or broken selector rod detent springs
2 Worn gear on pinion shaft
3 Excessive end float of pinion shaft gears
4 Worn bearings
5 Selector fork wrongly positioned
6 Gearshift mechanism worn

(d) Slipping out of third or fourth gears

1 Check 1, 4, 5 and 6 in (c)
2 Worn teeth on synchromesh sleeve
3 Excessive end float of main drive shaft gears

(e) Gearbox noisy in neutral

1 Worn bearings and bushes
2 Excessive end float of main drive shaft
3 Incorrect or insufficient lubricant

(f) Gearbox noisy in forward gears

1 Worn drive and pinion shaft bearings
2 Worn reverse idler or constant mesh gears
3 Incorrect or insufficient lubricant

(g) Oil leaks

1 Damaged or worn rear oil seal, scored shaft
2 Damaged joint washers or joint faces
3 Worn gearshift bushes
4 Loose cover nuts

CHAPTER 7

REAR AXLE AND SUSPENSION

7:1 Description

To divide the transmission and rear axle system into two reasonably logical sections it has been decided to treat the gearbox and final drive gears as a unit in **Chapter 6,** and to cover the rear axles, universal joints, rear hubs and the suspension layout in this Chapter.

The plan view in **FIG 7:1** shows how the rear axles and suspension components are arranged in vehicles with manual gearboxes. The two axle shafts run inside axle tubes 1, the outer ends of the shafts being supported by ballbearings. The splined ends of the shafts carry integral hubs and brake drums. The inner ends of the shafts are flat and slide in slots in fulcrum blocks. Each fulcrum block is mounted in a spherical seating in the differential side gears, this allows the shafts to swing relative to the side gears and still continue to drive the rear wheels as they move up and down due to road undulations. The outer ends of the shaft tubes are constrained to move in an arc by radius arms or spring plates 2. The forward end of each radius arm is mounted on the outer end of a torsion bar by means of serrations. The inner ends of each of the two torsion bars are also serrated and locate in an anchor block in the chassis.

Each rear wheel bearing housing is attached to the lower end of a telescopic damper 7. The upper end of each damper is connected to brackets bolted to the body. The inner ends of the axle tubes 1 can move inside hemispherical housings about an arc centred on each fulcrum block. Dirt is excluded by rubber dust sleeves 4.

An equalizer or compensating spring is also fitted as shown in **FIG 7:2**. This consists of a third torsion bar 44 mounted transversely above the rear axle. The ends of the torsion bar are mounted in rubber-bushed brackets 45 and 46 bolted to reinforced side panels. A lever 57 or 62 at one end of the bar points to the front of the vehicle and another at the opposite end points to the rear. These levers are connected by rods 51 or 52 to brackets 61 on the rear axle tube as shown in **FIG 7:11**. The connecting rods are mounted on the torsion bar levers by rubber bushes. The purpose of the compensating spring is to improve the rear suspension when the vehicle is fully laden. The rubber buffers 41 or 42 on the connecting rods bottom on the lower brackets and the transverse torsion bar stiffens the normal springing. The compensating spring does not operate when cornering or in the lightly laden condition.

For 1302 and 1303 models and all vehicles fitted with automatic transmission, the rear suspension is modified: the drive shafts are double-jointed and the rear wheels are located by additional diagonal arms, as shown in **FIG**

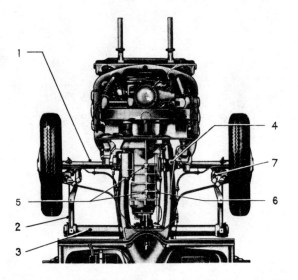

FIG 7:1 Plan view of the rear axle and suspension layout

Key to Fig 7:1 1 Axle tube 2 Radius arm (spring plate) 3 Torsion bar housing 4 Dust sleeve 5 Transmission drain plugs 6 Level plug 7 Telescopic damper

7:12. The compensating spring is deleted. This layout gives less change of rear wheel camber angle with suspension movement and so provides improved road-holding. Each drive shaft has two constant velocity joints, splined to permit axial movement and permanently lubricated like the roller and ball bearing in each hub unit. The differential and its casing are also modified.

7:2 Routine maintenance

The working parts of the rear axle on cars with manual gearboxes are lubricated from the oil supply in the main transmission casing. Drainage and replenishment are covered in **Chapter 6**.

7:3 Removing and servicing axle shafts

Two types of axle shafts (halfshafts) are used in these vehicles; the earlier type, shown in **FIGS 7:2**, **7:3, 7:4** and **7:5**, which are encased in axle tubes, and the later type, shown in **FIG 7:12**. This section details the method employed for servicing the earlier type, whilst **Section 7:10** covers the later type.

Axle shafts can be removed with the transmission in the car providing there is clearance to remove the retainer plate shown detached in **FIG 7:3**. Check this point before going too far, as the alternative is to remove the axles and transmission complete. The wheel bearing needs a special puller which fits between the races, but if the assembly is out of the car, the axle can be pulled off with the bearing in place.

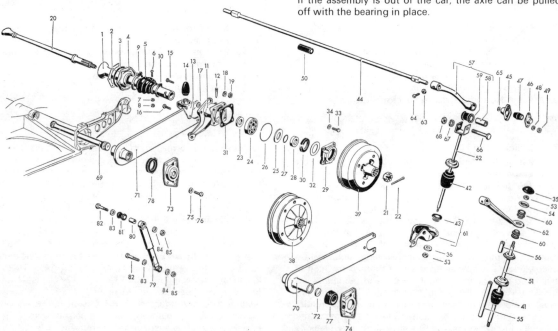

FIG 7:2 Components of rear axle and suspension showing the equalizer or compensating spring

Key to Fig 7:2 1 Axle tube 2 Gasket 3 Plastic insert 4 Axle tube retainer 5 Dust sleeve 6 Screw 7 Washer 8 Nut 9 Clip 10 Circlip 11 Bearing housing 12 Pin 13 Bracket 14 Bump rubber 15 Bolt 16 Bolt 17 Washer 18 Washer 19 Nut 20 Axle shaft 21 Axle nut 22 Splitpin 23 Spacer 24 Bearing 25 Shim 26 Seal 27 Seal 28 Spacer 29 Bearing retainer 30 Oil seal 31 Gasket 32 Oil flinger 33 Bolt 34 Washer 35 Rubber cap 36 Washer 38 Brake drum 39 Brake drum 41 Rubber buffer 42 Rubber buffer 43 Cap 44 Torsion bar 45 Bracket 46 Bracket 47 Bush 48 Washer 49 Nut 50 Sleeve 51 Rod 52 Rod 53 Nut 54 Washer 55 Sleeve 56 Sleeve 57 Lever assembly 58 Sleeve 59 Rubber bush 60 Rubber bush 61 Lower bracket assembly 62 Lever 63 Washer 64 Screw 65 Washer 66 Bolt 67 Washer 68 Nut 69 Torsion bar 70 Spring plate 71 Spring plate 72 Washer 73 Torsion bar cover 74 Torsion bar cover 75 Lockwasher 76 Bolt 77 Rubber bush 78 Rubber bush 79 Damper 80 Sleeve 81 Rubber bush 82 Bolt 83 Washer 84 Washer 85 Nut

If there is clearance for the retainer plate, proceed as follows:

1 Loosen the axle nuts while the car is on the ground. These are so tight that it is dangerous to try to slacken them initially while the car is on jacks or stands. Lift the car and then remove the axle nuts.

2 Pull off the brake drum after releasing the handbrake and slackening off the brake shoes. From the centre of the backplate remove the bearing housing cover (four bolts). Detach the brake pipeline and remove the backplate. Release the lower damper mounting. Refer to **Section 7:4** before releasing the spring radius arm from the housing flange.

3 Pull off the bearing. At the inner end remove the retainer (6 nuts) and pull off the axle tube, retainer, gasket and plastic insert as in **FIG 7:3**. The insert is the part with the radial slots.

4 Remove the circlip and thrust washer from deep inside the transmission case as shown in **FIG 7:4**. Pull out the axle, and if necessary, remove the differential side gear.

7:3 Removing axle tube from final drive casing. Gasket and split plastic insert are clearly shown

Servicing the dust sleeve:

One item which may need replacing is the rubber boot or dust sleeve 5 in **FIG 7:2**. The one-piece sleeve cannot be renewed without removing the bearing housing at the outer end of the axle tube. **This is pinned, and is also a press fit. It may be damaged if suitable equipment is not available.** To avoid the need to carry out such an operation it is possible to cut away the old sleeve and fit a replacement part which is split for easy fitting. This is done as follows:

Remove the clips and cut the defective sleeve to remove it. Clean the axle tube and the retainer. Note that all this may be done without removing the axle tube from the transmission, if necessary.

Use a little jointing compound on the mating faces of the new split sleeve after checking that the large end is the correct size for the retaining plate. The split in the sleeve should be horizontal and face to the rear. Do not tighten the screws or the clips until the axle is in a loaded condition with the vehicle on the ground. See that the sleeve is not twisted or strained and then tighten the screws and clips moderately.

FIG 7:4 Removing circlip and thrust washer from side gear

The axle tubes, shafts and side gears:

Inspect all parts for wear. The spherical surfaces of the transmission casing and the axle tubes must be smooth. Note the spherical plastic inserts which are sandwiched between the metal faces. Assemble the tube and retainer plate and check the end float or clearance. Too great a clearance will result in wear and noise. The latest figures for clearance are a maximum limit of .008 inch with the retainer plate nuts tightened to 14 lb ft. Select gaskets which will give the required clearance. A small hole near one of the stud holes signifies that the gasket is .010 inch thick. A thicker gasket has two holes. If it is necessary to fit the retainer plate without a gasket, jointing compound must be used. The reduction of axle tube end play can be done with the axle in the car.

Check the axle shafts, differential side gears and their thrust washers. The maximum permissible runout of the shaft at the point where the wheel bearing fits, is .002 inch.

FIG 7:5 Measuring clearance between axle shaft and fulcrum plates

FIG 7:6 Bearing cover removed from axle end, showing outer spacer, sealing ring, washer and bearing. Backplate fits on righthand flange

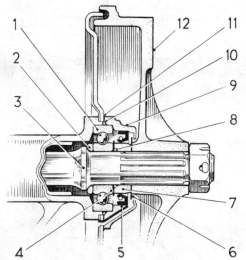

FIG 7:7 Section through rear hub and brake drum

Key to Fig 7:7   1 Ballbearing   2 Inner spacer   3 Axle shaft
4 Washer   5 Oil seal   6 Oil flinger   7 Outer spacer
8 Sealing ring   9 Bearing cover   10 Large sealing ring
11 Gasket   12 Brake drum

The colour groups are graded as follows:

Paint mark	Inner dia. of side gear	Outer dia. of shaft
Yellow	2.3600 to 2.3610 inch	2.3570 to 2.3582 inch
Blue	2.3610 to 2.3622 inch	2.3582 to 2.3598 inch
Pink	2.3625 to 2.3638 inch	2.3602 to 2.3610 inch
Green	2.3641 to 2.3649 inch	2.3614 to 2.3622 inch

Note that excessive clearance at the transmission end of axle shafts may lead to noisy operation.

The wheel bearings and oil seals:

If a suitable bearing puller is available, the wheel bearing can be removed after the brake backplate is taken off, and the axle shaft and tube need not be detached from the transmission. A view of the axle end is given in **FIG 7:6**, but note that the brake backplate and large sealing ring are not shown. **FIG 7:7** shows the large sealing ring 10 and paper gasket 11 which will be found when the bearing cover 9 is removed. After removing the cover and backplate, take off the outer spacer 7, the small sealing ring 8 round the shaft 3, and the washer 4. There is an oil flinger 6 like a large washer on the outside of the outer spacer. Extract the bearing 1 and the inner spacer 2, which is rounded on the inner face to fit the radius on the shaft. The cover has a lug and drilling on the lowest edge, and the gasket has a hole in it. This allows oil which passes the seal 5 to drain away behind the backplate.

Clean and examine the ballbearing when dry, renewing it if worn, or rough when spun. Renew the rubber sealing rings and the gasket. Renew the oil seal if oil leakage has been persistent or the lip is damaged but do not forget to insert the oil flinger washer into the cover first. Check the surface of the outer spacer where it contacts the lip of the seal. Remove scores and rust and polish with very fine emery cloth. Clean out the drain hole in the cover.

Check the splines on the shaft and in the brake drum and renew the parts if the splines are worn and slack. When renewing an oil seal, press it in with the sealing lip facing the bearing.

To reassemble, fit the radiused spacer on the shaft and press in the bearing. Fit the washer and small sealing ring, followed by the outer spacer with its chamfered bore contacting the ring. The bevel on the outer surface then acts as a lead when fitting the cover and oil seal. Oil this surface lightly and carefully fit the backplate and cover on new gaskets. Make sure the drain hole is at the bottom, and tighten the screws to a torque of 40 to 47 lb ft. Fit the drum and tighten the nut moderately. When the vehicle is back on the ground, tighten the nut to 217 lb ft and fit a new splitpin. Do not slacken the nut in an attempt to align the splitpin holes. Check the transmission oil. Bleed and adjust the brakes.

7:4 Removing transmission and rear axle

Two types of axle shafts (halfshafts) are used in these vehicles, depending on the year model. Earlier models have the axle shafts encased in rigid axle tubes while later models (from 1971) may be fitted with double-jointed axle shafts which are not encased in tubes (see **FIG 7:12**).

When working on the earlier type, it will be easier to remove the transmission and rear axle in one, whilst the later version of the axle shafts makes it possible to remove

Small errors may be corrected by straightening the shaft **cold**. At the transmission end, assemble the shaft in a side gear with the fulcrum plates, as shown in **FIG 7:5**. Check the clearance between the flats and the plates with feeler gauges. It should lie between .001 and .010 inch. If the clearance is excessive renew the parts or fit oversize fulcrum plates, which are marked with a groove on the face.

The widest rounded part of the flattened end of each shaft must not have a clearance in the side gear which exceeds .004 inch, with a minimum of .001 inch. On some shafts, one of these spherical surfaces is fitted with a spring-loaded ball which eliminates side clearance.

Shafts and side gears are mated in pairs and colour-coded in three groups, yellow, blue and pink, although there is also a pair coloured green for early models. The gears are marked with a spot in the recess, and the shafts by a painted ring six inches from the flattened end.

the transmission only, leaving the axle shafts, suspension and brake assemblies undisturbed.

Removing the earlier type:

If it is intended to dismantle the axle, loosen the axle shaft outer (brake drum) castellated nuts before the car is lifted on jacks or stands. **The nuts are very tight and the car might be pulled off the jacks if they are not slackened first.**

1 Disconnect the battery earthing strap. Remove the rear wheels. Remove the engine as instructed in **Chapter 1.**

2 Disconnect the rear brake hoses. Release the cables from the handbrake lever, remove the lever and then pull the cables from the guide tubes.

3 Loosen the clips round the axle dust sleeves. Remove the lower damper mounting bolts.

4 Refer to **FIG 7 : 9** and use a cold chisel to make a nick on the spring radius arm in-line with the groove already in the flange of the axle bearing housing. This operation is unnecessary if a complete axle assembly, or a new rubber front mounting, or a new subframe or new radius arm is to be fitted, as the geometry of the rear suspension will then need checking and adjusting. Otherwise the nicks will help to reassemble the parts in their original positions.

5 Disconnect the cable from the clutch operating lever on the transmission case and withdraw the cable and sleeve. Disconnect the cables from starter terminals 30 and 50.

6 Lift the rear seat and remove the inspection cover from the tunnel. Underneath is the gearshift coupling. Cut the locking wire from the rear screw and remove the screw. Move the gearlever until it is possible to withdraw the coupling from the gearshift rod.

7 Refer to the lefthand half of **FIG 7 : 8** and remove the nuts from the front mounting of the transmission. Just take the weight of the transmission on a trolley jack if available and remove the two transmission carrier bolts indicated by arrows in the righthand view.

8 Withdraw the assembly. Take every care not to bend or damage the main drive shaft. A good plan is to drill a hole in a piece of wood to take the tip of the shaft and bolt the wood across the transmission casing flange.

9 Working on the axle parts has been covered in **Section 7 : 3.** If it is intended to substitute an Exchange axle, note that the brake drums and cables remain on the axle, but the brake pipelines and clips on the axle tubes should be removed.

Removing the later type:

1 Remove the engine as detailed in **Chapter 1.**

2 Disconnect the axle shafts from the transmission by removing the socket head screws securing the inner constant velocity joints to the flanges on the sides of the transmission. Use a piece of wire to suspend each axle shaft away from the transmission.

3 Disconnect or remove the components mentioned in steps 5, 6, 7 and 8 covering the earlier type, and remove the transmission.

7 : 5 Installing transmission and axle

1 Lift the assembly into place and fit the two mounting bolts arrowed in **FIG 7 : 8,** after greasing them well. Now loosen the nuts attaching the rear carrier to the

FIG 7 : 8 Releasing transmission front mounting (left). Arrows indicate transmission carrier bolts (right)

FIG 7 : 9 Using chisel to mark radius arm (spring plate) before dismantling

rear rubber mountings. **This sequence must always be followed before the front mounting is secured.**

2 Tighten the nuts of the front mounting plate as shown in **FIG 7 : 8** on the left. Then tighten the rear mountings. This will avoid distortion and premature breakdown of the rubber in the mountings.

3 Restore the gearshift rod coupling under the rear seat. Make sure the pointed end of the securing screw fully engages the recess in the rod and then lock with wire. The correct assembly of the coupling is important because it is possible that a defect at this point could lead to reverse being selected at the same time as second gear, with disastrous results. It might also make it difficult to drop down to first or second gear.

4 Line up the nicks in the spring plates and the axle tube housings (if previously removed). These were made before dismantling as shown in **FIG 7 : 9.** As the holes in the spring plates are slotted, adjustment is possible. Tighten the fixing bolts to a torque of 80 lb ft. Securely tighten the lower bolts for the dampers.

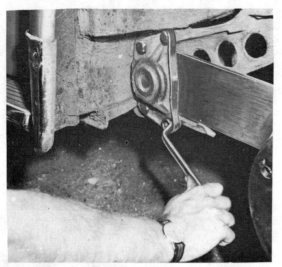

FIG 7:10 Removing torsion bar end cover

FIG 7:11 Connecting rod between axle and equalizer bar. Rod (top arrow), rubber buffer (middle arrow), and nut (bottom arrow)

5 Refit the engine as described in **Chapter 1**. Adjust the clutch pedal free play as instructed in **Chapter 5**. Bleed and adjust the brakes as explained in **Chapter 10**. If slackened, do not tighten the axle shaft outer (brake drum) castellated nuts until the car is standing on the ground. Use a torque figure of 217 lb ft. Tighten the clips of the dust sleeves on the earlier type of axle shafts after the car is on the ground. Make sure the sleeves are not strained or distorted.

6 On later type (double-jointed) axle shafts, refit the shafts to the transmission flanges and tighten the socket head screws to 25 lb ft.

7:6 Removing rear torsion bars

Before starting this operation the owner must realise that renewal of any of the parts of the suspension system or of the frame and transmission mountings means that the rear wheels will need re-alignment. If, however, it is only a matter of renewing a defective torsion bar, it is possible to reset the camber of the wheels by checking the angles of the two spring plates or radius arms which connect the axle tubes to the torsion bars. This check can only be carried out by setting the car so that the body sill is level and by using a spirit-level type of protractor for measuring accurate angles.

To remove a torsion bar proceed as follows:

1 Stand the car on level ground and adjust until the door sill is horizontal on both sides. As the rear wheel(s) must be removed, this implies that the car must be supported on blocks or stands. .

2 Disconnect the handbrake cables from the lever and withdraw them slightly to the rear.

3 With a cold chisel, mark a nick on the spring plate or radius arm in-line with the existing mark on the bearing housing at the outer end of the axle tube as shown in **FIG 7:9**. This will ensure accurate reassembly, because the mounting holes for the arm are slotted.

4 Remove the lower damper mounting bolt. Remove the three bolts securing the spring plate or arm to the bearing housing and pull the axle rearwards until it is clear of the slot in the arm. Remove the torsion bar cover as shown in **FIG 7:10**. Note the rubber bush. Some models have a longer outward extension of the arm at this point, a longer bush and a cover with a large central hole in it. The bush has four ribs on the outer face and is stamped 'OBEN' for top.

5 Pull the spring plate or arm off the torsion bar, levering it away from the stop rib on the mounting bracket. Remove about five of the screws attaching the rear wing(s) at the forward edge. Twist the wing to one side and withdraw the torsion bar. If the bar is broken, the inner part cannot be removed until the opposite torsion bar has been withdrawn and a long bar used to push out the piece.

6 Mark the bar(s) on the end so that it can be replaced on the same side as that from which it was removed. Bars which are stamped **R** for right and **L** for left on the outer end cannot be interchanged. These bars are pre-stressed in manufacture and must be fitted as marked. **It is most important to take the greatest care of torsion bars once they are removed. Do not mark or scratch them in any way or they may fail prematurely.** Make sure the protective paint remains intact as corrosion may also lead to failure. Replace a bar which is rusty or one which has splines with evident signs of wear.

7:7 Installing and setting torsion bars

It will be evident that the unloaded angle of the spring plate or radius arm will affect the camber of the rear wheel. This angle can be measured with an accurate protractor and adjustments made by rotating the torsion bar. The inner end of the bar has 40 splines so that rotation by one spline alters the angle by 9 deg. The outer end has 44 splines so that turning the radius arm in the opposite direction alters its angle by 8 deg. 10 minutes.

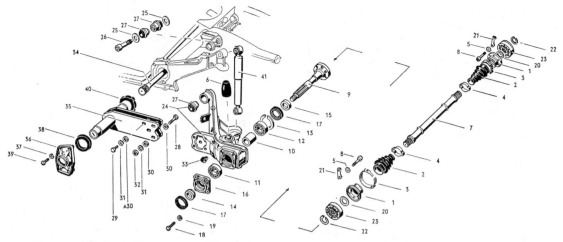

FIG 7:12 Components of double-joint rear axle and suspension used on later cars

Key to Fig 7:12   1 End cap   2 Dust sleeve   3 Clip   4 Clip   5 Washer   6 Bump rubber   7 Drive shaft   8 Bolt
9 Stub shaft   10 Spacer   11 Roller bearing   12 Ballbearing   13 Circlip   14 Sleeve   15 Sleeve   16 Bearing housing
cover   17 Oil seal   18 Bolt   19 Lockwasher   20 Dished washer   21 Tabwasher   22 Circlip   23 Constant velocity
joint   24 Diagonal arm assembly   25 Washer   26 Bolt   27 Rubber bush   28 Bolt   29 Bolt   30 Washer
31 Lockwasher   32 Nut   34 Torsion bar   35 Spring plate   36 Torsion bar cover   37 Lockwasher   38 Rubber bush
39 Bolt   40 Bush   41 Damper

The actual difference between the original position of the radius arm and its new position is therefore the difference between the two angles, which is 50 minutes. This is the smallest alteration possible and is a little less than one degree.

Install a torsion bar as follows:

1 Grease the splines and install the bar and radius arm (spring plate). Check that the door sill is still exactly horizontal.

2 Place a spirit-level type of protractor on the upper edge of the arm. Lift the arm very lightly to take up any play. Check the angle against the required figure. The arm must, of course, be otherwise free and not attached to the axle, nor against the stop on the bracket.

The specified spring plate settings are quoted in **Technical Data**.

Completing the installation of torsion bar and radius arm:

Having adjusted the setting of the radius arm to the correct position, proceed to complete the assembly as follows:

1 The cover or retaining plate over the outer end of the bar cannot be bolted down until the radius arm is over the stop rib along the bottom edge of the mounting bracket. It might be possible to use a jack to lift the arm until it can be tapped into place. The best way to tackle this operation is to make up a clamp from a length of screwed rod, one end of which hooks over the body mounting bracket above the middle of the arm. A loose hook fits under the lower edge of the arm, backed up by a nut on the screwed rod which forms the backbone of the clamp. Tightening the nut will slide the hook up the rod and raise the arm.

2 With the arm above the stop, press it home on the torsion bar. Coat the rubber bush with flake graphite, fitting the type which has four ribs so that the word 'OBEN' is at the top.

3 Fit the cover or retaining plate. Use two longer screws diagonally to pull the cover down until the other two can be inserted.

4 Clean the mating surfaces of the rear end of the arm and the axle bearing housing, swing the axle forward into the slot and align the nicks made before dismantling. Fit the bolts and new lockplates. Use a torque of 80 lb ft on the bolts.

5 Connect the handbrake cables to the lever and adjust according to the notes in **Chapter 10**.

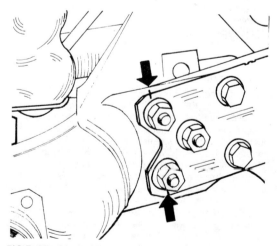

FIG 7:13 Mark the top and bottom faces of the spring plate and diagonal arm as indicated by arrows

At the beginning of this Section it was pointed out that renewal of many parts of the suspension and transmission system might affect the alignment of the rear wheels. After the radius arm setting is known to be correct it is essential to have the system checked by an optical alignment gauge if such renewal has taken place. This will ensure that details like the toe-in or toe-out of the rear wheels are correct according to the maker's specification for the model concerned.

7:8 Equalizer or compensating spring
Removal:

Disconnect the battery earthing strap, loosen the rear wheel bolts, lift the rear end of the vehicle and take off the wheels. There are two different types of connecting rod in use, these are shown on the righthand side of **FIG 7:2**. Unscrew the nut 53 at the lower end of the rod 51 or 52 and remove washer 36. At the top end depending on the type, unscrew nut 68, remove bolt 66 and washer 67, or remove rubber cap 35 and unscrew nut 53. Remove the connecting rods. From the outside of the side panels, remove the support brackets 46 and bushes 47. Withdraw the torsion bar 44 to the right. If necessary remove hard rubber washers and levers 57 or 62 from the torsion bar. The brackets 61, which are bolted to the axle tubes, are fitted with rubber guide inserts 43. These can be levered out if renewal is necessary. Inspect all rubber bushes for signs of deterioration and renew if necessary.

Installation:

If the levers were removed from the bar, slide the lefthand one into place, pointing to the rear. It is marked **L**. The righthand lever faces to the front. Tighten the clamp screws 64 and locknuts 63.

Insert the bar 44 from the righthand side and fit the support brackets 46 and bushes 47. Fit the spacer tubes 55 and 56 to the connecting rods and fit the rubber bushes 59 on each side of the eyes in the levers. The long rod goes on the lefthand side. Tighten the nuts 53 and fit the protective caps 35, or fit the bolts 66 and washers 67 and tighten the nuts 68. Insert the rods 51 or 52 into the axle brackets 61, fit the washers 36 and tighten the nuts 53 but do not do this until the top nuts have been fully tightened and the operator is satisfied that the top bushes locate on the levers correctly. Put on the wheels, lower the car, tighten the wheel bolts and reconnect the battery strap.

7:9 Rear dampers

The damper mounting can be seen in front of the rear axle tube in **FIG 7:11**. Standard dampers are not adjustable and it is difficult to test dampers without proper equipment. Clamping one end in a vice and moving the other by hand will show whether there is resistance, but it will not determine efficiency in operation. Trouble with poor road-holding and pitching over bad roads might be attributed to defective dampers. As they are not capable of being adjusted or topped up, the only cure is to renew them. If the dampers are used in conditions of tropical heat, continuous heavy loads or the likelihood of damage by stones, fit the special heavy duty dampers which are available. In this case, always fit a complete set of four. Where conditions are particularly bad it is recommended to fit the Koni adjustable type.

Removal:

Loosen the wheel nuts, lift the vehicle and take off the wheel. Remove the damper fixings at top and bottom and lift the damper away. Check the condition of the rubber bushes in the ends and renew them if the damper is fit for further service. If new dampers are to be fitted, make quite sure that they are the correct replacement type. Front dampers are not suitable.

Installation:

Fit the dampers in the reverse order of removal. Fit the spring washers and tighten the nuts to a torque of 43 lb ft.

7:10 Rear axle and suspension used on later cars
Removal and installation:

1 Loosen the rear wheel nuts, remove splitpin and slacken axle nut while the rear wheels are on the ground. Lift the car and remove rear wheels and axle nut.
2 Unscrew socket head screws 8 (see **FIG 7:12**) securing the end caps 1 to the constant velocity joints 23. Remove drive shaft 7 complete with constant velocity joints and dust sleeves 2. Cover the joints to prevent entry of dirt.
3 Pull off the brake drum after releasing handbrake and slackening off the brake shoes. Detach brake pipeline and handbrake cable. Unscrew bolts securing bearing housing cover 16 and brake backplate. Remove cover and backplate. Mark the top and bottom faces of the spring plate and diagonal arm with a cold chisel as indicated by arrows in **FIG 7:13**.
4 Unscrew nut and remove bolt securing damper 41 at lower end, then unscrew the nuts and bolts securing the diagonal arm 24 to the spring plate 35. Unscrew fitted bolt 26 securing diagonal arm to bracket on axle tube and remove arm. Remove spring plate and torsion bar 34 as described in **Section 7:6**.
5 Inspect the bearings for signs of wear or damage. If it is necessary to renew them, proceed as follows. Clamp the diagonal arm in a vice and knock out the stub shaft 9 using a hide-faced mallet. Extract the spacer ring 14, roller bearing inner race 11 and the sleeve 10. Extract the inner and outer oil seals and remove circlip 13. Press the ballbearing 12 out of the housing and use a copper drift to drive out the roller bearing outer race.
6 Inspect the bearings, seals, spacers, sleeves and stub shaft for signs of wear or damage and renew if necessary.
7 Press the ballbearings into the housing and refit circlip. Press the inner oil seal into the housing and repack with 60 grams of lithium grease. Push in sleeve then press in outer race of roller bearing. Position inner spacer on axle stub shaft then press shaft into ballbearing. Press the rollers and inner race onto shaft taking care to support the stub shaft flange. Press the outer oil seal into the cover and lightly smear with lithium grease. Refit the cover and tighten the screws.
8 Check the torsion bar as described in **Section 7:6** and install together with spring plate as described in **Section 7:7**. The spring plate setting is given as

part of **Technical Data** in the **Appendix**.

9 Fit the diagonal arm to the axle tube and secure bolt 26 by peening the lip of the bracket into slot in head of bolt after tightening to a torque of 87 lb ft. Install the brake backplate and bearing cover and tighten screws to a torque of 36 lb ft. Connect the brake hose and handbrake cable. Refit brake drum and replace slotted nut, but do not tighten yet. Bleed and readjust brakes as described in **Chapter 10.**

10 Remove protective cover from constant velocity joints and lightly grease the joints. Check that the flanges are clean and free from grease and refit axle shaft. Fit new tabwashers and tighten bolts to a torque of 25 lb ft. Lock bolts with tabwashers. Replace wheels and lower vehicle onto the ground. Tighten slotted nut to a torque of 217 lb ft and lock using a new splitpin.

7:11 Constant velocity joints

Removal:

Refer to **FIG 7:12.** Unscrew and remove the screws 8 securing the end caps to the joints, then swing the shaft downwards and remove it.

Detach the two clips 3 and roll back the rubber gaiters. Remove the circlip 22, and with a drift tap off the cap 1, from the joint ring. It should be noted that after this cap has been removed the inner race should not be pivoted more than 20 deg. otherwise the balls may drop out.

Slide the ring 23 upwards with the balls over the inner race. Press out the shaft from the inner race and remove the dished washer 20. The inner race must be suitably supported during this operation.

Check the shaft, joint and rubber gaiter and replace any part showing signs of wear or damage.

Slide new clips 4 over the shaft and then carefully avoiding the splines fit the gaiter.

Noting that the greater diameter of the ring 23 should be towards the gaiter, replace the dished washer 20 and press the joint onto the shaft. Fit a new circlip 22, making sure that it seats securely in its groove.

The constant velocity joint should be lubricated with 60 grammes of molybdenum disulphide grease, of which two thirds should be introduced between the ring, cap and gaiter, the remaining one third should be forced previously into the open joint. The joint faces between the seal and the cap as well as the gaiter cap and shaft should be clear of grease.

Replace and tighten the two clips, the operating parts of the clips should be located between the bores of the joint ring.

Squeeze the rubber gaiter by hand so as to press the grease into the joint from the rear. Refit the shaft and tighten the socket head screws.

Dismantling:

If it is required to dismantle a constant velocity joint, after removing it from the shaft as described earlier, the procedure is as follows:

Extract the inner race and the ball cage from the outer ring and take the balls out of the cage. Note that the inner and outer races are matched and should not be mixed. The six balls in each joint and the two races must not be renewed individually but only as a complete assembly.

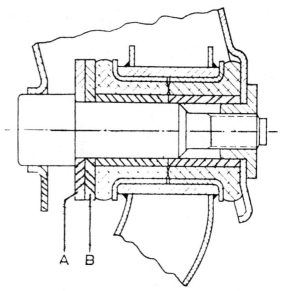

FIG 7:14 Showing the position of the shims for adjusting the alignment of the rear wheels

The inner race is separated by rolling it over the chamfers of the ball cage.

Carefully examine the two races, ball cage and the balls and replace the joint if there are signs of damage, corrosion or wear.

Fit the inner race to the cage by passing it over the two chamfers then insert the balls in the cage.

Fit the inner race into the outer race, noting that the chamfer on the inner diameter of the inner race (splines) should be towards the thrust washer and the larger diameter of the ring.

Refit the inner race with cage and balls, into the ring or outer race and see that when the inner race is inserted into the outer there is in each case a wide race at the same side as a narrow race. It will be necessary to manipulate the balls and the cage a little to achieve this insertion, after which the inner race must be pressed fully home.

The movement of the joint can be checked by ensuring that hand pressure will displace it throughout its full travel.

7:12 Alignment of the rear axle

The only adjustments required on the double jointed rear axle are associated with the toe-in of the two road wheels. Note that two shims are always fitted at the outside of the radius arm.

The correct alignment of the rear wheels should be set to an accuracy of within 10' to 15'; to enable these values to be obtained the following checks and adjustments are provided in the rear axle system.

(a) By means of the two shims at A and B (see **FIG 7:14**) the radius arm can be displaced laterally and so adjust the alignment between the flanges of the half shafts.

(b) The outer part of the radius arm is attached to the spring plate by four bolts which pass through elongated holes in the double plate and so enable alignment to be adjusted by displacement of the radius arms.

(c) The rear flexible engine mounting can be displaced laterally and so enable the engine/differential assembly to be centred.

Since the alignment of the rear wheels and the spacing of the half shaft flanges are inter-dependent, it is essential during adjustments to the rear suspension system to make simultaneous checks on both the alignment and the setting of the radius arms. To check this accurately requires special equipment, so that if the components cannot be reassembled exactly to the marks made on dismantling, or if any parts have been renewed, the alignment is likely to need adjustment by a VW agent.

7:13 Fault diagnosis

(a) Noisy axle

1 Worn wheel bearings
2 Excessive clearance of transmission universal joint
3 Excessive clearance of axle tube spherical joint
4 Worn shaft and hub splines, loose nut

(b) Excessive backlash

1 Worn axle shaft, trunnion pads or side gear
2 Worn shaft and hub splines, loose nut

(c) Oil leakage

1 Defective seals or gaskets
2 Overfilling transmission oil

(d) Poor handling, bad road-holding

1 Torsion bars 'settled' or broken
2 Worn torsion bar splines
3 Radius arm (spring plate) setting incorrect
4 Wheel alignment incorrect
5 Dampers ineffective
6 Bump rubbers defective or missing
7 Equalizer spring defective
8 Faulty transmission mountings
9 Loose radius arm to housing fixings

CHAPTER 8

FRONT SUSPENSION

8:1 Description

The principles underlying the VW suspension system have remained unchanged since its inception, but there have been many detailed improvements over the years. The cutaway views in **FIG 8:1** show the components of the assembly for a LHD installation, but it is only the alterations in the steering layout which need to be considered when dealing with RHD cars.

The assembly consists of two tubular beams 15, rigidly joined together and bolted across the front of the chassis frame. Shaped sideplates form the top anchorages of the telescopic dampers 12. Independent suspension is provided by a pair of trailing torsion arms 14 which pivot on bearings 6 and 8 inside the axle beam tubes. At these ends the torsion arms are coupled to the multi-leaf torsion bars 7 which are housed in the tubes. As each torsion bar assembly is held against twisting by an anchor block in the middle of each tube, this gives the effect of two torsion bars from one assembly, making four bars in all. The outer ends of the torsion arms are joined to the steering knuckle and stub axle 13 by ball joints 2, the top one being mounted in an eccentric bush which permits adjustment for camber angle.

A stabilizer bar 11 is attached to the lower torsion arms by rubber bushes and clips to prevent roll. Telescopic hydraulic dampers 12 are fitted with bump rubbers.

The one-piece hubs and brake drums run on taper roller bearings.

8:2 Routine maintenance

The vehicle must be lifted until the front wheels are off the ground for the lubrication service to be effective.

The introduction of ball joints reduced the number of grease nipples to the four shown in **FIG 8:2**, and these must be lubricated every 6000 miles, or once a year if that mileage is not reached.

Wipe the nipples free from dirt before applying the gun and continue pumping until fresh grease can be seen exuding from the seals. If grease gets on the tyres or brake hoses, wipe it off immediately as it will cause deterioration.

Every 30,000 miles the front hubs should be dismantled and the old grease cleaned out. The bearings must then be packed with fresh grease and each hub reassembled

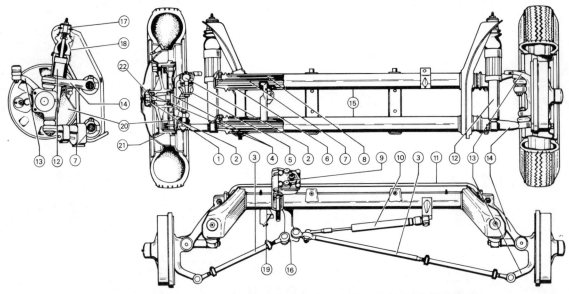

FIG 8:1 Layout of front suspension system using ball joint links (LHD illustrated)

and adjusted as instructed in **Section 8:3**. Do not put grease in the caps.

For all front lubrication use a multi-purpose, lithium based grease.

Other maintenance jobs which will ensure trouble-free motoring will be attention to tyres and tyre pressures, the checking and adjustment of toe-in and a check of all the dust seals round the joints.

8:3 Servicing front hubs and drums

Removing ballbearing hubs:

1 Prise off the hub caps after removing the wheels. Before the lefthand cap can be removed it will be necessary to take out the cotter pin which passes through the squared end of the speedometer cable.

2 Slacken the pinch bolt which clamps the spindle nut and then unscrew the nut. The lefthand stub has a lefthand thread. Pull off the brake drums after backing-off the brake shoes.

Clean inside the drums and examine the braking surfaces. If they are scored or out-of-true the drums can be refaced. Do both drums and then fit oversize brake linings. Clean the backplate free from abrasive dust.

Hub bearings:

It will be necessary to remove the bearings from the hub for cleaning and packing with fresh grease, or for renewal in the case of defects.

Dismantle as follows:

1 Pulling off the drum will bring the outer taper roller bearing with it. At the inner end of the hub will be found the outer race of the inner bearing and the oil seal.

2 Draw the inner race off the stub axle, followed by the spacer. Note that the oil seal lip runs on the outer surface of the spacer.

3 Do not disturb the outer races of the bearings unless they are defective. Clean all the parts and examine for cracks and pitting. If required, press out the outer races and oil seal, working from the opposite end in each case.

Reassemble as follows:

1 If new outer races are to be pressed into the hub, they must be a tight fit. Slackness here will allow the races to move in the hub, causing wear which will lead to the scrapping of the hub and drum.

2 Fit the spacer first, after checking the sealing surface, which must be highly polished and free from cracks or pitting. Drive the inner race onto the axle with a tubular drift.

3 Renew the oil seal if lubricant has been leaking into the brake. The lip and spring face into the hub. Pack the hub space between the outer races with multi-purpose lithium grease.

4 Grease and fit the inner cage and rollers, then the oil seal. Fit the drum. Grease and fit the outer cage and rollers and then drive home the inner ring of the outer race, being careful not to damage the rollers and races with excessive force.

5 Fit the washer and spindle nut. The bearings are adjusted so that there is a very small amount of free play. **There must not be any preloading or the bearings will be damaged.** First tighten the spindle nut to a torque of 11 lb ft, which will take up all slack.

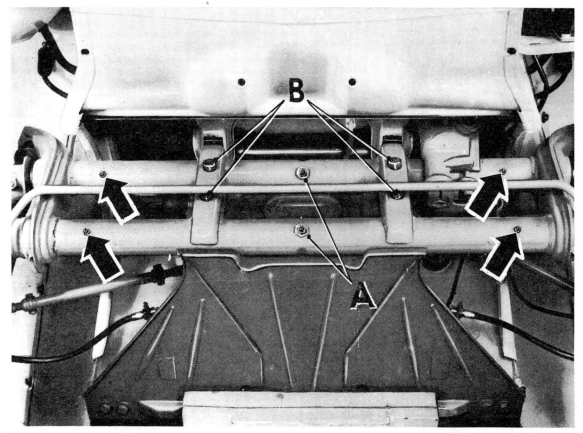

FIG 8:2 Arrows show torsion arm grease nipples. Central torsion bar fixings at **A**, axle beam to frame fixings at **B**

Then turn the nut back so that there is end play of the hub. This can be checked by dial gauge and should lie between the limits of .001 and .005 inch. At the higher figure there will be perceptible play in the hub but this is permissible and need only be reduced if there has been noise from the front wheels. When the adjustment is correct, tighten the clamping bolt to a torque of 7 lb ft. **Replace the hub cap but do not fill with grease.**

Note that all old grease must be removed, particularly if the grade is not known. Test the bearings after cleaning and drying them. Do not try to renew individual parts such as rollers or cages alone.

8:4 Servicing suspension

The front axle assembly is shown in **FIG 8:1** where the following features can be seen. The main axle tubes 15, ball joints 2, taper roller bearings 4 and the top eye fixing of the dampers with rubber rings 17 and a progressive bump rubber stop 18.

Dismantling without removing axle beams from vehicle:

1 Lift the vehicle and remove the wheel(s). Detach the brake hose at the bracket and seal the brake pipeline with a bleed screw dust cap.

2 Remove the outer steering ball joint from the steering arm, referring to **Chapter 9** for details of the best method to use. Never hammer on the end of the ball pin thread 1 in **FIG 8:3**.

3 Remove the nut at the top of the damper above item 17. A thin 42 mm spanner will hold the hexagon just above the rubber stop 18 to prevent the damper from turning.

4 Remove the brake drum and backplate, referring to **Section 8:3** and **Chapter 10**.

5 Remove the nut 3 from the ballpin of the upper joint in **FIG 8:3**. Loosen the large nut 2. This is part of a tapered eccentric bush used to adjust camber.

6 Remove the lower ball joint nut 3. Both ball joint nuts are self-locking and can be used again. With the upper ball joint out of the way, press out the lower ballpin using a long threaded bolt with a nut and large washer fitted as an abutment against the underside of the upper eye in the steering knuckle. In case of difficulty refer to the instructions on removing steering ball joints in **Chapter 9**.

Clean and inspect the parts. **Bent steering knuckles and steering arms must not be straightened.** If the fit of the inner bearing races on the stub axle is impaired, renew the steering knuckle.

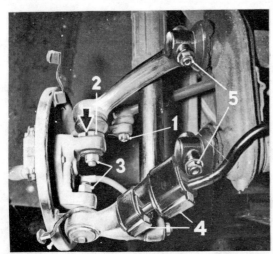

FIG 8:3 Front suspension assembly. Arrow indicates notch in eccentric bushing

Key to Fig 8:3   1 Steering ball joint nut   2 Hexagon of eccentric bushing   3 Steering knuckle ball joint nuts 4 Stabilizer bar clips   5 Arm to torsion bar locking screws and locknuts

Upper and lower ball joints:

These can be serviced after removing the torsion arms as in **Section 8:5**. Before attempting to remove the rubber dust seals it is important to remove all external dirt. If the seal has been damaged and road grit has entered the joint, fit a grease nipple in place of the plastic plug and force grease through until clean grease emerges. Use narrow feeler gauges to check the clearance of the ball in the joint. Clearance new is .020 inch with a wear limit of .080 inch. If the upper joint needs renewal the eccentric bushing 2 can be pressed off the ballpin. To reassemble, fit and secure the dust seal using 1 mm wire or a spring ring according to the method used. Fit the plastic clip and make sure the ring does not twist. Force in grease until the seal is full, remove the grease nipple and fit a new plastic plug.

The ball joints are pressed into the torsion arms, being knurled to ensure a tight press fit. Never try to refit a joint once it has been removed but fit a new one. If the torsion arm eye is oversize, an oversize joint is available which is marked with two notches instead of one.

To press out the upper joint, fit a nut to the ballpin to prevent it from coming out of the eccentric bush. Press in a new joint after lining up the joint notch with the notch in the torsion arm. Press out the lower joint. If the ballpin comes out first, follow up by pressing out the socket. Line up the notches when fitting new joints.

Reassembling:

This is carried out in the reverse order of dismantling. Fit the steering knuckle and ball joints to the torsion arms. Notice the notch in the eccentric bush which is arrowed in **FIG 8:3**. This must be fitted so that it faces forward. The bush can be turned by the large hexagon so that the camber angle of the wheel can be adjusted as discussed in **Chapter 9**.

Use self-locking nuts on the ballpins, tightening the 10 mm nuts to a torque of 29-36 lb ft and the 12 mm nuts to 36-50 lb ft. Install the dampers as instructed in **Section 8:7**. Tighten the tie rod ball joint nuts and lock with new splitpins. Fit the brake backplate and brake drum and install the hoses free from twist. Adjust and bleed the brakes. Adjust the wheel bearings as instructed in **Section 8:3**. Adjust toe-in and camber as instructed in **Chapter 9**.

8:5 Removing torsion arms

The bearings for torsion arms are an outer needle roller bearing 6 and an inner plastic and metal bush 8 as shown in **FIG 8:1**. Removing and pressing in these bearings to the correct depth requires the use of special equipment. It is recommended that the axle beam assembly is removed as in **Section 8:8** and the work entrusted to a VW agent.

Torsion arms are removed as follows:

1 Disconnect the damper from the lower arm. Remove the knuckle complete with brake drum, and if the lower arm is to be removed, disconnect the stabilizer bar and damper as instructed in **Section 8:7**.

2 Loosen the locknuts and unscrew the setscrews 5 in **FIG 8:3**. These lock the arms to the torsion bars. The arms can now be drawn out of the axle tubes and the dust seals removed if necessary.

Clean and check the bearing surfaces for wear. Wear limit in the bushes is .009 inch. Excessive wear in the needle bearings can be cured by fitting oversize bearings.

Check the arms for cracks and distortion. **Do not try to straighten bent arms**. Renew the dust seals if they are defective and reassemble the arms to the axle tubes using lithium grease.

8:6 Removing torsion bars

The torsion bars consist of leaves of flat strip steel stretching from end to end of the axle beams. The outer ends are clamped in the torsion arms and the centre of each bar assembly is locked against turning. Remove torsion bars as follows:

1 Remove the torsion arms from one side as instructed in the preceding Section.

2 Unscrew the locknuts and setscrews indicated at **A** in **FIG 8:2**. These secure the central parts of the torsion bars.

3 Move to the side where the torsion arms are still installed and pull both them and the bars out of the axle tubes. Note that it is not necessary to mark the bars for correct reassembly if they are completely detached. The direction in which they have been twisted has no effect on their life.

Clean the bars and examine them carefully for cracks or breaks. Fit new bars if necessary. Coat them well with grease before inserting and check that the correct assembly of leaves is being fitted. The number of leaves is ten.

Line up the recesses in the bars before fitting the setscrews and locknuts. Replace all the parts in the reverse order of removal.

8:7 Servicing stabilizer bar and dampers

A stabilizer bar is secured to the lower torsion arms by rubber-lined clips 4 in **FIG 8:3**. When both front wheels move in the same direction the bar is inoperative, but it reduces roll when one wheel moves up much more than the other, for example, when cornering.

Removing stabilizer bar:

Lift the vehicle and take off the front wheels. The clips round the rubber bushes are secured by clamps on the underside. Bend up the tabs on the inner ends of the clamps and drive them off in an outward direction by using a piece of flat steel bar and a hammer. Open up the clips and remove the plates, stabilizer bar and rubber bushes. Renew any defective parts.

Refitting stabilizer bar:

Fit the rubber bushes to the bar and lift into place. Fit the clips with the tapered slot narrowing towards the outer ends of the bar. Compress the clips with a powerful wrench so that the clamps can be fitted. Drive the clamps inwards, tab first until they are positioned and then turn up the tabs to lock them in place.

Damper servicing:

The dampers are of the double-acting telescopic type and are not adjustable. If the front end of the car pitches badly over bumpy roads or if, after bouncing the front end, the movement is not damped out almost immediately, then the dampers need checking. It is not enough to set the dampers vertically in a vice and test the resistance to movement up and down by hand. This will show that some damping is taking place but it is no check of efficiency.

Removal:

Remove the wheel and the outer tie rod ball joint as instructed in **Chapter 9**. Removal of the ball joint will ensure that the tie rod is not bent. Also remove the lower eye from the torsion arm and unscrew the top nut while holding the large hexagon above the rubber buffer stop 18 **FIG 8:1**. Lift away the damper.

Testing:

Adequate testing can only be carried out on special equipment, but if there is no resistance to movement when the damper is compressed and extended, it is certainly due for renewal. Otherwise, if there has been any doubt about the damping effect, the only cure is proper testing or renewal. Slight leakage of fluid is not necessarily a serious matter if the damper is working. There is no provision for topping up, but there is an adequate reserve supply in the damper.

When renewing dampers, fit a pair and ensure that they are the correct type for the front axle. Rear dampers cannot be used. Check the damper rings 17 shown in **FIG 8:1** and rubber buffer stop 18. It is possible to unscrew the top stud off the piston rod after pulling down the buffer. Check the rubber bush in the lower eye and have it renewed if necessary. A VW agent can fit a new oversize mounting pin to the lower torsion arm if the old one is worn or broken.

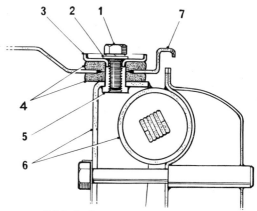

FIG 8:4   Body to axle beam mounting

Key to Fig 8:4   1 Body mounting bolt   2 Lockwasher
3 Spacer   4 Rubber packing pieces   5 Threaded bush
6 Axle beam   7 Body

In conditions of tropical heat, high loading and possible stone damage there are heavy duty dampers available, but all four dampers must be renewed. For very arduous conditions the Koni adjustable damper is recommended.

Refitting dampers:

Lightly grease the lower pin, fit the damper and tighten the securing nut lightly. At the top end, fit the lower damper ring on the buffer stud with the spigot upwards. Feed the piston rod through the mounting bracket and fit the top damper ring with spigot downwards. Fit the top plate and nut. Tighten this nut fully, then tighten the lower nut to a torque of 22-25 lb ft.

8:8 Removing complete front axle

With some variations according to model, do the following:

1 Loosen the front wheel fixings, lift the car and place firm supports clear of the front axle and then remove the wheels.
2 Disconnect the hoses from the brake backplates or from the brackets. Plug the hoses with wooden plugs.
3 Remove cotter pin from speedometer drive in lefthand hub and pull cable out from behind stub axle.
4 Disconnect steering damper from bracket. Remove the long tie rod and steering damper.
5 Pull off fuel hose and plug it, then remove the fuel tank as described in **Chapter 2**. Remove steering column as described in **Chapter 9**.
6 From under bonnet remove the two body mounting bolts 1 in **FIG 8:4** which screw into the upper axle beam. Remove the four axle mounting bolts **B** in **FIG 8:2** after supporting the axle so that it cannot fall. Lift the axle away.

Dismantling of the axle has been covered in preceding Sections devoted to the individual assemblies. If the axle beam has been bent or damaged, remember that it is a welded assembly and must be renewed. **Do not try to straighten bent tubes.**

8:9 Installing complete front axle

Before installing the axle assembly fit the lower rubber packing pieces 4 to the threaded bushes 5 in **FIG 8:4**. Lift the axle assembly into place and fit the upper packing pieces, the spacers 3 and the bolts 1 with new spring washers. Tighten to 14-21 lb ft after fitting the four front mounting bolts and tightening them to 36-43 lb ft.

Install the steering column and steering gear as described in **Chapter 9**.

Tighten the tie rod ball joint nuts and fit new cotter pins. Fit the steering damper to the bracket using a new lockplate with its open end pointing to the front. Tighten bolt to 18-22 lb ft and bend up lockplate.

Connect up the brakes, taking care that hoses are not twisted (see **Chapter 10**). Bleed and adjust the brakes. Check front wheel alignment as in **Chapter 9**.

8:10 The speedometer drive

Removing the cable:

Loosen the knurled nut and free the drive from the back of the speedometer, then to gain access to the hub drive, remove the outer hub cap from the lefthand front wheel.

Pull out the cotterpin or circlip in the squared end of the drive cable and pull the cable out of the stub axle.

Pull the cable out of the guide channel and grommet on the body.

Fitting the cable (see **FIG 8:5**):

Taking care not to kink the cable, pass it through the grommet and locate it in the guide channel. Insert the squared end into the speedometer and tighten the knurled nut.

Push the other end of the cable into the steering knuckle using a new rubber sleeve 4 and drive in the metal sleeve 3. Do not lubricate these parts.

Fit the cotterpin 6 or circlip into the squared cable end outside the hub cap 7 as shown.

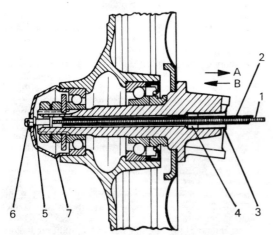

FIG 8:5 Fitting the speedometer drive

Key to Fig 8:5 1 Cable   2 Synthetic casing   3 Metal sleeve   4 Rubber sleeve   5 Cable drive end   6 Cotterpin or circlip   7 Cap

Note that the speedometer cable must lie behind the left tie rod on lefthand drive cars, but on righthand drive models it is in front of the tie-rod.

In order to allow for expansion under heat, the fitting of the synthetic drive casing is important. Refer to the illustration and pull the casing 2 in the direction of arrow A until resistance is felt, then push back as shown by arrow B about 6 to 7 mm (.23 to .27 inch).

A ticking noise in the drive or an oscillating speedometer needle can usually be rectified by careful attention to this latter operation and careful routing of the cable to avoid sharp bends and kinks.

8:11 MacPherson strut-type front suspension

This type of suspension was adopted on some models late in 1970 and will need little by way of explanation. The front wheels are suspended on combined spring and damper assemblies which are supported at their top ends on the vehicle body and at the bottom on transverse arms which are articulated to a front axle mounting through damper blocks and bracket rings which require no maintenance.

The suspension elements include a double acting shock absorber, supported at the top by helical variable-rate springs and bolted at the bottom to the stub axles and steering knuckles.

Dished washers at the top ends seat against the body, through sliding and rotating washers in metal/rubber bearings, so that the springs can follow all the rotational movements of the suspension elements. Upward movement is limited by a hollow variable-rate rubber damper and downward movement by a rubber stop on the damper.

A stabilizer, or anti-roll bar is mounted through rubber bushes to the frame and to the transverse arms and helps to control body sway when cornering.

The front axle mounting is an H-shaped element, attached to the frame at four points, and the transverse arms are articulated to this through a metal/rubber block with an eccentric washer and bolt by means of which the camber angle of the wheels can be adjusted. This angle is $1° + 20' - 40'$ with a maximum difference between sides of 30'.

Steering knuckle:

The suspension strut was modified in 1974 to bring the steering axis outside the tyre centreline. The steering knuckle on this type bolts to the side of the strut (see **FIG 8:8**), and the ball joint is mounted in the track control arm and enters a hole in the bottom of the steering knuckle, being retained by a clamp bolt.

1 Jack-up the car and remove the road wheel.

2 On the lefthand wheel remove the speedometer cable (see **Section 8:10**).

3 Disconnect the track rod ball joint (see **Section 9:7**).

4 Pry off the brake hose retaining plate.

5 Remove the brake assembly and bearings (see **Section 8:3** and **Chapter 10**).

6 On pre-1974 models bend down the locking tabs 31 and remove the bolts 32 (see **FIG 8:6**) and remove the steering knuckle.

7 On 1974 models and later, loosen the clamp bolts for the control arm ball joint and pull the control arm down out of the steering knuckle.

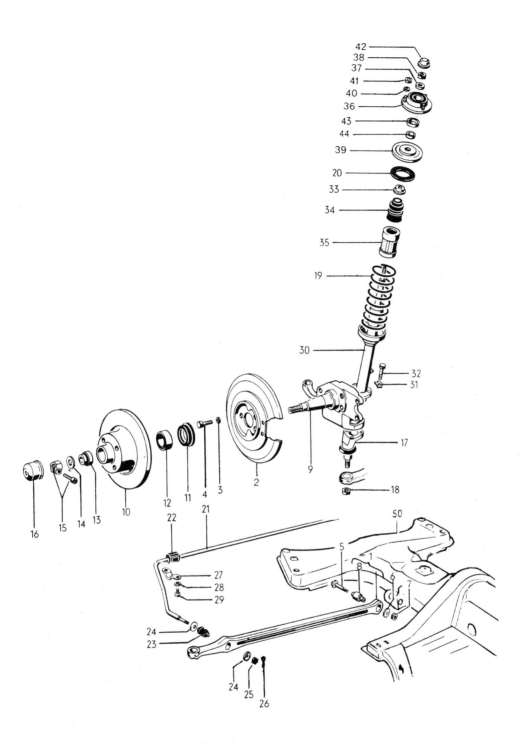

FIG 8:6 Front suspension, 1302 and 1303 models, early type

Key to Fig 8:6 1 Control arm   2 Backplate   3 Washer   4 Bolt   5 Bolt   6 Washer   7 Nut   8 Bush   9 Stub axle
10 Hub/disc   11 Seal   12 Bearing   13 Bearing   14 Washer   15 Clamp and bolt   16 Cap   17 Swivel pin   18 Nut
19 Spring   20 Thrust washer   21 Anti-roll bar   22 Rubber bush   23 Bush   24 Washer   25 Nut   26 Splitpin   27 Bracket
28 Washer   29 Bolt   30 Cylinder   31 Washer   32 Bolt   33 Seal   34 Rubber buffer   35 Tube   36 Top mount   37 Washer
38 Nut   39 Spring seat   40 Washer   41 Nut (self-locking)   42 Dust cap   43 Nut   44 Seal   50 Central support

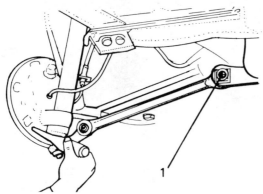

FIG 8:7 Front suspension, showing the eccentric mounting for camber adjustment 1

8 Remove the two steering knuckles to strut retaining bolts and remove the knuckle.

Refitting is the reverse order of the removal, noting that on early assemblies new lockplates must be fitted and the steering knuckle retaining bolts torque tightened to 29 lb ft (4 kgm); on later models the two mounting bolts are torque tightened to 61 lb ft (8.5 kgm) and the ball joint clamp bolt to 25 lb ft (3.5 kgm).

Adjust the wheel bearings, camber and toe-in.

Checking the front axle:

This should preferably be carried out by a service station using optical equipment, but if this is not possible the following method should prove satisfactory if a suitable angle checking tool is available. First of all the following conditions must be established.

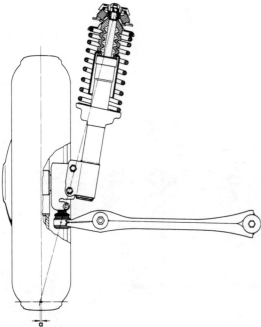

FIG 8:8 Modified steering knuckle on later suspension struts

Tyres correctly inflated, steering linkage in good order and the car on a flat level surface. Wheel bearings correctly adjusted and the suspension settled down with normal loading.

Camber:

This is best checked with the car raised on a jack. Use a spirit level to set the car horizontal from side to side.

Apply the tool against the wheel rims and mark the points of contact with chalk. Read off the camber angle.

Rotate the wheel one half turn and place the tool again at the chalk marks and repeat the check. The mean camber angle is obtained from a comparison of the two readings.

Any adjustment required to obtain the correct camber angle is obtained by turning the eccentric 5 and 6 in **FIG 8:6** as necessary. See also **FIG 8:7**.

Wheel alignment:

With the two road wheels in the straight-ahead position measure the distance between the two rims at the front and at wheel centre height. Mark the reference points with chalk.

Roll the car forward for one half turn of the wheels so that the chalk marks are now at the back of the wheels and measure the distance between them.

The second measurement should be greater than the first by .03 to .01 inch (.8 to .4 mm). For those owners with an angular checking tool the angle should be 30' ± 10'.

To make an adjustment, unscrew the nuts of the bolt for the locking collar and the nut of the cone ring on the two steering rods, then turn the two steering rods in the same direction to obtain the desired dimension. Lock and recheck.

8:12 Suspension units

Removal:

The steering knuckle and brake assembly can be left on the car.

Disconnect the suspension strut from the steering knuckle as described in **Section 8:11**.

On early models re-install one bolt to support the steering knuckle.

Support the unit and remove three self-locking nuts 41 securing the top of the suspension unit, but do not move the centre nut 38.

Using a suitable compressor, compress the helical spring and then remove the nut 38 from the screwed end of the damper piston rod using a ring spanner and Allen key. Slowly release the spring and remove the damper components.

Refitting:

This is a reversal of the removal procedure with particular attention to the following points.

Install the rubber buffer 34 and protective sleeve 35 (see **FIG 8:6**) on the piston rod and place the unit and spring in the spring compressor.

Compress the spring until $\frac{5}{16}$ to $\frac{3}{8}$ inch (8 to 10 mm) of the plain part of the piston rod protrudes above the spring seat 39.

Install the top mounting 36 and using the ring spanner and Allen key torque tighten the nut 38 to 50 to 61 lb ft (7 to 8.5 kgm) on early models, 43 lb ft (6 kgm) on later models.

Fill the spaces in the top mounting around the ball-bearing with lithium-base grease, and fit the dust cap 42.

Bolt the top of the unit to the body with new self-locking nuts.

8:13 Fault diagnosis

(a) Wheel wobble

1 Unbalanced wheels and tyres
2 Worn steering ball joints
3 Incorrect steering angles
4 Weak, broken or incorrectly angled torsion bars
5 Worn hub bearings

(b) Erratic steering

1 Check 1, 2, 3 and 4 in (a)
2 Bent torsion arms
3 Wear in ball joints
4 Unequal torsion bar angles on opposite sides
5 Uneven tyre wear or pressures
6 Defective dampers
7 Incorrect steering angles
8 Worn tension arms and bearings, worn kingpins

(c) Rattles

1 Worn steering ball joints
2 Lack of lubrication
3 Loose damper mountings, rubber bushes faulty

(d) Excessive pitching and 'bottoming'

1 Dampers inoperative
2 Bump or buffer rubbers missing or faulty
3 Broken torsion bar leaves

NOTES

CHAPTER 9

THE STEERING

9:1 Description

The steering gear fitted to 'Beetles' and Karmann Ghias is the worm and roller type as shown in **FIG 9:1**. This illustrates the rigid column type. A roller 24 is mounted on a needle roller bearing 25 and runs on shaft 26. The roller engages with the worm which is integral with worm shaft 13 this gives an almost frictionless response to any movement. Backlash between the roller and worm can be taken out by an adjusting screw 15. Backlash of the worm shaft can be eliminated by an adjusting screw 17 for the lower bearing 14 in the steering gear housing. The roller 24 and shaft 26 are mounted on a roller shaft 19 to which the drop arm 21 is attached at the lower end. The other end of the drop arm is attached by ball joints 43 to separate track rods 74 and 75 (see **FIG 9:3**). The outer ends of the track rods are connected by ball joints 76 and 77 to the steering knuckles. A steering damper 87 mounted on the axle tube is attached to the longer tie rod just above the steering drop arm. This damps out road shocks to the steering wheel.

In 1968 a safety steering column was introduced, this is illustrated in **FIG 9:2**. The outer column 48 is attached to a bracket 62 fixed to the underside of the front luggage compartment bulkhead. The two attachment bolts 65 screw into tapped holes in two discs. The discs are secured to the bracket 62 by plastic shear pins. If in the event of a collision the driver is thrown forward onto the steering wheel the plastic pins shear and the discs together with the attachment bolts move forward through slots in the mounting bracket. A special section 39 is fitted between the steering box and the lower end of the steering column, this is designed to collapse progressively upon impact, thereby minimising injury to the driver.

The safety measures described do not affoot the steering characteristics in any way. However it is most important that the collapsible section 39 and bracket 62 together with its discs and shear pins are not damaged. In the event of the slightest accident these components must be examined and renewed if necessary.

Cars from 1975 onwards fitted with strut-type front suspension have rack and pinion steering (covered in **Section 9:10**) in place of the worm and roller type.

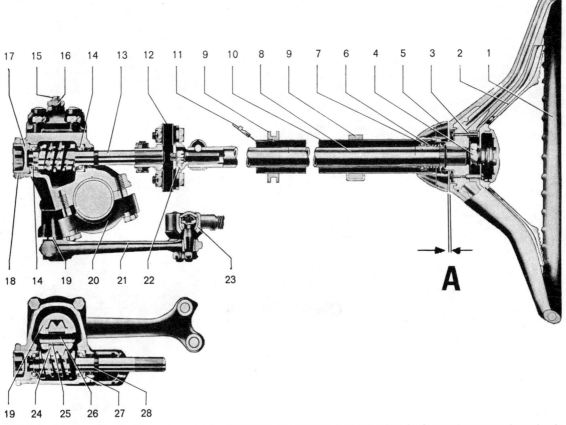

FIG 9:1 Components of roller and worm type of steering gear. The two plastic plugs in the gearbox cover show that it is the latest type which is packed with grease

Key to Fig 9:1   1 Steering wheel   2 Horn ring   3 Horn contact pin   4 Steering wheel nut   5 Direction indicator switch
6 Spring   7 Ballbearing   8 Inner steering column   9 Rubber mounting for outer column   10 Outer column
11 Horn connection   12 Flexible coupling   13 Worm shaft   14 Ballbearing   15 Roller shaft adjusting screw
16 Locknut   17 Worm shaft adjusting screw   18 Locknut   19 Roller shaft   20 Clamp to axle tube   21 Drop arm
22 Earth connection   23 Track rod ball joint   24 Roller   25 Needle bearing   26 Shaft for roller   27 Shim
28 Mark to indicate central position

9:2 Routine maintenance

The latest types fitted with worm and roller steering gear have two filler holes in the cover. These holes will be sealed with plastic plugs. This type of gearbox is filled with 160cc of special transmission grease on assembly, and there is no need for regular inspection and replenishment. However the tightness of the two plastic plugs should be checked periodically.

The track rod ball joints do not require lubrication but the rubber dust seals should be checked and renewed if damaged.

The remaining lubrication points which affect the steering gear are shown in **Chapter 8.**

Adjustments:

Normally there is no need to adjust the steering gear. Wear at various points in the steering and suspension assembly may make adjustment or renewal necessary.

Parts of the suspension system which will affect the steering are covered in **Chapter 8.** All other adjustments will be fully covered in the following instructions.

9:3 Removing steering wheel and column:

1 Disconnect the battery earthing strap, refer to **FIG 9:2.** Prise off the horn switch cover with a screwdriver and disconnect the cable from the switch.

2 Remove the steering wheel nut and spring washer and draw off the steering wheel.

Replace the steering wheel in the reverse sequence after putting some universal grease in the top bush.

The direction indicator switch is located just below the hub of the steering wheel, make sure the brass washer cut-out is exactly opposite and away from the lever with the front wheels in the straight-ahead position. The tongue of the cancelling ring 67 must engage in the cut-out. Fit two-spoke wheels so that the spokes are horizontal with the wheels set straight-ahead. One spoke should point downwards on three-spoked wheels. Tighten the nut to a torque of 36 to 43 lb ft.

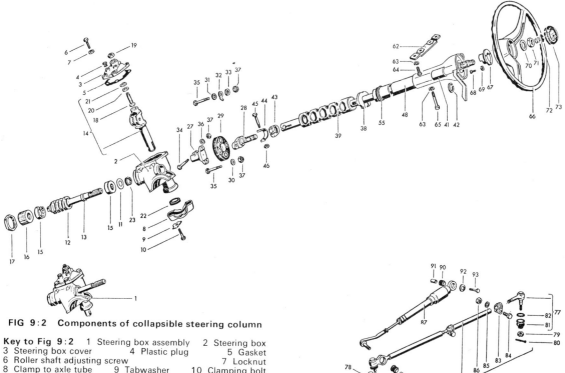

FIG 9:2   Components of collapsible steering column

Key to Fig 9:2   1 Steering box assembly   2 Steering box
3 Steering box cover   4 Plastic plug   5 Gasket
6 Roller shaft adjusting screw   7 Locknut
8 Clamp to axle tube   9 Tabwasher   10 Clamping bolt
11 Washer   12 Worm shaft   13 Bearing inner race
14 Roller shaft assembly   15 Ballbearing
16 Adjusting screw   17 Locknut   18 Pressure pad
19 Locknut   20 Washer   21 Lockwasher   22 Seal
23 Seal   27 Flexible coupling yoke, lower
28 Flexible coupling yoke, upper   29 Flexible coupling
30 Washer   31 Washer   32 Earth tab   33 Washer
34 Pinch bolt   35 Bolt   36 Washer   37 Stiff nut
38 Thrust plate   39 Collapsible section   41 Bush
42 Circlip   43 Clamp   44 Clip   45 Clamp bolt
46 Nut   48 Outer column   55 Rubber mounting
62 Mounting bracket   63 Lockwashers   64 Screw
65 Bolt   66 Steering wheel   67 Cancelling ring
68 Screw   69 Lockwasher   70 Washer
71 Steering wheel nut   72 Horn switch
73 Motiff and cover

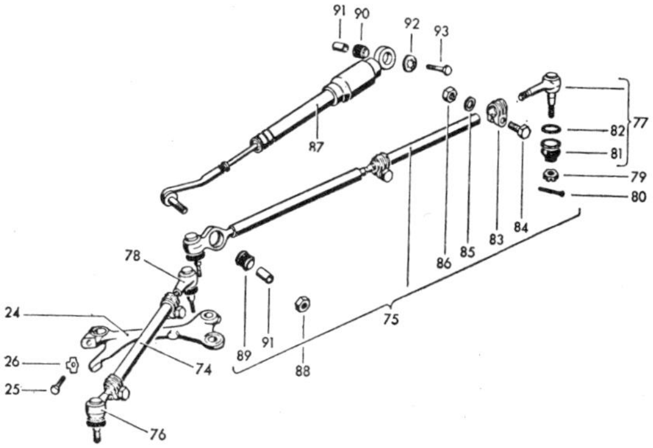

FIG 9:3   Components of track rod assembly

Key to Fig 9:3   24 Drop arm   25 Bolt   26 Tabwasher
74 Track rod   75 Track rod assembly   76 Ball joint
77 Ball joint   78 Ball joint   79 Slotted nut   80 Splitpin
81 Rubber cover   82 Washer   83 Clamp   84 Bolt
85 Washer   86 Nut   87 Steering damper   88 Nut
89 Sleeve   90 Sleeve   91 Bush   92 Washer   93 Bolt

Removing rigid steering column:

1 Pull off the horn cable from the connection 22 on the
coupling low down on the inner column. This
coupling is item 12 in **FIG 9:1**. Remove the upper
clamp screw and clip from just above this coupling.

2 On models without a steering/ignition lock, loosen
the wheel nut slightly and pull the column out of the
tube. On cars fitted with a lock, take off the wheel
Loosen the indicator switch screw and take off the
switch, disconnecting the cables and pulling them
slightly out of the instrument panel. Pull out the column
complete with bearing. If it is necessary to drive the
bearing out through the lock shells on the column be
careful not to damage it. Press the circlip off and
remove the brass washer, thrust spring and support
ring. Check the condition of the ballbearing. To remove
push upwards and out.

Refitting rigid steering column:

Before reassembling, check the steering column for
alignment. If there is a top bush instead of a ballbearing,
there must be no more than .03 inch clearance between
the wheel hub and bush. Press in a new bush so that
.04 inch projects from the outer column. Clean up the
horn contact surfaces.

Refit all the parts in the reverse sequence. The top ballbearing is packed with special grease and needs no
maintenance. On cars with a steering lock, drive the
bearing into the tube and replace the supporting ring
with flange upwards. Fit the spring and brass washer and
secure with the circlip. Set the brass washer as instructed
at the end of the notes on removing and replacing the
steering wheel. Set the space between the hub and the
indicator switch to .08 inch as indicated at **A** in **FIG 9:1**.
Fit a new lockplate to the screw in the clip at the bottom
of the column.

Note that assemblies which have a bush at the top of the column may have a plastic bush instead of the original type. This is half the width. Renew the earlier bush by fitting two plastic ones. The wheel hub must not touch the column tube. If it does, the position of the steering gear must be adjusted.

Removing collapsible steering column:

1 Disconnect the battery earthing strap. Remove petrol tank as described in **Chapter 2.**
2 Remove the steering wheel as described in **Section 9:3**. Extract circlip and plastic bush. Loosen the indicator switch and remove two screws securing retainer plate indicated by arrow **A** in **FIG 9:4**.
3 Insert key into ignition switch, turn the key slightly and pull the lock cylinder out of the housing after depressing the retaining spring through slot at arrow **B**. The steering column is locked by a pin which is attached to a sleeve. Extract sleeve using a suitable tool.
4 Unscrew clamp bolt 45 (see **FIG 9:2**) and remove clamp 43. Knock down tabs and remove thrust plate 38. Unscrew retaining bolts 65.
5 Pull the steering column assembly upwards until the lower end is clear of the front bulkhead.

Refitting collapsible steering column:

1 Check that the screws 64 securing the mounting bracket 62 are tight and that the open ends of slots in the bracket are facing forwards.
2 Push the steering column assembly through the rubber mounting 55 in the front bulkhead. Fit a new clamp 43 and locate flexible coupling yoke 28 in the bore at the lower end of the steering column.
3 Fit the clip 44, bolt 45 and nut 46, but do not tighten fully at this stage. Reconnect the horn cable.
4 Check that the front wheels are centralized and that the worm is at the midpoint of travel. Centralize the steering column then position the clamp 43 correctly and tighten bolt 45 fully.
5 Fit a new thrust plate 38 and lock the tabs. Refit steering lock, retainer plate and steering wheel in the reverse sequence. Check that the direction indicator switch is central. Tighten the steering wheel nut 71 to a torque of 36 lb ft. Position the indicator switch cover so that the clearance between the cover and steering wheel boss is between .078 and .118 inch. Tighten cover screws to 7 lb ft.

9:4 Removing and refitting steering gear

1 Jack up the front of the car and support on blocks. Remove the front wheels. Refer to **FIG 9:1**. Unlock and remove the nuts from the inner ball joints 23 of each track rod. Press out the threaded ballpins from the drop arm 21. Do not hammer on the end of the pin in order to loosen it. Hold a heavy steel block against one of the drop arm eyes and hammer on the opposite side of the eye. This should jar the tapers apart. The correct method is to use an official extractor.
2 Pull off the horn wire from the steering column tube contact.

3 Remove the screw from the clip at the lower end of the column and pull the column upwards to free it from the steering gear shaft.
4 Remove the clamp 20 from the steering gearbox where it is mounted on one of the suspension cross-tubes. Mark the position of the gearbox on the tube. Remove the steering gear.

Refitting steering gear:

It is assumed that the assembly has been checked and serviced according to the instructions in **Section 9:6**. Then proceed as follows:

1 Refit the steering gearbox in the original marked position. The steering column of the rigid type must not touch the column tube. It will be found that there are two welded stops to help in positioning the gear.
2 Fit new lockplates on the mounting clamp screws and tighten when the alignment is satisfactory.
3 Check the toe-in or tracking of the front wheels as instructed in **Section 9:8. Whenever the steering gearbox is removed or its position adjusted, it is essential to check the tracking.**

9:5 Dismantling steering gear

Before venturing to dismantle and reassemble the roller and worm type of steering gear shown in **FIG 9:1** it must be pointed out that accurate setting of the roller and the worm is a task for a competent engineer who is prepared to make up the measuring devices. The method will be given in the following instructions, but anyone who has doubts about his ability to carry out the adjustments in a satisfactory way is strongly recommended to entrust the work to a VW Service Station.

Dismantling:

1 Drain out the oil and clamp the box to a piece of tubing held in a vice. Unlock and remove the drop arm clamping screw and pull off the arm 21.
2 Remove the cover (four screws) after taking off the adjuster locknut and turning the screw 15 inwards.
3 The splines on the roller shaft 19 are likely to damage the casing oil seal when the shaft is pushed upwards and out. Service Stations use a piece of very thin-walled tubing slipped over the splines as a protection against such damage. When the shaft is removed, release the adjusting screw at the top by removing the circlip. The screw is fitted with a washer. **No further dismantling of the roller shaft is permissible.**
4 At the lower end of the casing, unlock and unscrew the worm adjuster 17. Pushing on the shaft by hand will press out the worm and lower ballbearing. The upper ballbearing is removed by driving both bearing and oil seal inwards with a drift. There will be a shim 27 behind the bearing.

Clean all parts and check for wear or damage. Renew bearings with pitted races and renew oil seals if leakage has been troublesome. Renew the worm and the roller shaft assembly if wear and play is apparent. End float of the roller must not exceed .0016 inch. Do not fit the steering worm oil seal until after the steering worm assembly has been adjusted.

9:6 Reassembling and adjusting

To understand the adjustments necessary on this type of steering gear it must be appreciated that the steering mechanism in the box is only free of play for a small range of movement on either side of the central or straight-ahead position. On increasing the lock some play becomes noticeable when the car is stationary but this cannot be felt when under way. Those adjustments which can be made without dismantling the assembly will be covered at the end of this Section.

1 Fit the upper ballbearing to the worm with the original shim or one approximately .012 inch thick and insert in the casing. Insert the lower ballbearing. Do not fit the oil seal.

2 Screw in the lower adjusting screw for the steering worm and tighten fully, then slacken until the worm can just be turned freely by hand without end float. Tighten the locknut 18.

3 Fit the adjusting screw into the roller shaft followed by the washer and circlip. There should be no end play in the adjusting screw but it should be free to turn. Washers are available in various thicknesses to enable the required conditions to be met. Assemble the shaft to the cover by screwing in the adjusting screw all the way. Before introducing the shaft into the casing, insert a guide with a tapered lead so that it will expand the oil seal and allow the shaft splines to pass through without damage to the seal. Set the roller shaft arm so that it is at right angles to the worm. Tighten the four screws to 14 to 18 lb ft.

4 Fit the drop arm and tighten the clamping screw. Turn the worm shaft fully in both directions and then set it in the midway position. The groove in the end of the shaft should then be vertical.

5 Make up a protractor scale measuring about fifteen deg. on either side of zero and arrange to clamp it in the slot of the drop arm so that it is in line with the arm but pointing in the opposite direction. The centre of the particular scale must coincide with the centre line of the roller shaft. Make up a pointer which can be clipped to the casing and yet be capable of radial movement.

6 Move the drop arm to and fro to the extent of the free play between roller and worm, halve it and set the pointer at zero on the scale in that position. Screw in the roller shaft adjusting screw in the cover about four turns and turn the worm shaft until the pointer reads 11 deg. to left or right of zero. Move the drop arm quickly to and fro to set the amount of play between the roller and the worm and then turn the adjusting screw until there is no perceptible play at the drop arm. Hold the screw and tighten the locknut. Turn the steering onto the other lock and check the angle at which free play becomes noticeable.

7 The range without free play should be equal on each side of the central position at an angle of 11 deg. ± 2 deg. on each side. This applies to **new** worm and roller assemblies only. After use, adjust to 5 deg. on each side. A deviation of more than 2 deg. to one side calls for correction of the worm position by shimming. The assembly must be dismantled and shims selected as follows: When steering lock with no free play is greater on the left side of the degree scale, fit a thinner shim. If on the opposite side, fit a thicker shim. Shims

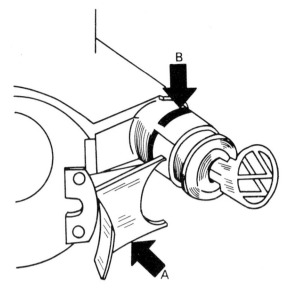

FIG 9:4 Removing steering lock. Arrow **A** indicates retainer plate. The lock cylinder can be removed by depressing retaining spring through slot indicated by arrow **B**.

are available in thicknesses from .20 mm to .50 mm in steps of .050 mm.

8 Press in the worm shaft oil seal. Remove the four cover screws, coat them with sealing compound and tighten to 14 to 18 lb ft. Refit assembly to car and fill with 160 cc of the correct grade of grease before fitting the cover.

Checking and adjusting whilst in car:

Check with the wheels on the ground and the front wheels straight-ahead. Turn the steering wheel with gentle finger pressure to feel the free play before resistance becomes noticeable. The total range of free play in the central position should not exceed 1 inch at the steering wheel rim. Excessive play is eliminated in the following sequences, but first be certain that the play is not in the track rod ball joints or the swivel pins.

To take out end float in the worm shaft, lift the front wheels clear of the ground and make sure that there is no stiffness in the rest of the steering gear due to lack of lubrication. Turn the steering wheel on right or left lock and loosen the locknut on the worm adjusting screw at the lower end of the steering gearbox. Tighten the screw until no play can be felt when turning the worm to and fro at the coupling. Hold the adjusting screw and tighten the locknut.

Turn the steering from lock to lock to check for tightness at any spot. Slacken the adjustment if any is felt.

To eliminate play between the roller and the worm keep the car wheels on the ground. There should be no play between the roller and worm when the steering is in the central position. Turn the steering wheel 90 deg. to left or right. Loosen the roller shaft adjusting screw locknut. Slacken the screw about one turn and then tighten it again until the roller can be felt to contact the worm. Hold the screw and tighten the locknut to 16 to 18 lb ft.

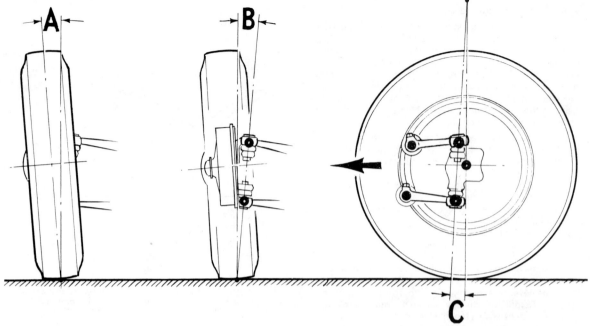

FIG 9:5 The angles which determine steering behaviour. **A** is the camber angle, **B** is the kingpin inclination, and **C** is the castor angle

Check by turning the steering wheel 90 deg. to each side. Play at the wheel rim must not exceed 1 inch. If there is more play on one side adjust the roller to the worm at 90 deg. on that side.

Check the toe-in as instructed in **Section 9:8.** Carry out a road test. Take a sharp corner at 10 to 12 mile/hr and let the steering wheel return virtually unaided. It should do this to within 45 deg. of the central position. If it does not the roller is too tight and damage could ensue. Readjust at once.

Position of free play between roller and worm:

This cannot be adjusted by altering the roller shaft or worm shaft adjusters. Any defect of this nature can only be cured by following the instructions given in 'Reassembling'.

9:7 Track rods and steering damper

Servicing track rods:

The ball joints fitted to the ends of the track rods may be locked in place with clips and pinch bolts as shown in **FIG 9:3** or by two nuts. The sealed ball joints are packed with grease and these do not need attention. The condition of the rubber seals is vitally important. Sealed joints must be renewed if the seal is damaged and every care must be taken not to squeeze grease out of them when they are being handled or taken off.

Removing:

1 Raise the front of the vehicle and remove the wheels. Detach the steering damper 87 and unlock and remove the nuts securing the ball joint pins to the drop arm 24 and steering arms.

2 Press the ballpins out with a special extractor made for the job. Do not hammer on the threaded end of the pin if the extractor is not available. It helps to jar the tapers loose by hammering on one side of the eye while a heavy steel block is held against the opposite side.

3 Before unscrewing the ball joints from the rods it is useful to record the position approximately, so that the joint can be refitted in much the same place. This will save time when checking the tracking.

Check the rods 74 and 75 for damage. Bent rods must not be straightened but renewed. Check each ball joint by moving the pin about. It must do so without roughness and without shake. The thread on the pin must be undamaged. Joints can be renewed individually.

Replacing track rods:

Install both rods so that the ball joints with lefthand threads are on the lefthand side. These are sometimes marked with a paint spot. Tighten the ballpin nuts and lock them, then slacken the clips 83 or nuts securing the joints to the track rods. Move the joints until they are aligned with each other at both ends of a rod and tighten the nuts or clips. Refit the steering damper and check the tracking according to the instructions in **Section 9:8.**

Removing steering damper:

Remove the bolt 93 from the bracket end and the nut 88 from the track rod end and remove the damper 87. Check by pushing the plunger in slowly and steadily. The resistance should be uniform throughout the travel. Renew the damper if there are 'flat spots'.

The rubber bushes 89 and 90 may need renewal. First press out the metal sleeve 91 followed by the rubber bush.

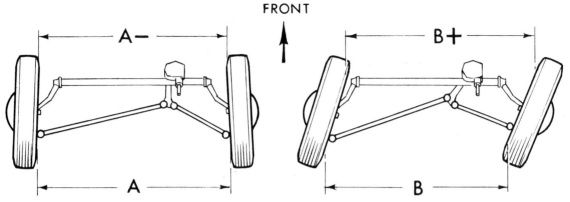

FRONT

FIG 9:6 Front wheel tracking. With front wheels straightahead, toe-in means that dimension **A**—is less than **A**. On large steering locks this becomes toe-out as indicated on the right. **B+** is then greater than **B**

Press in a new bush and then use a tapered and shouldered pilot to press in the metal sleeve. Put a smear of rubber grease on the pilot to assist penetration. Do not forget the bush and sleeve in the track rod and make sure the attachments are sound.

Refitting steering damper:

Tighten the inner nut at the track rod eye to 18 to 22 lb ft and secure with a locknut. Fit the bolt at the bracket end, using a new lockplate. Fit the plate with the open end pointing forward and the short angled end on the bracket. Tighten bolt to 18 to 21 lb ft and lock.

9:8 Steering geometry and tracking

If steering is to be smooth, accurate and without strain then several conditions must be met. These are, that lubrication is regular and adequate, that all parts are correctly adjusted, that the steering angles have not been thrown out by accident damage, that the tyres are not excessively out of balance and that they are running at the correct pressure. Tyre wear must be even, the dampers must be in working order and the tracking or toe-in must be correct.

Correct steering angles are specified by the manufacturers and they will be found in Technical Data. **FIG 9:5** shows the camber angle, the kingpin inclination and the castor angle in diagrammatic form. Wear and damage will affect these angles and may result in hard steering, excessive tyre wear, pulling to one side, front wheel 'shimmy', poor road holding and poor cornering.

Camber angle and kingpin inclination reduce the effect of road shocks on steering and keep down tyre wear, especially when cornering. Castor angle is noticeable because it induces the steering wheel to return unaided to the central position after passing through a sharp bend. Not enough castor angle makes the vehicle wander about over potholes and bad roads or under the influence of side winds. Too much increases the effort needed to deflect the wheels from the straight-ahead position.

Rough checks can be made to establish whether the angles are seriously out, but accurate measurements must be made by optical alignment gauges as used in service stations. The required conditions are that the vehicle is on a level, horizontal and smooth surface. The tyres must be at the correct pressure and the front wheel

bearings correctly adjusted. The steering gear must be properly adjusted, the vehicle must be unladen except for the spare wheel and a full tank and the suspension must be well bounced before testing.

Given these conditions, the camber angle can be roughly checked by dropping a plumb line from the top bulge of a front tyre and measuring the distance from the line to the bottom bulge. A simple drawing on a large sheet of paper will enable the dimensions to be set out and the angle measured with a protractor. It is advisable to check by rolling the car forward for half a turn of the wheels, measuring again and taking the average. This method will enable a check to be made of the angles on each side.

Adjusting the tracking or amount of toe-in:

The front wheels are not parallel when at rest but 'toe-in'. This is done so that the wheels are parallel when under way because all the play which is present in the steering gear and suspension is taken out by the rolling resistance of the wheels. **FIG 9:6** shows the amount of toe-in is the difference between measurements **A** and **A**—. Due to the geometry of the steering gear the wheels actually toe-out when they are turned for cornering at sharp angles as shown in the righthand view. This angle must also be checked in cases where there is trouble with the steering.

To carry out a rough check of the toe-in, satisfy the test conditions and then measure the distance between the rims at **A** and **A**— at wheel centre height above the ground. Roll the car forward for half a wheel and measure again in order to compensate for uneven rims. The difference between measurements **A** and **A**— is the amount of toe-out or toe-in.

Adjustment is made by altering both track rod lengths an equal amount. Set the wheels straight-ahead by halving the steering wheel turns from lock to lock. The ball joints at each end of the track rods must be released by slackening the clips or unlocking and turning the nuts. Turn each track rod in the required direction to rectify any error. **Turn both rods in the same direction and by an equal amount or the position of the steering wheel spokes will be altered.** Tighten the ball joint clips or nuts after setting the points at each end of a rod in the same plane.

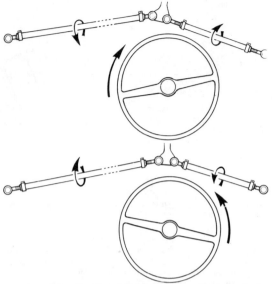

FIG 9:7 Setting the steering wheel spokes correctly on vehicles with two adjustable track rods. The arrows indicate the direction in which to turn the rods to bring the spokes to the horizontal position

Adjusting the camber angle:

Assuming that accurate measuring facilities are available, it is possible to adjust the camber angle. The adjustment is made by turning an eccentric bush which can be seen in **FIG 8:3** in **Chapter 8**. To adjust by means of the eccentric bush do the following:

1 Place the vehicle on a smooth level surface with the tyres correctly inflated and the front wheels exactly in the straight-ahead position.

2 Loosen the self-locking nut which secures the upper ball joint pin to the steering knuckle. Note the notch in one face of the hexagonal part of the eccentric bush. Initially, this notch is assembled in the straight-ahead position. For adjustment purposes it can be turned no more than 90 deg. in either direction. When satisfied with the setting, hold the hexagon and tighten the ball pin nut to a torque of 29 to 36 lb ft.

Steering wheel spokes at an angle

This condition must not be cured by turning the wheel on the column splines. Adjustment is made by altering the length of the track rods, one rod being lengthened and the other shortened by equal amounts. The principle is clearly shown by the arrows in **FIG 9:7**. If the rods are turned equal amounts in opposite directions, the toe-in will remain unaltered.

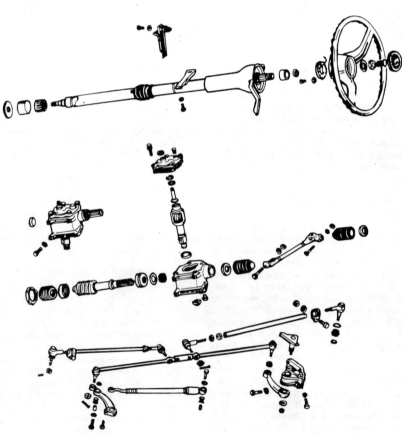

FIG 9:8 Exploded view of the components of later type steering layout

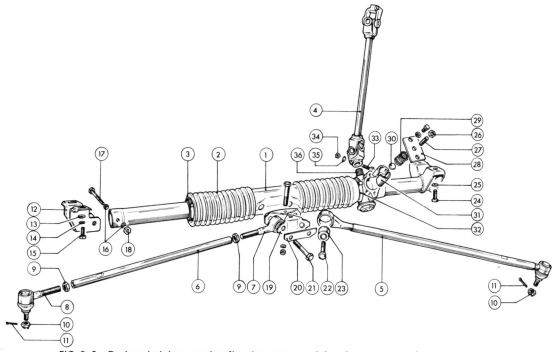

FIG 9:9 Rack and pinion steering fitted to some models using strut-type front suspension

Key to Fig 9:9 1 Rack housing 2 Rubber boot 3 Boot clip 4 Steering column shaft 5 Lefthand track rod (non-adjustable) 6 Righthand track rod (adjustable) 7 Inner tie rod 8 Outer tie rod 9 Tie rod locknut 10 Ball joint nut 11 Splitpin 12 Mounting bracket 13 Flat washer 14 Spring washer 15 Bolt 16 Washer 17 Bolt 18 Nut 19 Tie rod bracket 20 Lockplate 21, 22 Tie rod bolt 23 Bush 24 Mounting bolt 25 Washer 26 Adjusting screw locknut 27 Adjusting screw 28 Cover plate 29 Spring 30 Thrust washer 31 Thrust pad 32 Boot clip 33 Pinchbolt 34 Locknut 35 Washer 36 Pinion splines

9:9 Steering gear, later type

From the operating point of view this is unchanged, but to conform with the altered front suspension layout the box has been slightly modified with a new body shape. The roller shaft has been strengthened, with the roller being carried on two ballbearings and a re-designed steering arm

Steering column:

This also has been re-designed to suit the new layout as will be seen from the exploded view in **FIG 9:8**. It is connected to the steering worm through a cranked and jointed shaft including two universal joints. In the event of a frontal impact the jointed shaft can disengage and so prevent the force of the impact from being transmitted to the two-spoked safety steering wheel.

Linkage:

This is in three parts. The central steering rod which transmits the steering motion to the two adjustable outer track rods is attached to the steering drop arm and the relay arm.

The relay or reaction arm is articulated through a metal/rubber bush to a bearing bracket bolted to the frame. Two adjustable stop screws are mounted on the bracket to limit the total steering deflection.

The steering damper is mounted on rubber bushes to the steering arm and the chassis.

Subject to the changes shown in the illustration, the instructions given earlier in this chapter should enable the operator to remove and refit the steering system.

9:10 Rack and pinion steering

Some models using strut-type front suspension are fitted with rack and pinion steering as shown in **FIG 9:9**. Because of inherent self-damping qualities in this type of system, the hydraulic damper fitted to other models is not incorporated. The system requires no lubrication but can be adjusted if rattling or vibration is evident when considerable mileage has been covered.

Rack adjustment:

Remove the blanking plug from the adjusting screw access hole in the spare wheel well. With the car standing on level ground and the tyres correctly inflated, loosen the locknut and turn the adjusting screw until it contacts the thrust washer. The adjusting screw and thrust washer are shown at 27 and 30 in **FIG 9:9**. When correctly adjusted, the steering must not feel excessively stiff and must self-centre as the car rolls forward. Hold the screw in this position, tighten the locknut and then recheck the adjustment.

Tracking:

Adjusting the front track to set the front wheels at the correct toe-in is described in **Section 9:8**, the only difference being that when rack and pinion steering is fitted, only the righthand track rod can be adjusted to set toe-in within specification. To adjust the track rod, loosen both nuts 9 (**FIG 9:9**) and use a spanner or a pair of grips to turn the rod as necessary until the track is correct. On completion, hold the track rod against rotation and tighten both nuts to 2.5 kgm (18 lb ft).

Removing and refitting:

To remove the rack and pinion assembly, raise the front of the car and firmly support on axle stands. Remove the front wheels. Working under the front of the car, push back the steering column shaft lower rubber boot to expose the lower universal joint shown in the illustration. Unscrew and remove the shaft pinchbolt, nut and washer. (These are shown at 33, 34 and 35 in **FIG 9:9**.) If necessary, turn the steering wheel until these items are exposed for ease of removal.

Refer to **FIG 9:9**. Bend open the locking plate 20 and unscrew the bolts 21 and 22 which secure the inner ends of the tie rods. Remove the bolts and disconnect the tie rods from the steering rack. Remove the nuts and bolts which secure the ends of the housing 1 to the brackets on the body side members. Use a large screwdriver or a suitable lever to separate the lower universal joint from the pinion (see 36 in **FIG 9:9**). Remove the rack and pinion assembly from the car.

Refitting is the reversal of removal, tightening the bolts 15 and 24 (**FIG 9:9**) to 4 kgm (29 lb ft), nut 18 to 2 kgm (14.5 lb ft), bolts 21 and 22 to 5.5 kgm (40 lb ft) and the pinchbolt nut 34 to 2.5 kgm (18 lb ft).

9:11 Fault diagnosis

(a) Wheel wobble

1 Unbalanced wheels and tyres, pressures uneven
2 Looseness in steering gear and connections
3 Front end damaged, incorrect steering angles
4 Incorrect toe-in adjustment
5 Worn or slack hub bearings
6 Faulty dampers

(b) Steering wander

1 Check 2, 3 and 5 in (a)
2 Smooth front tyres, pressures too high or too low

(c) Heavy steering

1 Check 3 in (a)
2 Low or uneven tyre pressures
3 Faulty steering gear adjustment
4 Lubrication neglected
5 Front suspension worn or out of alignment
6 Steering gearbox mounted out of line
7 Faulty steering damper
8 Weak or broken torsion bars
9 Steering column bent

(d) Lost motion

1 Loose steering wheel, worn splines
2 Worn ball joints and suspension pivots
3 Drop arm loose on shaft
4 Steering gearbox mounting loose
5 General wear and faulty adjustment of steering gearbox

(e) Steering pulls to one side

1 Check 3 in (a) and 2 in (c)
2 One front brake binding
3 Broken or sagging rear suspension
4 Bent front axle tubes

CHAPTER 10

THE BRAKING SYSTEM

10:1 Description

All models except 1968-69 1200 'Beetles' are fitted with a dual braking system. The purpose of this is to provide the maximum safety in the hydraulic braking system. This is done by separating the front and rear hydraulic brake circuits and supplying pressure to each by separate sections of the dual master cylinder, as shown diagramatically in **FIG 10:13**. The lefthand view shows the master cylinder supplying the needs of both circuits. The centre view shows what happens when the front brake hydraulic circuit fails due to leakage of hydraulic fluid. The floating piston A is pushed to the left by the fluid between the pistons, so that it cannot force fluid into the faulty circuit. The rear circuit continues to function with an increase in pedal travel. The righthand view shows the action when the rear brake hydraulic circuit develops a leak. Piston B moves to the left until it contacts piston A which then provides fluid pressure to the front brake circuit. The brake pedal pushrod is on the right. Note how the fluid reservoir is divided into two compartments so that loss of fluid in one circuit does not affect the other. A warning lamp is fitted to the dashboard on some models, if the lamp lights when the brakes are applied the hydraulic brake circuit should be checked immediately, as one of the two brake circuits may have failed.

The layout of the hydraulic braking system is given in **FIG 10:1**. This shows drum brakes at the front and a single circuit master cylinder as fitted to 1200 'Beetles' prior to 1970. On models with dual braking circuits, the front and rear brakes have separate circuits as previously described.

Fluid reservoir 25 ensures that the braking system of pipes and cylinders is always full of fluid. Pressure on the brake pedal moves piston 37 down the bore of body 30, forcing fluid past valve 31 and into the pipelines connected to the brakes as illustrated in **FIG 10:1**. Typical front and rear drum brakes are shown in **FIG 10:2**. There have been changes in brake design which will be seen on some models as a different mounting angle for the components and varying arrangements of the brake shoe pull-off springs. None of these will affect the description of the system.

Both front and rear drum brakes are fitted with a single shoe-expanding cylinder as shown in section in **FIG 10:3**. The cylinder 5 carries two pistons 10, each provided with a sealing cup 8. Fluid under pressure from the master cylinder enters each wheel cylinder from behind the backplate and forces the pistons apart, thus pressing the shoes 2 into braking contact with the drums. An adjustment for lining wear is provided by two screws

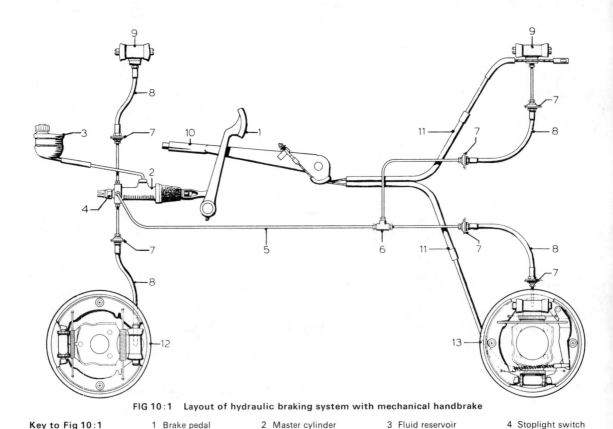

FIG 10:1 Layout of hydraulic braking system with mechanical handbrake

3 and nuts 4. The serrated nuts can be turned with a screwdriver, either through the drum or through the backplate according to model.

On the rear brakes, the handbrake mechanism can be seen as cable 22, pushrod 19 and lever 21, to provide a mechanical means of expanding the shoes.

Disc brakes on the front wheels will be covered in **Section 10:8.**

10:2 Routine maintenance

Topping up hydraulic reservoir on drum brakes:

The reservoir is located behind the spare wheel in the front compartment as shown in **FIG 10:4**. Clean all round the cap thoroughly so that dirt cannot enter when the cap is unscrewed. Check the fluid level. The reservoir must always be at least threequarters full and when topping up the level must be to within $\frac{1}{2}$ to $\frac{3}{4}$ inch of the top. **Use only genuine high quality brake fluid. Never put mineral oil in the system as this will ruin all the rubber seals. Be careful not to spill the fluid on paintwork.** Before restoring the cap, check the vent hole in it. This is sometimes blocked when a vehicle has been repainted.

If the reservoir needs frequent topping up there is a leak in the system. This must have immediate attention as further neglect might have dangerous consequences. The most likely places for leaks are at the pipe joints and past the sealing cups in the cylinders. Flexible hoses must also be checked.

Topping up hydraulic reservoir on disc brakes:

The reservoir will be found to the rear of the front compartment on the lefthand side on cars with dual braking systems. The double reservoir will be recognized although it has only one filler cap. Top up with a heavy duty brake fluid suitable for disc brake systems, filling the reservoir to the level of the joint round the container.

Adjusting hydraulic drum brakes:

Before adjusting, check the front wheel bearing play. Apply the brake pedal several times to centralize the shoes. Raise the vehicle and release the handbrake. Remove the wheel caps.

The adjustment is made through a hole in the drum or holes in the backplate which are sealed by plastic plugs as shown in **FIG 10:5**. Consult **FIG 10:2** to determine the correct way to move the serrated adjusting nuts when taking up slack. Turn one nut, using the screwdriver as a lever, until a light drag on the drum can be felt. Repeat on the other nut, then back off both nuts by three to four teeth until the wheel will turn freely. Repeat on the other three wheels. **Never adjust one wheel alone.** Test by applying the brake pedal hard several times then check the adjustment. Do not forget to replace the plugs in the backplate holes to exclude dirt.

FIG 10:2 Front brake (left), rear brake (right). Large arrow points to front of car, small arrows show direction to turn adjusting nuts to reduce lining clearance

Adjusting hydraulic disc brakes:

As disc brakes are self-adjusting the only cause of excessive pedal movement is leakage, or wear of the rear brake linings. Adjust the rear brakes in the manner suggested in the preceding instructions for drum brakes.

Adjusting the handbrake:

Adjust as shown in **FIG 10:6.** The screws are accessible through slots in the boot. Clear the screws and loosen the locknuts then jack up the rear wheels. Tighten the adjusting screws so that the wheels are still free with the handbrake released. Pull the lever on two notches and check that there is equal resistance to turning the rear wheels. At four notches the wheels should be immovable by hand. Tighten the locknuts and replace the boot. The cover flaps for the slots in the boot must be pushed inwards. Check the adjustment after a road test.

Dual braking system warning lamp:

Periodically check the bulb by pressing the lamp housing with the ignition switched on. If the lamp fails to light, renew the bulb.

10:3 Servicing master cylinder

Removing master cylinder:

The master cylinder is mounted in front of the pedal cluster. Disconnect the stoplight cable from the switch 29 in **FIG 10:7.** Remove sealing plug 26 and pipeline from reservoir. Disconnect the three brake pipes from the front end of the cylinder and plug the pipes carefully. Bleed screw valve caps make useful plugs. Disconnect the pushrod 40 from the brake pedal, loosen the brake pedal stop plate and remove the pushrod. Do not attempt to alter the length of the pushrod.

Remove the flange bolts and take out the master cylinder from the front.

Replacing master cylinder:

Replace the distance tubes in the front crossmember. Check the pushrod against **FIG 10:8.** The type shown must not be altered and if a new rod is fitted the length indicated must be made the same as the old one. Install the master cylinder complete with pushrod and boot. Bolt the cylinder in place and reconnect the pushrod. Always fit a new lockplate to the pushrod pin.

The next step is to ensure that there is .04 inch of free play between the spherical end of the pushrod and the bottom of the recess in the master cylinder piston as indicated at **A** in **FIG 10:7,** when the brake pedal is at rest. Adjustment is made by moving the pedal stop plate. As the clearance is difficult to check at the pushrod end, it is sufficient to arrive at a free movement of the top of the brake pedal pad of approximately $\frac{1}{2}$ inch. Afterwards, check the clutch pedal free play as outlined in **Chapter 5.** Connect up the pipelines and the stoplight cable, fill the reservoir with fluid and bleed the brakes. Test on the road and check the stoplight.

Dismantling and reassembling master cylinder:

These instructions apply to all models, but those with dual braking systems will need to refer to **FIG 10:9** to identify the extra parts.

The essential point when dealing with all internal parts of the hydraulic system is to maintain absolute cleanliness of the components and the fluid. The efficiency of the rubber sealing cups is dependent on such cleanliness, as grit will destroy the sealing effect and may permanently score the cylinder bores. Any leaks in the hydraulic braking system can be dangerous. **When cleaning all parts use only clean brake fluid or methylated spirits; any other solvents may cause a breakdown of the rubber cups.**

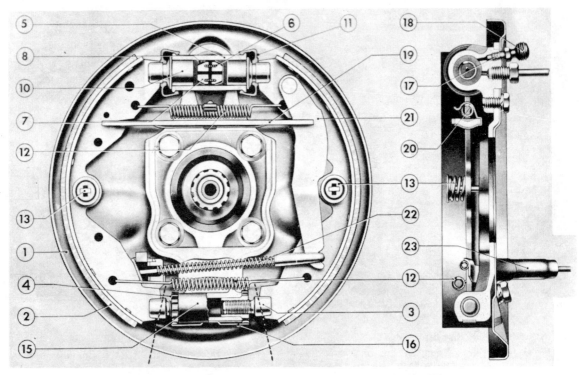

FIG 10 : 3   Rear brake showing wheel cylinder and adjuster in section

Key to Fig 10 : 3   1 Backplate   2 Brake shoe   3 Adjusting screw   4 Adjusting nut   5 Wheel cylinder housing
6 Cup expander spring   7 Cup expander   8 Cup   10 Piston   11 Boot   12 Shoe return spring
13 Shoe locating spring and washer   15 Anchor block for adjusters   16 Leaf spring   17 Bleed screw   18 Dust cap
19 Handbrake pushrod   20 Clip   21 Lever   22 Handbrake cable   23 Brake cable guide tube

FIG 10 : 4   Master cylinder fluid reservoir in front compartment

Dismantle the master cylinder as follows:

1 Remove the rubber boot 27 and prise out the locking ring or circlip 41.
2 Remove the stop washer 28 and shake out the piston 37, followed by spring 32 and check valve 31. The check valve differs on some models and earlier types may have a flanged metal cup with an internal rubber valve and there will then be a rubber seating washer at the bottom of the bore. This can be removed.
3 **On cars with dual braking system,** remove stop-screw 21 in **FIG 10 : 9** and then extract all the internal parts in the order shown.

Clean and examine all the parts for wear and deterioration. In **FIG 10 : 7** will be seen a small port 33 in front of the primary sealing cup 36. This must always be uncovered when the piston is fully retracted to enable fluid from the reservoir to recharge the system if necessary. Check that the port is clear and free from burrs. There are two ports in the master cylinder of a dual braking system. The piston(s) must be a suction fit in the master cylinder bore when clean and dry.

Always renew the rubber sealing cups on the piston(s) and the seating washer for the earlier check valve. Renew the check valve if there has been faulty operation. The parts are available in kits. Note that all the cups can be interchanged on the dual system with the exception of the cup for the rear circuit piston.

Reassemble the parts in the correct order, coating the piston(s) with genuine VW Brake Cylinder Paste. Be careful not to trap or turn back the lips on the cups. See that the circlip seats properly. On dual circuit master cylinders, place the cup washer, support washer, spring plate and spring on the front piston. Hold the cylinder with open end down and feed in the parts so that they do not fall off. To the rear piston fit the cup washer, primary cup, support washer, stop sleeve, spring and stroke-limiting screw and insert into cylinder. Fit stop washer and spring ring. Use the pushrod to press the front piston forward, well clear of the hole for the stopscrew, which can then be fitted complete with sealing washer. Install stoplight switches and tighten to 11-14 lb ft. Fit the rubber boot with the breather hole underneath.

The residual pressure valves 19 which are shown in the illustration are used on early systems which have drum brakes all round. They are fitted to maintain some pressure in the system. Later master cylinders have restriction drillings for all models, but the master cylinders must only be used in their correct application. With drum brakes all round the master cylinder is marked by a countersink in the mounting flange adjacent to the supply line boss. The disc brake type is marked with a V-notch on the side of the mounting flange, near the mounting bolt hole.

10:4 Removing drum brake shoes

Front shoe removal:

1 Jack up the front end and remove the wheels. Remove the hub caps, noting that it is necessary to remove the cotter pin which passes through the squared shaft of the speedometer drive before the front lefthand cap can be prised off.
2 Slacken the screw and remove the nut. The lefthand axle has a lefthand thread.
3 Back off the brake shoes before pulling off the drums. Brush dirt from inside the drums and examine for wear. Worn drums can be reground by VW agents and oversize brake linings must then be fitted. Attend to the hub bearings as instructed in **Chapter 8**.
4 Although **FIG 10:3** shows the rear brake, front shoe details are much the same, with the exception of the handbrake fittings. First remove the locating springs and washers 13 by pressing and turning through 90 deg. Remove the pins. Remove the lighter return spring 12 and pull one shoe outwards until it is released from the slot in the adjusting screw 3. The shoe can then be released, which will make it possible to remove the second shoe. Take particular note of the way the return springs are fitted.
5 Brake linings are due for renewal if they are down to .1 inch thickness. It is not advisable to try rivetting on linings oneself, as replacement shoes have linings which are accurately bedded to the shoes and are concentric to the drums. **Never renew one set of linings alone and make sure the material of the linings is the same on all four brakes.**
6 While the shoes are off, make sure that the brake pedal cannot be depressed. If the wheel cylinders are not to be dismantled, put a clamp or a loop of wire over the pistons 10 to ensure that they cannot be ejected by use of the brake pedal. Another method is to put a

FIG 10:5 Adjusting shoe clearance through backplate

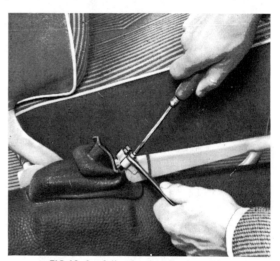

FIG 10:6 Adjusting handbrake cables

clamp on the flexible hose behind each brake backplate.

7 When replacing the shoes, be careful to fit the return springs correctly. Fit one end of the lower spring only, at first. Fit the stronger return spring at the cylinder end as shown in **FIG 10:2**. Shoes which are notched near the spring holes must be fitted with the notches at the cylinder end.
8 Fit the shoes into the slots in the pistons and then into the slots of the adjusters. Check that the angled ends of the shoes and the adjusters coincide and line up with the dotted lines drawn on **FIG 10:3**. Hook the return springs in from the front and make sure that they do not contact other parts.
9 Fit the retainer pins and locating springs and washers. Check the oil seal and grease the hub and bearings according to **Chapter 8**. Fit the brake drum centralize the shoes and adjust the wheel bearings. Adjust the brakes and then bleed the system as instructed in **Section 10:11**.

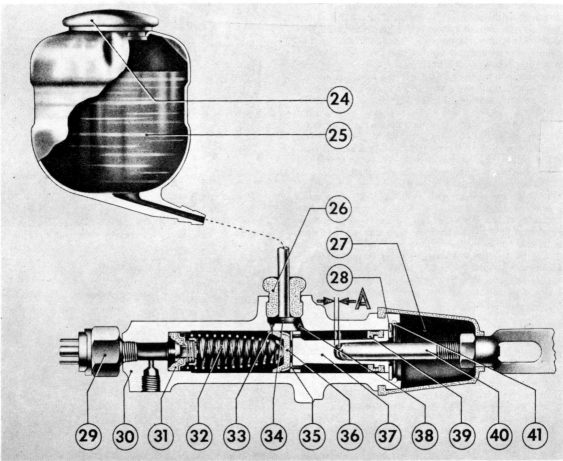

FIG 10:7 Section through master cylinder. When at rest there must be clearance at **A** between pushrod **40** and piston **37**

Key to Fig 10:7   24 Cap   25 Fluid reservoir   26 Supply pipe sealing plug   27 Boot   28 Piston stop washer
29 Stoplight switch   30 Master cylinder   31 Check valve   32 Spring   33 Small bypass port   34 Washer
35 Piston washer   36 Primary cup   37 Piston   38 Intake port   39 Secondary cup
40 Pushrod from brake pedal   41 Circlip

Rear shoe removal:

Before starting on this operation the owner must realise that the rear axle nuts are tightened to a torque of 217 lb ft. **It is dangerous to try to loosen these nuts with the vehicle on jacks or trestles. Always slacken and tighten the nuts when the vehicle is on the ground.**

1 After slackening the axle nuts, lift the rear of the vehicle and remove the wheels. Release the handbrake and back off the shoe adjusters. Remove the axle nuts and brake drums.

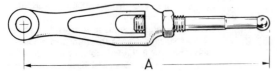

FIG 10:8   Master cylinder pushrod. Length **A** must be transferred to replacement rod

2 Remove the springs and cups 13 in **FIG 10:3** and then the retaining pins. Unhook the lower return spring on cars. Unhook brake cable 22.

3 Pull the shoes outward to remove them from the adjuster slots and lift them away complete with lever and pushrod 19.

4 Put a clamp or wire loop over the pistons 10 so that they cannot be ejected by pressing the brake pedal. Alternatively, put a clamp on the flexible hose behind the backplate.

5 The handbrake lever can be detached if necessary by removing the anchor pin circlip.

6 Clean all parts and check linings and drums for wear. Have the drums reground by a VW agent if badly scored or out of true. Fit the same type of lining material to both brakes. Do not fit new linings to one side only. Refer to the preceding instructions for front brakes.

7 Replace the shoes in the reverse order, fitting the return springs correctly and making sure they cannot

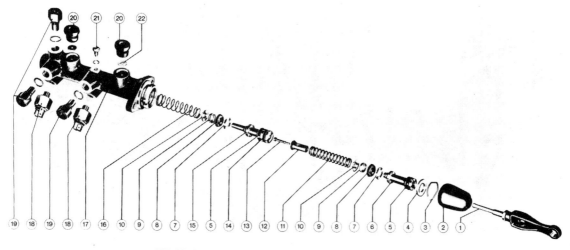

FIG 10:9   Components of dual-circuit master cylinder

Key to Fig 10:9
1 Pushrod   2 Boot   3 Circlip   4 Stop washer   5 Secondary cup
6 Piston for rear circuit   7 Cup washer   8 Primary cup   9 Support washer   10 Spring washer
11 Spring for rear circuit   12 Stop sleeve   13 Stroke limiting screw   14 Seal   15 Piston for front circuit
16 Spring for front circuit   17 Master cylinder   18 Stoplight switch   19 Residual pressure valve   20 Sealing plug
21 Stop screw   22 Washer for plug

contact other parts. Make certain that the shoes and angled slots in the adjusters line up as shown by the dotted lines in **FIG 10:3.**

8 Fit the drums and nuts but do not tighten fully until the vehicle is standing on the ground. Then tighten the axle nuts to a torque of 217 lb ft. If the cotterpin holes do not line up, tighten still further. **Do not slacken off.** Adjust the foot and handbrakes and bleed the system as described in **Section 10:11.** Carry out a brake test on the road.

10:5 Removing and servicing wheel cylinders

If wheel cylinders need renewal make sure that each replacement cylinder has the same bore as the original one.

To remove wheel cylinders proceed as in the previous section on removing brake shoes. When the shoes are off, disconnect the flexible hoses as outlined in **Section 10:7.** Remove cylinder mounting and bleeder screws and take away the cylinders.

Service each cylinder by cleaning the exterior thoroughly. Using every care to maintain all internal parts in a state of absolute cleanliness, remove the dust-excluding boots and withdraw both pistons with pushrods 10 in **FIG 10:3.** Take out the cups 8, the cup expanders 7 and the spring 6. **Clean the parts in methylated spirit or clean brake fluid and no other.** When dry and clean, the pistons must be a suction fit in the cylinder. Always renew the rubber cups. Renew the cylinder and pistons if worn or scored.

Reassemble in the reverse order, coating the pistons with genuine VW Brake Cylinder Paste. When fitting the rubber cups be careful not to trap or turn back the lips. Connect up the hoses in the manner described in **Section 10:7.** Adjust and bleed the brakes and test on the road.

10:6 Dismantling drum brakes

Follow the instructions in preceding **Sections 10:4** and **10:5.** After the wheel cylinder is removed from a front brake, unscrew the adjusting screws and nuts and remove the leaf spring clicker. Remove the three back-plate mounting bolts and lift the backplate away.

To remove a backplate from the rear axle, remove the brake cable retainer. Remove the adjusting screws and nuts. Take off the leaf spring clicker. Remove the four bolts from the bearing house cover round the axle shaft and pull off the backplate.

When replacing a front backplate clean the contact surfaces of plate and stub axle. Tighten the mounting bolts to 29 to 32 lb ft. Tighten the wheel cylinder mounting bolts on recent models to a torque of 40 to 42 lb ft.

Replace the backplate on the rear axle but clean all the contact surfaces first. Before fitting the bearing housing cover check the oil seal and bed it correctly in its recess. Renew both gaskets for the cover and spacer. The oil drop lug on the housing cover must point downwards. Tighten the mounting bolts to 29 to 32 lb ft. The adjuster screw leaf spring can be set slightly if more tension is required. Apply some universal grease sparingly to the adjuster threads. When fitting the brake drum check the position of the oil deflector.

Finally, adjust all brakes, bleed the system and test on the road.

10:7 Brake hoses and pipelines

Brake hoses must not be painted or left in prolonged contact with oil, grease, paraffin or fuel.

To remove a hose, take off the wheel. Unscrew the union nut securing the metal pipeline at the inner end, release the retainer and pull the hose from the bracket. Unscrew the hose at the backplate. On rear hoses release the union nuts at both ends.

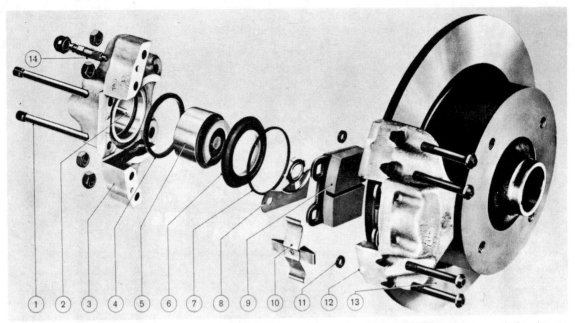

FIG 10:10 Components of ATE disc brake. Pad 9 may have one lug and a single pin 1. There may be no pin 2 and parts 8 and 10 may differ in shape. There may be one or two bleed screws 14

Key to Fig 10:10   1 Friction pad retaining pin   2 Pin (pressed in)   3 Inner caliper housing   4 Rubber seal
5 Caliper piston   6 Outer seal   7 Spring ring   8 Piston retaining plate   9 Friction pad   10 Spreader spring
11 Fluid channel O-ring   12 Outer caliper housing   13 Brake disc   14 Bleed screw

Fit hoses with the axles free from load. **Most failures are due to twisting when installing or to chafing against nearby objects.** It is most important to ensure that neither of these defects can affect braking safety.

Install each hose without twist so that it hangs down. Check that the hose cannot be strained at any steering angle or position of the suspension. It must not chafe against any part of the car when the vehicle is under way with the suspension moving up and down to the fullest extent. Tighten the hose and union hexagons to a torque of 10 to 14 lb ft.

Brake pipelines are of $\frac{3}{16}$ inch steel tubing and are subject to corrosion and to damage by stones after long periods of use. Check all sections and renew any which are faulty. The ends are double flared. Moisten these flares with a little brake fluid before tightening the union nuts. Check that the pipes are firmly clipped to the chassis.

10:8 Disc brakes

ATE:

The construction and operating principles of the disc brakes can be followed by referring to **FIG 10:10**. Note, however, that one type of brake is fitted with pads 9 having one lug for a single retaining pin 1. This means that spreader spring 10 has been changed in design and the shape and fitting of retaining plate 8 has been modified. None of these changes affects the following notes on the operation of the brakes.

The brake disc 13 revolves between a caliper assembly consisting of housings 3 and 12 bolted together. Each

housing has a cylinder bore fitted with a piston 5 bearing on the back of a friction pad 9. A seal 4, fitting in a groove in each cylinder bore, surrounds each piston to prevent leakage of fluid. It also acts as a piston return spring as seen in **FIG 10:11** where it is shown deflected under braking and returning to its normal shape when braking pressure is released. This action retracts the piston a small amount to give a little clearance between the friction pad and the disc. This clearance is maintained at all times and means that disc brakes do not require adjustment for wear of the pads. A bleed screw 14 enables air in the system to be eliminated. **FIG 10:12** shows how the caliper is mounted on the stub axle unit.

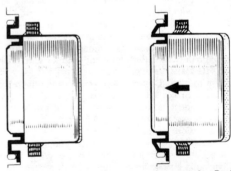

FIG 10:11 Disc brake piston at rest on left. Brake applied on right. Note how square-sectioned rubber seal is deformed. When brake is released seal returns to normal shape to retract piston

Girling:

The Girling calipers fitted to the 1303S models operate in a similar manner but the pads are retained by a U-shaped retaining pin locked in position by a clip. The caliper has two bleeder valves of different lengths, the long valve being fitted at the top.

Noise damping plates are fitted behind the pads.

To service the rear drum brakes and the hydraulic circuits the owner should refer to **Sections 10 : 2 to 10 : 7.**

10 : 9 Disc brake maintenance

ATE :

The only routine maintenance required is a check on the thickness of the friction pads at least every 6000 miles and renewal if the friction material is less than 2 mm or $\frac{5}{64}$ inch thick. The spreader spring must be renewed at the same time and the parts are available in kit form.

To remove the pads, remove the wheel and clean the caliper housing, particularly round the area of the pads. With a suitable pin punch, knock out the retaining pin(s) 1 from the outside face of the caliper. Remove spreader spring 10 and scrap it. Use a stout wire hook to extract the pads. As each pad is removed scratch it on the back with symbols to denote which brake it came from, right-hand or lefthand and whether it is an inner or an outer pad. This will ensure correct replacement if the original pads are to be used again. Clean out the slots in the caliper, but do not use a screwdriver to dislodge dirt.

Before either old or new pads can be fitted, the pistons 5 must be pushed back in the bores. This raises two problems. The first is that fluid will then rise in the master cylinder reservoir in the front compartment. If the reservoir is full, syphon some fluid off, not by mouth suction because the fluid is poisonous, but by a flexible squeeze bottle and a piece of tubing. Keep the bottle exclusively for this purpose and no other. The second problem is to press the pistons back into the bores without damaging seals and piston or bore surfaces. A wooden lever carefully shaped might be used, or a clamp adapted for the purpose. Do not use sharp-edged screwdrivers or other such tools.

FIG 10 : 12 Bleeding a brake system. Tube connects bleed screw to liquid in container. Unscrew bleed screw with spanner. Arrows indicate securing bolts

Now remove the piston retaining plates 8 and clean the pad contact surfaces of the caliper housings with methylated spirits. Do not use other solvents such as fuel which could damage the rubber seals. The outer seal 6 may be found to have deteriorated after a long period of use. This can be renewed by following the instructions in **Section 10 : 10.**

To install the pads, first fit the retaining plates 8. The modified design of plate is much simpler than the one shown but the angled edge is a feature of both types. This angled edge must be upwards as shown, and must fit snugly in the piston cutaway. The lips must fit firmly into the recess in the piston. Old pads will probably be all right, but check that new ones slide freely in the caliper housings. A touch with a file will help to ease tight pads.

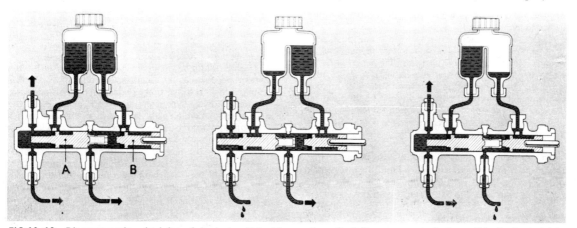

FIG 10 : 13 Diagrammatic principles of dual-circuit braking system. On left, movement of piston **B** by brake pedal is transmitted to piston **A** by fluid between. Fluid under pressure flows to three outlets, two on the left to front brakes, one on right to rear brakes. Central view shows failure in front brake circuit, piston **A** moves to stop on left, piston **B** provides pressure to rear circuit. On right, failure of rear brake circuit, piston **B** contacts piston **A** to provide pressure to front circuit only

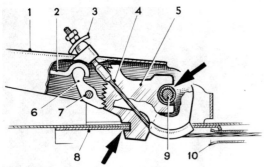

FIG 10:14 Handbrake lever assembly. Top arrow shows segment slot engaging pivot pin bush. Bottom arrow shows notch in segment engaging edge of frame aperture

Key to Fig 10:14 1 Handbrake lever 2 Pushbutton control rod 3 Compensating lever 4 Handbrake cable 5 Ratchet segment 6 Pawl 7 Pawl pivot pin 8 Frame 9 Lever pivot pin 10 Cable guide tube

Fit the pads and start the retaining pin(s) in the holes. Fit the spreader spring and drive the pin(s) home using a hammer and not a pin punch to avoid damage to the split retaining sleeves. Depress the brake pedal hard before using the car on the road. This will settle the pads with the correct clearance. Then check the fluid in the master cylinder reservoir and top up if necessary.

Girling:

Check the thickness of the pads at 6000 mile (10,000 km) intervals. The minimum pad friction material thickness allowed is 2 mm ($\frac{5}{64}$ inch). Mark pads for installation in the same position if they are to be re-used. If any pad requires renewal, all four pads must be renewed at the same time. Always use a new spreader spring and U-retainer locking clip.

To remove the pads, remove the retainer locking clip and pull out the U-shaped retainer. Remove the caliper (see **Section 10:10**) but do not disconnect the hydraulic pipe line, suspend the caliper from the steering tie rod with a stiff wire hook. Rotate the pads through 90 deg. and remove them. Push the noise damping plates to the middle of the caliper and remove.

Clean all parts thoroughly and blow any dust away with an air line. Observe the same precautions as already described for ATE discs, and calipers. Check the disc for run out. To install the pads, place the noise damping plates in position with their arrows pointing in the direction of forward wheel rotation. The longer bleed valve is at the top of the caliper. The grooved face of the pad is towards the disc. Refit the caliper (see **Section 10:10**) and tighten the retaining bolts to 30 lb ft (4 kgm).

Fit a new pad spreader spring, refit the U-shaped retainer and fit a new locking clip. Bend the straight leg of the clip through 45 deg. Depress the brake pedal several times to seat the pads, and top up the reservoir.

10:10 Disc brake servicing

Removal:

1 Let the unit cool down before starting work. Remove the caliper as a unit and never try to separate the housings.

2 Remove the wheel, disconnect the flexible hose at the inner end and plug the metal pipeline. The bleeder screw cap will do.

3 Bend up the lockplate and remove the two securing screws arrowed in **FIG 10:12**. Scrap the screws and lockplate. Lift off the unit.

Checking disc runout:

This can be done by removing the friction pads. First check and adjust the front wheel bearings if necessary. Clamp a dial gauge so that it can be brought to bear on the surface of the disc near the outer edge, but on the working face. Turn the disc slowly without pushing it in and out or rocking it. The maximum permissible runout is .008 inch. Fit a new disc if this runout is exceeded or if the working faces are deeply scored or cracked. Carry out a road test.

Installing caliper unit:

1 Make sure the mounting surfaces are clean and the splash shield is undamaged. Adjust the front wheel bearings if necessary.

2 Secure the caliper unit in place with new screws and lockplate and tighten to 30 lb ft (4 kgm). The screws must be genuine parts of K10 grade. The bleed screw, if only one is fitted, must be at the top. Lock the screws.

3 Connect the flexible hose, bleed the brakes as in **Section 10:11** and replace the dust cap on the bleed screw(s). Depress the brake pedal hard, several times, and then carry out a road test.

Master cylinder:

The one fitted to cars with disc brakes has a slightly modified check valve to ensure that the system has a little residual pressure at the moment after the pedal is released. A drilling in the valve then allows the pressure to drop, because disc brake systems must be free of pressure when at rest. Master cylinders fitted with this type of check valve are marked with a blue strip bearing the words 'Anschluss mit Spezial-Bodenventil'.

10:11 Bleeding the brakes

The following method will apply to all hydraulic systems. Use **FIG 10:12** for reference purposes.

The operation is necessary when there is air in the system because air is compressible and it will give a 'spongy' feeling to the brake pedal, which may also have excessive travel. Whenever any work is done on the braking system which calls for removal of the hoses, pipelines or cups from the wheel cylinders, then air will enter. This is bled out of the system in the following way:

1 Secure the services of a second operator. Have ready an extra supply of clean brake fluid of the correct grade. This must be either genuine VW or Lockheed Brake Fluid. Remember that fluid will be used from the reservoir shown in **FIG 10:4** and the level must be maintained throughout the operation. If the level falls so low that air can enter the master cylinder then the whole process must start from the beginning again.

2 Provide a clean glass container and a length of tubing which will fit over the bleed screw. The location of the bleed screw for disc brakes can be seen in **FIG 10:12**.

On drum brakes it is close to the union where the hose or pipeline enters the wheel cylinder, behind the backplate. Remove the bleed screw caps.

3 Start with the brake which is farthest from the master cylinder. Fit the tubing to the bleed screw and immerse the free end in a small quantity of fluid in the jar. Open the bleed screw about one turn.

4 The second operator must now depress the brake pedal quickly for a full stroke and allow it to return slowly. Air bubbles will stream from the immersed end of the tubing.

5 When air bubbles no longer come out, ask the second operator to hold the pedal down at the end of a full stroke while the bleed screw is tightened. Repeat the process on all the other brakes in turn. Fit the caps to the bleed screws to exclude dirt. Check the fluid level in the reservoir.

It is not advisable to use the fluid in the jar for topping up. It will be aerated and may not be perfectly clean. If it is known to be clean it may be used again after it has been standing for twenty-four hours. Never leave brake fluid uncovered, as it will absorb moisture.

10:12 The handbrake

Removing lever:

Refer to **FIG 10:14**. Take out the front seats and rear floor covering. Pull off the lever cover. Remove the nuts from the cable ends 4 and lift off the compensating lever 3. Remove circlip and push out lever pivot pin 9. Without pressing the release button move the lever rearwards until it can be lifted out complete with ratchet segment 5. Now press the button to release the segment. If the lever is dismantled, clean all the parts, renewing any which are worn and then reassemble with grease.

Installing lever:

Fit the half-round slot in the segment over the tube in the lever which takes the pivot pin as shown by the top arrow in **FIG 10:14**. The teeth of the pawl should engage properly and the rounded end must be positioned in rod 2 as shown. Fit the lever from above while steering the cables into position. Take care to engage the slot in the segment with the edge of tunnel 8 as indicated by the lower arrow. Install the lever pivot pin with a little grease lubrication. Remember to fit the circlip. Fit the compensating lever, attach the cables, adjust the brakes and lock the nuts. Replace the cover, the rear floor covering and the seats, then road test to check the handbrake.

The handbrake cables:

These can be removed after the rear wheels and brake drums have been removed as instructed in **Section 10:4**. Remove the cable from the handbrake lever. Remove the rear brake shoes, detach the cable, remove the cable retainer from the backplate and pull the cable out of its guide tube from the front end. To install a new cable, check the length against the old one. Use Universal grease on the cable before pushing it into the guide tube. When all operations are completed, check the action of the handbrake on the road.

10:13 Fault diagnosis

(a) 'Spongy' pedal

1 Leak in the system
2 Worn master cylinder
3 Leaking wheel cylinders
4 Air in the fluid system
5 Linings not firmly bedded to shoes
6 Insufficient fluid in reservoir

(b) Excessive pedal movement

1 Check 1, 4 and 6 in (a)
2 Excessive lining wear
3 Too much free movement of pedal
4 Check valve in master cylinder defective
5 Linings excessively worn, clearance needs adjusting

(c) Brakes grab or pull to one side

1 Distorted discs or drums
2 Wet or oily pads or linings
3 Brake backplate loose
4 Worn suspension or steering connections
5 Mixed linings of different grades
6 Uneven tyre pressures
7 Broken shoe return springs
8 Seized cable
9 Seized wheel cylinder piston
10 Loose caliper fixings

(d) Pedal must be pumped to get braking

1 Air in system
2 Check valve in master cylinder faulty
3 Weak spring in master cylinder

(e) Brakes get hot when not used

1 Small drilling in master cylinder blocked by main cup
2 No free play of master cylinder pushrod
3 Weak or broken shoe return springs
4 Tight wheel cylinder pistons
5 Rubber cups swollen due to wrong brake fluid

NOTES

CHAPTER 11

THE ELECTRICAL SYSTEM

11:1 Description

During 1967 the various models, with the exception of the VW 1200, were produced with 12-volt electrical systems. These used the original 6-volt wiring harness, which had particularly heavy cables to carry the high amperages common to 6-volt systems. This ensures that the 12-volt wiring is of ample capacity to carry any demands for current which may be made on it. The negative terminal of the 36 Ah battery is earthed as before. On cars, the battery is housed in a plastic container under the rear seat, and the top acts as a tray to prevent damage from spilled electrolyte.

The battery is charged by controlled output from the belt-driven generator, the controlling unit being a regulator. The regulator is sealed and must be renewed or adjusted at an official Service Station if faulty. It is mounted on Beetle cars under the rear seat or on the generator. On Karmann-Ghia, the regulator is mounted on the lefthand side of the engine compartment.

The Bosch generator, type G(L)14V.30A.20 is fitted to most vehicles and gives a higher output at lower speeds. For example, it will provide 30 amps at 25 mile/hr.

The regulator is a Bosch type VA.14V.30A, incorporating double contacts in a voltage regulator and a 'Variode' semi-conductor element in series with the control winding to influence the output curve. The usual type of cut-out relay is also fitted. The regulator is mounted under the rear seat.

From 1973, some models are fitted with a Bosch alternator rated at 50 amperes. A Motorola alternator is fitted to vehicles destined for the USA and this is also rated at 50 amperes. A separate regulator is installed to match either type of alternator.

The starter motor is mounted on the transmission casing and its shaft carries a sliding pinion. The pinion is moved into mesh with the ring gear on the flywheel by a solenoid and lever which come into action as soon as current is supplied. When the pinion is fully engaged the starter circuit is completed and the flywheel is turned. When the engine fires, an over-running clutch prevents the pinion from being spun too fast and a spring returns it to rest.

The Bosch starter is a more powerful type, designated EF(L)12V0.7PS. This ensures greater starting torque, assisted by a larger flywheel ring gear with 130 teeth instead of the original 109.

Wiring diagrams for 6- and 12-volt installations are given in the Appendix. Models may have small variations in equipment but the basic wiring will remain the same throughout and can be taken as a guide.

Instructions for electrical tests are given for the benefit of the owner who can use accurate test meters and there are some mechanical faults which can be rectified by a reasonably skilled person.

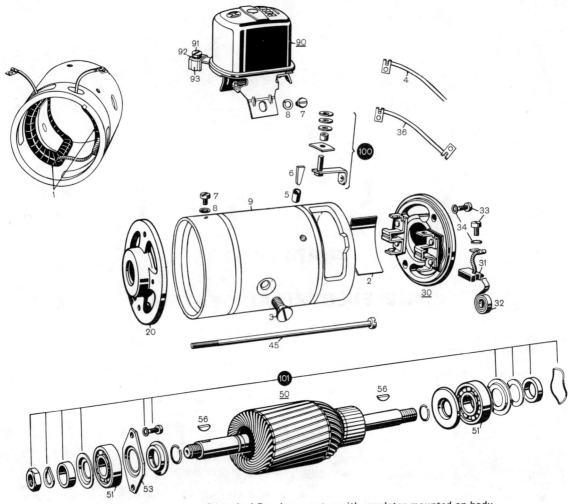

FIG 11:1 Components of a typical Bosch generator with regulator mounted on body

Key to Fig 11:1   1 Field coil   2 Insulating strip   3 Screw   4 Cable   5 Insulating bush   6 Key   7 Screw   8 Lockwasher
9 Body or frame   20 Drive end plate   30 Commutator end plate   31 Carbon brush   32 Brush spring   33 Screw   34 Lockwasher
36 Cable   45 Screw   50 Armature   51 Ballbearing   53 Bearing retainer   56 Woodruff key   90 Regulator (with parts 91 to 93)
91 Screw   92 Spring washer   93 Terminal bracket   100 Terminal assembly   101 Armature assembly

11:2 Battery maintenance

The negative terminal of the battery is earthed. The terminals and cables must be clean and dry. Brush away all corrosion, scrape the terminals and cable clamps to a bright metal surface and coat them with petroleum jelly before refitting. Make sure the battery is securely clamped.

Heavy demands are made upon a battery, particularly in the winter, and periodic attention is essential. On 'Beetles' the battery will be found under the rear seat. On Karmann Ghias the battery is in the rear compartment on the righthand side.

With the cover removed, check the level of the electrolyte and top up if required, using distilled water. Some batteries have indicators. On those without, top up to a level slightly less than $\frac{1}{4}$ inch above the plates.

Never add neat acid, and only top up with dilute sulphuric acid if some has been lost by spilling. To prepare the electrolyte, add sulphuric acid very slowly to distilled water. **Never add water to acid as this is highly dangerous.** Stir the liquid and test with an hydrometer until the specific gravity is 1.285 when cool. Do not use rainwater or tap water.

The state of charge of the battery can be checked with the hydrometer. Remove the filler plugs and use the bulb to suck up enough electrolyte to lift the float. When fully charged the reading should be 1.285, when half-discharged 1.20 and when fully discharged 1.12. **A discharged battery must be recharged at once.** Never leave a battery in a discharged condition or it will become sulphated. If it is to be left unused for long periods, give it a freshening charge every six weeks.

Testing each cell with a voltmeter is not a real test of a battery. This method is only satisfactory if it is done while the battery is made to deliver a heavy discharge, and most garages have suitable equipment. The voltage of all cells should be 2. Any cell which is .2 volt less than the average is probably defective. If the voltage drops below 1.6 volts during a heavy discharge test, the battery is discharged. Charge again at a rate which is 10 per cent of the capacity. A 66 amp/hr battery will thus be charged at 6.6 amps. Remove all the filler plugs and keep naked lights away. Rapid charging of a sound battery is permissible in an emergency, but it is not recommended at frequent intervals.

Remove the negative cable from the battery when working on the cables of the electrical system. Short circuits may cause serious damage, particularly if there is spilled fuel about.

11 : 3 Generator maintenance

There is no provision for regular lubrication. The ball-bearings are packed with high-melting point grease. Repack with fresh grease during a major overhaul, say at 20,000 miles. Never use ordinary grease.

Routine maintenance is confined to examination of the brushes and to the adjustment of the driving belt as instructed in **Chapter 4.**

Brushes:

To check the brushes remove the cover(s) from the rear end of the generator body. This will reveal the apertures at the righthand end of body 9 in **FIG 11 : 1**. Through these will be seen the brushes 31 and springs 32. Hook up the springs with a piece of bent wire and pull the brushes out of the holders. Try to keep them the right way round for correct replacement. It is possible that the latest models may not have a cover band.

The brushes must slide freely in their holders. If, after cleaning with a fuel-moistened rag, a brush still sticks, ease the sides by rubbing on a smooth flat file. If the brushes are soaked in oil or are so worn that they no longer bear on the commutator, they must be renewed. A very short brush also leads to low spring pressure. If the springs are weak they must be renewed. Check the condition of the commutator and recondition it as follows:

Commutator:

This is the segmented copper cylinder at the righthand end of part 50 in the illustration. The copper should be clean and smooth and the insulation between the segments must not stand proud or the brushes will not make electrical contact with the copper. If the commutator is only discoloured it can be polished by cleaning with a fuel-moistened cloth, pressing with a piece of wood. Then it should be rotated while holding a piece of very fine glasspaper in contact. Clean away all dust.

If the commutator is burnt and obviously worn, the generator must be dismantled and the armature run between centres in a lathe. A light cut with a very keen tool should be taken, removing as little metal as possible. Finally polish with very fine glasspaper. **Do not use emerycloth.** After this, the insulation between the segments must be undercut as shown in **FIG 11 : 2**. Grind the sides of a fine hacksaw blade until it is the width of the insulation then carefully cut between each pair of segments to a depth of approximately $\frac{1}{64}$ inch.

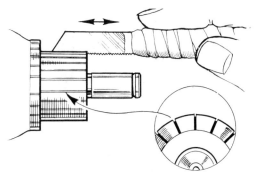

FIG 11 : 2 Undercutting commutator insulation with hacksaw blade ground to width between copper segments

11 : 4 Generator and regulator testing

Visual indication of generator current is given by the red warning lamp on the instrument panel. A burnt-out bulb can be renewed as shown in **FIG 11 :14**.

Assuming that the bulb is working it should light up when the ignition is switched on and go out when the generator is charging the battery. If the bulb continues to glow even though the generator and regulator are known to be in order, there must be an excessive voltage drop between the regulator terminal B+ and the bulb. Check the connections as follows:

1 Run the engine at a fast-idle and switch on the head-lamps, screen wiper and indicators.

2 Connect a little over four yards of heavy insulated cable to terminal B+ on the regulator. Bare the insulation from the free end.

3 With the help of an assistant to watch the warning lamp, contact the following points in sequence: Lighting switch terminal 30. Fuse box terminal 30. Ignition/starter switch terminal 30. Fuse box terminal 15/54.

4 If the warning lamp stops glowing when one of the connections is made the poor connection causing the voltage drop lies between the last point of contact and the previous one. Look for loose connections, faulty cables and defective contacts in switches. If the warning lamp continues to light up with the engine running fast, test the generator as follows:

Note that cables to the generator and regulator must not be connected or disconnected with the engine running. When the engine is stationary, disconnect cable B+ or 51, as a shortcircuit will damage the regulator. Be careful not to interchange the cables to D+ (or +) and F (or DF) as this will also damage the regulator.

Note that even if the warning lamp goes out when engine speed rises, it does not guarantee that the regulator is in order or that the battery is being charged properly.

Carry out the tests with two accurate moving-coil meters, a 0-30 voltmeter and a 50-0-50 ammeter.

Testing no-load voltage:

1 Disconnect the cable from terminal B+ (or 51) on the regulator. To the same terminal, connect the positive lead of the voltmeter and earth the negative lead of the meter.

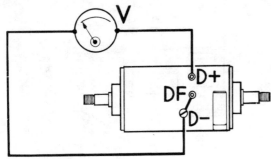

FIG 11:3 Checking generator output without regulator.
Connect voltmeter between generator D + and earth

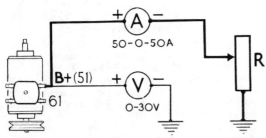

FIG 11:4 Checking regulator operation independently of the state of battery charge

2 Start the engine and increase the speed until the needle no longer rises. On 6-volt systems this no-load voltage should be 7.4 to 8.1 volts, or 6 to 7 volts on early generators. Shut off and watch the needle. Just before the engine and generator stop turning, the needle should drop suddenly to zero, indicating that the cut-out points in the regulator are opening correctly. If the cut-out points do not open the regulator will become very hot and the battery will become discharged through the generator.

3 On 12-volt systems using regulator VA.14V.30A, a tachometer is required as well as the meter. Use the greatest care not to shortcircuit the field coils when carrying out this test. Disconnect the two leads from the generator. Earth terminal DF. Connect the voltmeter across terminal D+ (or 61) and earth, start the engine and gradually increase speed. With a cold generator running at 1450 rev/min the output should be 14 volts. **Complete this test in a few seconds or the field coils may burn out. FIG 11:3** shows how the connections are made. For the owner with limited facilities it is suggested that he makes a test set from a 12-volt headlamp bulb and arranges two test leads from it. Then apply the two leads across earth and the D+ terminal on the regulator under the rear seat and run the engine up to speed, but not excessively. The bulb will light if the generator is working. Do not alter the length of the wiring from regulator to generator as cable resistance is matched with the 'Variode' device in the regulator.

Checking charging current:

1 Disconnect battery earthing strap. Disconnect cable from B+ on regulator. Insert an ammeter between the disconnected cable and the B+ terminal. Reconnect the battery strap.

2 Run the engine at a fast-idle. Switch on the lights and other current users. If the ammeter does not record on the positive side then the regulator is defective.

3 Reduce engine speed slowly to idling and watch the meter needle. It should cross the zero mark to the discharge side. Just before the speed drops to idling the needle should flick back to zero, which shows that the cut-out points in the regulator have opened. If, with the engine stopped, a heavy discharge is still indicated, remove the battery lead at once as the battery is discharging through the generator due to the cut-out points being welded together. The regulator must then be serviced or renewed. This test does not show whether the current control of the regulator is correctly set for battery charging at the required rate.

Checking regulator:

This should form part of the generator tests, before the generator is removed for servicing. The initial instructions refer to the 6-volt regulator.

Refer to **FIG 11:4** when making the connections. Equipment required will be a 0-30-volt meter, a 50-0-50 ammeter and an adjustable resistance capable of passing 50 amps. Carry out the test on 6-volt systems as follows, with the generator in the vehicle if desired:

1 Use heavy cables which are as short as possible. Disconnect cable from B+ (or 51) terminal on regulator. Connect the resistance in series with the ammeter and a good earth on the generator. Make the best connections possible, as extra resistance will give faulty readings.

2 Connect the positive terminal of the voltmeter to the same regulator terminal and earth the other side.

3 Run the generator at approximately 4000 rev/min, remembering that this speed is not the same as engine rev/min. Set the resistance to show a reading of about 45 amps on the meter. The voltage indicated should be at least 6 to 7.5 volts on the 6-volt system. Renew the regulator if the reading is not within the limits. **Repair or adjustment is a job for an authorized Service Station.**

On 12-volt systems the regulator is sealed and no attempt should be made to adjust it. **Repair and adjustment must be left to an official Service Station.** It is possible to make a simple test to determine whether the regulator is working if the generator and battery are known to be in good order. Remove the rear seat to reach the regulator. Connect a moving coil 0-20 volt meter across regulator terminal B+ and a good earth. Battery voltage should be indicated. Run the engine and increase the speed. The meter reading should rise as the generator is cut-in by the regulator, but only by a small amount.

Repeating an earlier warning, connections to the generator and the regulator must be made with the engine stopped and cable B+ (or 51) disconnected. A shortcircuit will make the regulator unserviceable. Interchanging the cables to D+ (or +) and F (or DF), may affect the polarity of the generator.

11:5 Removing and installing generator

On 6-volt generators disconnect the battery earthing strap and the cables to the regulator terminals. Release the regulator from the generator body. Disconnect the two cables D+ (or +) and F (or DF) from under the regulator. On 12-volt generators simply remove the two cables.

Remove the air cleaner and carburetter. Take off the fan belt and remove the generator retaining strap. Remove the cooling air thermostat by undoing the screws with a socket inserted through the holes in the lower air deflector plate under the engine. Detach the warm air hoses from the fan housing, remove the two fan housing screws at the sides and lift the housing, referring to **Chapter 4** if necessary. Remove the four screws from the fan housing cover and lift the generator and fan away.

Installing the generator:

Reverse the removal instructions. When the regulator is mounted on the generator the thick cable from one of the brushes is connected to D+ (or +) under the regulator. The thin field coil cable must be connected to the F (or DF) terminal under the regulator. If a new regulator has been fitted without curing any defects in the system, the generator is at fault. Bear in mind, however, that reversed generator leads may have reversed the generator polarity. Refer to the next section on generator servicing for instructions on restoring correct polarity.

11:6 Generator servicing

The general instructions given here are applicable to the 12-volt as well as the 6-volt generator. In the same way the illustration of the components of the generator may be used as a guide, although some differences in the terminal construction may be found. Remove, dismantle and service the 12-volt generator in the sequence suggested, but note that when testing the resistance of the field coils, the correct figure is 3.5 ohms.

The largest permissible eccentricity of the commutator is .001 inch. The armature must not contact the field coil polepieces and the maximum permissible eccentricity of the laminations is .002 inch.

If it is obvious that the generator is defective due to electrical faults or serious mechanical wear it is recommended that it should be entrusted to the skilled care of an official Service Agent. Quite the best way of overcoming serious defects in the generator is to make use of the manufacturer's exchange scheme.

Use **FIG 11 :1** for reference purposes. The illustration shows the Bosch generator but the VW generator will be found to resemble it fairly closely. The most likely differences will be in the bearing assemblies, so make a careful note of the sequence of circlips, washers, seals and spacers which will be found on the armature shaft or in the end covers.

Note that the generator and regulator must both be of the same make.

To dismantle a generator, do the following:

1 Remove the driving pulley and the fan. Disconnect the field coil terminal 100 from the holder of the positive brush.

2 Remove the two long through-bolts 45. Prise out the keys 56 and remove any burrs from the shaft of armature 50. Tap off the end cover 30.

3 At the other end, tap off cover 20 which will bring the armature with it. Check the position of the various washers, seals and spacers at the commutator end. Press the armature shaft out of the bearing in the end cover 20.

4 To remove the bearing in the end cover at the fan end, remove the two screws from retainer plate 53. Clean all parts except the windings with fuel and dry thoroughly, preferably with compressed air.

Check the condition of the brush gear and commutator as described in **Section 11 :3**. Inspect the field coils and connections for breakdown of insulation. Check the dry bearings for cracks, pitting or roughness when spun. Check the armature laminations for the bright marks of actual contact with the field coil polepieces. **Never attempt to straighten a bent shaft or machine the armature laminations.** Test the armature and the field coils.

Armature testing:

Badly burned spots between the commutator segments indicate broken windings. Shortcircuits can be checked on a device called a growler which is part of Service Station equipment.

Field coil testing:

Test coils 1 with a battery and test lamp, trying each one for an open circuit. Test for earthing by putting a 230-volt test lamp across one end of each coil and the body of the generator.

Testing for a shortcircuit needs either an ohmmeter or an ammeter. Compare the readings of resistance. To use the ammeter connect a 6-volt battery in series with the meter and check the current consumption of each coil. If the difference is more than half an amp there is a shortcircuit in one of the coils.

Reassembling generator:

Fill the bearings with high-melting point grease and no other. Reassemble in the reverse sequence to dismantling.

It is possible for a generator to have reversed polarity due to crossed leads or shortcircuits. Before installing an overhauled generator, motor it for a short time, using a battery of the correct voltage. Connect terminal F (or DF) to earth, the positive terminal of the battery to D+ (or +) and the negative battery terminal to earth or D—.

Fit the fan and cover so that there is the correct clearance given in **Chapter 4.** Tighten the fan nut to a torque of 40-47 lb ft.

The generator is cooled by air from the fan housing. The fan cover plate has a slot on the periphery for the cooling air intake, and it is most important to fit this cover to the fan housing with the slot at the bottom.

Finally, fit the pulley, adjust the belt tension and make the connections to the regulator. The red cable goes to terminal 51 and the blue cable to terminal 61.

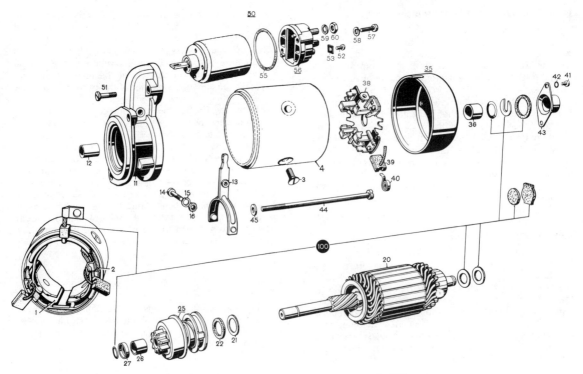

FIG 11:5   Components of Bosch starter motor in EEF series

Key to Fig 11:5   1 Field coil   2 Insulating strip   3 Screw for polepiece   4 Cover   11 Intermediate housing
12 Bush for transmission casing   13 Pinion engaging lever   14 Screw   15 Lockwasher   16 Nut   20 Armature   21 Shim
22 Packing ring   25 Pinion assembly   26 Bush   27 Stop ring   35 Commutator end cover   36 Bush   38 Brush plate assembly
39 Carbon brush   40 Brush spring   41 Screw   42 Spring washer   43 End cap   44 Screw   45 Washer   50 Solenoid assembly
51 Screw   52 Screw   53 Lockplate   55 Packing ring   56 Switch cover   57 Screw   58 Lockwasher   59 Lockwasher
60 Nut   100 Kit of parts

11:7 Starter motor, description and maintenance

The illustration shown in **FIG 11:5** is of the 6-volt starter but will be found to be applicable to the 12-volt starter. Use the instructions given when servicing the 12-volt starter and note the following extra information.

The brush contact surface of the commutator should have a uniform grey-blue appearance and must be free from grease or oil. Maximum permissible runout is .002 inch. Use only genuine replacement brushes and fit a complete set when renewal is necessary.

Heavy brush arcing is caused by the commutator being out-of-round, by the brushes being worn or jammed or the springs weak, by unsoldered connections to the segments or by protruding insulation between the segments.

When cleaning the dismantled parts, do not immerse the armature or the drive pinion assembly in solvents such as petrol. It must also be remembered that solvents will remove the lubricant from porous self-lubricating bushes.

The starter motor is flange-mounted on the righthand side of the transmission housing. In the transmission housing is an outrigger bush for supporting the extended armature shaft. The starter pinion meshes with a flywheel ring gear with 130 teeth. The outrigger bush has a bore of 10.89 mm. There is a non-repeat lock in the ignition switch to prevent any attempt to actuate the starter while the engine is running. Before the starter can be operated again the ignition key must be turned right off. As mentioned earlier there are both Bosch and VW starters fitted to the various models. **FIG 11:5** shows the Bosch starter in exploded form. The pinion and solenoid assembly on VW starters will be found to be different in design but similar in operating principles. If care is taken to note the sequence for removing the various shims, washers and locking rings from the armature shaft, there should be no difficulty in dismantling and reassembling either make.

Routine maintenance:

The plain bushes which are used as bearings do not require regular lubrication. When the starter is due for overhaul, the bush at the commutator end can receive attention and when the starter is removed at any time, the outer bush in the transmission casing can be checked for wear and lubricated with grease.

The brushes should be checked every 6000 miles. Remove the brush inspection covers on the VW starter or the end cover 35 in **FIG 11:5** on the Bosch starter. Pull on the brush leads to check that the brushes 39 slide freely in their holders. Check the length of each brush.

If the flexible lead is almost in contact with the metal brush-holder it is time for renewal. While the brushes are out, examine the commutator. If badly burned or worn it will be necessary to remove the armature 20 to have the commutator skimmed. If the segments are just dirty or oily, clean them by rubbing a cloth dampened with fuel against them with a small piece of wood. Check that the springs 40 are not weak or broken. The renewal of brushes is covered under 'Starter motor servicing'. When refitting the brushes into their holders, make sure the flexible connectors are so placed that the brushes can move freely.

11 : 8 Starter motor servicing

Removal:

1 Disconnect the earthing strap from the battery.
2 Disconnect the cables from the two terminals on the solenoid.
3 Remove the bolts and nuts from the mounting flange and withdraw the starter.

Dismantling:

Refer to **FIG 11 : 5** and proceed as follows:

1 Release the connector strip from the solenoid 50 and remove screws 51 to release the solenoid from the intermediate bracket. Lift the solenoid until its slotted pullrod is clear of lever 13 and remove.
2 Remove end cap 43 and the sealing ring. Prise out the lock ring from the shaft and pull off the shims. Remove bolts 44 and end cover 35. This will also release the brush-holder plate 38, but lift the brushes before pulling the holder off the armature shaft.
3 Separate the starter body from the intermediate housing 11. Remove the pinion assembly. Remove the shift lever bolt 14 to release lever 13. A defective pinion assembly must be renewed complete.

These instructions will also be applicable to 12-volt starters.

Removing and dismantling VW starter:

1 Remove the connector strip from the solenoid, remove the two nuts and withdraw the housing with insulating disc. Remove the nut from the field coil lead and take off the specially shaped rubber seal.
2 Disconnect the connector strip at the end plate and remove the cap from the commutator end. From the end of the shaft, remove the circlip and the steel and bronze washers. Remove burrs from the shaft.
3 Lift off the two segmental brush covers, lift the brushes and wedge in position. Remove the two long through-bolts. This will enable the intermediate bracket at the drive end to be lifted off together with the armature. Keep a careful note of the position of the various washers.
4 Disconnect the field coil lead from the brush-holder and lift off the end plate. Remove the brake washer and thrust ring.
5 At the pinion end remove the spring clips and pivot pins from inside the bracket, pull out the insulating plate and turn the contact plate of the pointed solenoid

core through 90 deg. Withdraw the armature, shifting linkage and solenoid core as a unit. Take off the circlip and retaining washers from the drive end of the shaft. Take the armature in one hand and the pinion in the other. Pull the shift collar about $\frac{3}{16}$ inch from the over-running clutch and remove the drive assembly by turning clockwise and jerking slightly. Remove the shift collar and the five steel balls from the over-running clutch. The clutch cannot be dismantled.

Checking for defects:

Clean the parts in fuel but do not immerse the armature or field coils in it and keep it away from the porous bush at the commutator end. If the drive pinion is oily or has been reluctant to engage in cold weather it can be washed in fuel. Excessive oil in the starter may be traceable to a defective crankshaft oil seal or a main drive shaft oil seal.

Renew brushes by soldering the new leads into place one at a time. If the commutator is worn and out of round it can be skimmed in a lathe. Mount the shaft between centres and take light cuts with a keen tool. Do not reduce Bosch commutators below a diameter of 1.35 inches. After machining, or if the insulation stands proud between the copper segments, undercut the insulation about $\frac{1}{64}$ inch, using a ground-down hacksaw blade as shown in **FIG 11 : 2**. Maximum permissible runout is .002 inch.

Test the field coils 1 in **FIG 11 : 5** for open circuit by using a 6-volt battery and a test lamp with prods. Place the prods at the ends of each coil. If the outer insulation is in order it is rare to find a shortcircuit. Tests for short-circuits need special equipment.

Test for earthed coils by using test prods and a 240-volt lamp. Put one prod on a coil end and the other to the frame or body. Make sure that electrical connections between the coils are sound.

An electrical test for earthed armature windings can be made with test prods and a 240-volt lamp. Put one prod on the armature laminations and the other to each commutator segment in turn. Check the condition of the soldered joints at the risers of each segment. Sometimes the solder becomes overheated and is flung off.

Check the bearing bushes for play. After protracted use it is always advisable to renew these bushes. Before fitting new ones, soak them in hot engine oil for some hours. Press into place using a mandrel the same diameter as the armature shaft.

Check the solenoid connections by testing to earth with a 240-volt lamp and test prods. It is possible for excessive tightening of the terminal nuts to damage the insulation. The pull-in and hold-in windings of the Bosch solenoid can be checked for power and consumption by an official Service Station. **If defective, a solenoid must be renewed complete.**

The VW solenoid should move the pinion .240 inch. If less than this, the reason may lie in worn linkages or excessive end float of the armature. The permissible end float of .004 to .012 inch can be obtained by shimming. If, when holding the VW armature, the pinion cannot be turned anticlockwise, the over-running clutch is tight on the shaft. The clutch must be renewed as a unit. If the pinion does not spring right back to rest it may be due to sticking of the solenoid core or linkage, or the pressure spring in the over-running clutch may not be engaging.

FIG 11:6   Correct setting of solenoid actuating rod on Bosch starter motor

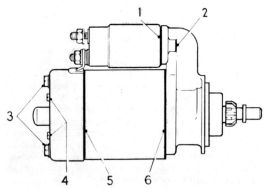

FIG 11:7   To seal starter motor against water and grit, use sealing compound at points indicated. Use compound D.14 at point 1, and compound D.1a under screw heads at 2, 3 and 4, and at joints 5 and 6

To test a 6-volt VW solenoid use a 6-volt battery and an ammeter reading to 50 amps. Insert the ammeter in a lead from the positive battery terminal to terminal 50. Connect the negative battery terminal to the pull-in winding terminal, when the meter should record a drain of 35-40 amps. To check the hold-in winding connect the negative battery terminal to the coverplate, when the meter should record a drain of 10-12 amps. Renew a defective solenoid.

11:9 Starter motor assembling

If the solenoid on a recent Bosch starter has been renewed, check the dimension indicated in **FIG 11:6**. When the core is drawn right in the distance from the face of the solenoid body to the outer end of the operating slot must be .748 ± .004 inch. Loosen the locknut and turn the rod to adjust.

Assembling Bosch starters:

Refer to **FIG 11:7** for details of the places where effective sealing is necessary to prevent the entry of water and road grit.

Assemble the armature and drive pinion to the intermediate bracket. Fit the stop ring and circlip, locking the stop ring in place by peening with a small chisel. Lubricate all moving parts and the shift lever with universal grease. Check that the support washer and seal between the starter body and the intermediate bracket are correctly fitted and assemble the parts together, using VW sealing compound D1a. Apply a touch of special Bosch grease to the shaft at the commutator end. Excessive lubricant at this point is liable to cause trouble with an oily commutator.

Fit the brushes and the brush holder. Apply sealing compound VW/D1a as indicated and fit the end cover. Apply sealer to the long through-bolts and fit them. Before fitting the cover fit the shims and lockwasher to the end of the shaft and check the armature end float, which should be between .004 and .012 inch. Fit the end cap with seal and put sealer under the screw heads.

To fit the solenoid, apply a strip of VW sealing compound D14 to the outer edge of the end face. Pull on the drive pinion and hook the solenoid operating slot over the lever. Put sealer on the solenoid fixing screws. Connect the field coil connector to the solenoid.

To install the starter motor, first put universal grease in the bush in the transmission casing. Apply VW sealing compound D1a between the intermediate bracket and the transmission. Insert the long screw in the bracket and fit the starter to the transmission. Connect the leads, making sure the terminals are clean and tightened securely but not excessively.

Assembling VW starters:

The steel balls of the drive assembly can be held in place with high-melting point grease. Lightly grease all moving parts. Push the over-running clutch into place by jerking slightly to ensure that the inner spring passes over the shoulder of the pinion and engages the groove. Pull the clutch forward to check the engagement of the spring. Fitting the circlip is easier if a tapered mandrel is available.

Fit the linkage and solenoid core to the shift collar and insert the driving end of the armature in the intermediate bracket. Turn the solenoid contact plate through 90 deg. and insert the insulating plate above it, and up to the stop. Fit the two pivot pins and secure with the spring clips. Fit the thrust ring and brake washer in the commutator end plate. Fit the body to the end plate so that the nose enters the groove in the plate. Connect the field coil lead to the positive brush-holder. Insert the armature assembly and fit the through-bolts, making sure the washers and shims are correctly positioned. Install the solenoid with the terminal in perfect contact and the profiled rubber seal seated properly.

Make sure all parts are sealed against the ingress of water and dirt, including the brush inspection covers and the end cap. Renew parts which do not seat properly. Use **FIG 11:7** for reference.

Fit the starter motor to the transmission casing in the manner described for the Bosch starter.

11:10 Headlamp servicing and adjustment

Some vehicles are fitted with headlamps incorporating parking lights and renewable bulbs with twin filaments to give main and dipped beams. Other vehicles are fitted with sealed-beam headlamps in which the front glass and reflector are sealed and form the bulb with the filaments inside. Failure of a filament in this type means that the complete unit must be renewed.

On the earlier type with separate bulb it is essential to handle the bulb with a piece of cloth or paper and not the bare fingers. Never attempt to clean the reflecting surface and do not touch it with the fingers. If the reflector loses its shine it must be renewed.

Renewing headlamp bulb:

1 Loosen the screw at the bottom of the rim. Take out the light unit by lifting the bottom to unhook the rim at the top.
2 From the back of the reflector, remove the bulb-holder by turning to the left, as in **FIG 11 : 8**. Pull the connector off the base of the bulb.
3 Fit the new bulb, holding it with a piece of cloth or paper. When installing, the lug in the bulb-holder must engage the notch in the reflector. The contact strip must press firmly on the base of the parking light bulb.

Renewing headlamp glass:

1 Remove the light unit as just described. Take out both bulbs.
2 Note the long springs holding the reflector in the rim. Hold down one end of a spring firmly and release the other end. Be careful when doing this, as a flying spring might cause an accident.
3 Clean up the threaded ends of the adjusting screws and remove them. Take out the retaining ring with reflector, glass and seal. Do not finger the reflecting surface.
4 Fit the new glass and sealing ring with the 'TOP' mark correctly positioned. Fit the reflector and retaining ring with the sealing ring between the rim and the retainer.
5 Fit the adjusting screws and peen the ends. Fit the retaining springs. Fit the light unit and adjust the beam as instructed later. Do not fit headlamps of one make with parts of another make.

Renewing sealed-beam light unit:

Loosen screw in lower edge of trim ring (see **FIG 11 : 9**) and remove ring. Remove the three screws securing sealed beam unit retaining ring and take off ring. Remove sealed beam unit and disconnect socket.

When refitting sealed beam unit, engage three lugs in support ring. Check headlamp beam setting.

Karmann Ghia lamps:

The preceding instructions will be applicable to renewable-bulb and sealed-beam headlamps on Karmann Ghias.

Headlamp beam setting:

This must be done in accordance with the Lighting Regulations of the country concerned. Basic setting on righthand-drive vehicles is done as follows:

FIG 11 : 10 shows the layout of aiming points on a vertical surface which is symmetrical about the centre line of the vehicle and at right-angles to the centre line. The vehicle must be standing on level ground 16 feet 5 inches away from the aiming surface, or 25 feet for sealed-beam lamps. Tyre pressures must be correct, and the rear seat must be weighted with one passenger or 154 lb.

Dim the headlamps and cover one. Aim the other by turning the two adjusting screws indicated in **FIG 11 : 11**. The top screw **B** is used for vertical aiming and the lower screw **A** for horizontal aiming. On renewable bulb headlamps the object is to get the horizontal borderline between light and dark to coincide with the horizontal line marked by the crosses. The point of the angle between

FIG 11 : 8   Headlamp assembly (non-sealed beam type)

FIG 11 : 9   Headlamp assembly (sealed beam type)

light and dark should coincide with the cross. On sealed-beam headlamps use the lower diagram in **FIG 11 : 10** and get the top edge of the high-intensity zone on the horizontal line and the righthand edge 2 inches to the left of the vertical line.

The setting of headlamp beams is so important in the interests of all road users that it is recommended to entrust the work to a Service Station equipped with the necessary devices, unless the greatest care is taken to ensure accurate results which conform to the Regulations.

11 : 11 Fuses and warning lights

A box containing ten or twelve fuses, according to model, is mounted either under the instrument panel near the steering column or, in the case of 1303 models, under the centre of the dash. In both cases the fuses are accessible from inside the car.

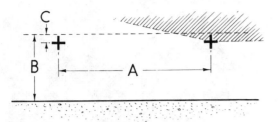

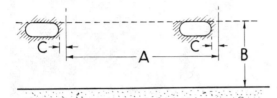

FIG 11:10 Headlamp beam setting on renewable-bulb type (top) and on sealed beam type (bottom). **A** is distance between lamp centres, **B** is height of lamp centres above ground level, and **C** is 2 inches

FIG 11:11 Turn screw **A** for horizontal beam setting. and screw **B** for vertical setting

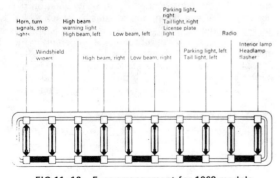

FIG 11:12 Fuse arrangement for 1968 models

There have been many changes in the arrangement of the fuse box so that it is not possible to detail which circuits are protected by which fuse for every model: two typical arrangements are shown in **FIGS 11:12** and **11:13**. In some cases the circuits protected are detailed on the transparent cover of the fuse box. If not, and in the absence of the driver's handbook, it is not difficult to locate fuses, if necessary, by removing each in turn and checking to see which items are inoperative with the fuse removed. A spare fuse position may be provided in the box to be used for optional additions such as a radio.

The fuses are mainly 8 amp with, usually, two 16 amp fuses protecting higher current items such as the wiper motor. Always carry one or two spare fuses of each capacity. Never use tinfoil, wire, or any other substitute in place of a blown fuse; the fuse is designed to be the weakest link in the circuit and if it has blown because of, for example, a short circuit, using an unsuitable substitute may lead to damage elsewhere in the wiring.

If a fuse blows, make a quick check for any obvious cause before renewing it. If the replacement blows there is a fault which should be traced and rectified. The most likely causes are a loose connection or damaged insulation causing a short circuit, or an internal fault in a unit such as a flasher relay.

Apart from the main fuse box, additional line fuses are located elsewhere on some models. An 8 amp fuse in a holder on the fan housing above the generator protects the reversing light circuit. On some semi-automatic transmission models the control valve circuit has a fuse near the ignition coil; if it blows the gears cannot be selected. An 8 amp fuse under the rear seat protects the heated rear window on some models.

Panel lights and warning lights:

On most models, access to the instrument lights and warning lights, can be gained by removing the cover at the rear of the front luggage compartment, revealing the back of the instrument panel as shown in **FIG 11:14**. The bulb holders are a push fit in the instruments. In addition to the lights shown, Karmann Ghia models have an extra bulb to illuminate the clock.

On 1303 models the re-designed facia necessitates a different procedure. Two narrow, rectangular cover strips, one at each of the instrument panel insert carrying the switches, can be carefully pulled off to reveal four screws. Alternatively, there may be an individual plug covering each screw. After removing these screws and a fifth screw near the centre of the panel, below the speedometer, the panel can be eased out of the facia. It is then possible, working through the opening, to push the speedometer out of its mounting, disconnecting the speedometer cable if necessary by unscrewing the knurled ring. The speedometer is a push-fit in the facia, retained by its rubber sealing ring. The instrument light and warning light bulbs are carried in push-fit holders in the back of the speedometer, as on earlier models. The switches on this model are retained in the panel insert by integral plastic tabs which must be depressed to release the switch. The clock, if fitted, is a push-fit retained by a rubber seal, like the speedometer.

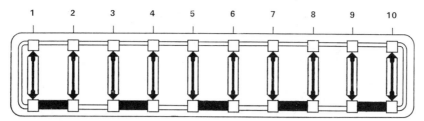

FIG 11:13   Fuse arrangement for 1969-70 Beetles. The items shown in brackets are not fitted to every vehicle

Key to Fig 11:13   1 Horn, indicators, fuel gauge (dual circuit brake warning light), (automatic), (heated rear window)
2 Windscreen wipers, brake lights   3 Main beam warning light, main beam lefthand   4 Main beam righthand
5 Dipped beam lefthand   6 Dipped beam righthand   7 Parking light lefthand, tail light lefthand   8 Parking light
righthand, tail light righthand, licence plate light   9 (Hazard warning light system), interior light (headlamp flasher)   10 (Radio)

11:12 Direction indicators and hazard warning lights

Hazard warning lights:

A hazard warning light system is fitted to 1970 Beetles and Karmann Ghias. This system operates with the ignition switched on or off. A relay is incorporated in the flashing direction indicator circuit. When the warning light knob is pulled out, the relay operates and all four direction indicators flash at the same time. A lamp in the warning light knob indicates that the system is operating. The wiring diagram is given in the Appendix.

Flashing direction indicators:

Before renewing an apparently defective flasher unit, check that it is making a good earth connection with the vehicle body. The location on many models is as shown at **A** in **FIG 11:14**. Note that some models have units which are screwed in place while others are clipped to the body panel by a spring tongue in the base. These will readily slide out when pulled. The front unit of the pair fitted to Karmann Ghias is the headlamp flasher relay.

On 1303 models the flasher unit is plugged into the top of the fuse box which is mounted under the centre of the dash. Removal of two screws allows the fuse box to be lowered and angled for access to the unit.

Failure of the flashers may be due to a blown fuse. The warning light on the dash will flash faster than usual if one of the flasher bulbs has failed. If both flashers on one side fail, the warning light will not operate, but do not forget that it is possible for the warning light to have burned out.

Before removing a flasher unit, take the earthing strap off the battery. Then remove the three leads, noting how they are connected. Screw the unit out of the mounting bracket or slide it free on models where it is clipped in place.

Defective units cannot be repaired. When refitting a unit make quite sure that it is correctly connected and is effectively earthed to the frame. The headlamp flasher relay on Karmann Ghias can be serviced in the same way.

Self-cancelling indicator switch:

Below the cables leaving the switch under the steering wheel hub is a screw which clamps the switch to the column. The clearance between the switch and the hub must be .080+.020 inch and this can be set by moving the column tube up or down. To set the switch so that it cancels correctly, slacken the clamping screw and turn the switch in the required direction. If the wheel is removed at any time, set the front wheels straight-ahead and fit the brass washer so that its recess points to the right. Fit the steering wheel with the spokes horizontal and the spoke recesses for the horn ring towards the driver's seat. The tongue on the cancelling ring must then engage with the brass washer.

11:13 Horn and windscreen wipers

The horn is mounted under the lefthand wing, except on the Karmann Ghia which is fitted with a pair in the spare wheel compartment. If a horn does not operate or has a poor note, check the security of the mounting and

FIG 11:14   Location of instrument and warning lights behind panel. A is the flasher unit. Access is gained by removing the front luggage compartment (boot) lining forward of the instrument panel

Key to Fig 11:14   1 Fuel gauge light   2 Speedometer light
3 Headlamp warning light   4 Oil pressure warning light
5 Flashing indicators   6 Generator warning light

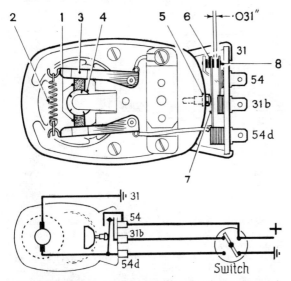

FIG 11:15 The early type windscreen wiper motor and wiring diagram. Note contact clearance. Refer to wiring diagrams for applicable connections

Key to Fig 11:15 1 Carbon brushes 2 Brush tension spring 3 Brush holder 4 Commutator 5 Self-parking plunger 6 Moving contact 7 Moving contact spring blade 8 Fixed contact

see that the horn does not touch the body. Also check the earthing and current supply from the horn button or ring. High resistance of dirty contacts and connections will be a contributory cause of trouble with the horn.

An attempt to adjust the horn must be made with great care. If the vibrating contacts inside the horn are kept in contact for too long with current passing, they will be damaged and the fuse will be likely to blow.

The adjusting screw on all vehicles except Karmann Ghias is on the back of the horn. Turn it fractionally in either direction and test with a quick operation of the horn button or ring. Continue until the best note is achieved. If it is impossible to find a position which gives a loud clear note, the horn must be renewed. After adjustment, the adjusting screw must be sealed with paint or shellac to prevent the ingress of water.

Before removing the horn, take out the fuse on the extreme left. On Karmann Ghias, disconnect the cable from terminal 87 on the relay to be found behind the instrument panel. This is the front of two units between the speedometer and the clock. Loosen the rubber boot in the front panel, lift out the spare wheel and disconnect the cable. Remove the securing screws and lift out the horns complete with boot. On all vehicles, make sure the horn is properly earthed, that it does not touch the body, and on Karmann Ghias, that the rubber boot is correctly positioned. Also on Karmann Ghias, there is a horn relay clipped into a hole in the side panel in the front compartment. To remove the relay, take out the fuse on the extreme left and then disconnect the four cables from the relay. Slide the relay upwards to detach it.

Horn controls can be examined by prising off the cap. Make sure all contact parts are clean and bright, and any springs correctly located.

The windscreen wipers:

These are operated by a linkage connected to a motor mounted on a frame behind the instrument panel in the front compartment.

The automatic parking action cannot work if the blades stop outside the area at the end of the return stroke, where switching takes place. If the blades are frozen to the screen or obstructed by piled snow it is possible for the motor to be burnt out. If the battery is flat and the arms have stopped midway, it is essential to move them to the parked position.

Apart from the renewal of wiper blades, there are several points which need lubrication after long service and the wiper motor brushes and commutator will also need cleaning and checking.

To remove the motor and linkage, take off the wiper arms by loosening the clamp screws. Disconnect the battery earthing strap. From the outside of the body, remove the hexagon nuts, washers and seals from the wiper arm and shaft bearings. Remove the cover from the back of the instrument panel and disconnect the lead to the wiper motor. Remove the glove box. On models since 1973 the wiper motor and frame are in the fresh air box. Remove the bolt securing the triangular wiper bracket to the body. The bracket carries the motor and linkage complete. To remove the motor, disconnect the driving link, loosen the shaft securing nut and motor nut. Removal of the connecting rod will enable the wiper arm bearings to be checked and renewed if necessary. If the plastic bushes in the linkages are worn, renew the links complete and fit them with the hollow side facing the triangular frame. When fitting the wiper bearings the pressed lug on the frame must engage the groove in the bearing.

Servicing wiper motor:

Refer to **FIG 11:15** and take off the cap by releasing the clip or removing a screw. Unhook the brush-holder spring 2 and swing the holders 3 outwards. Use long-nosed pliers to remove and insert brushes 1. Clean the commutator 4 with a fuel-moistened cloth. When the brush-holders are restored to the working position, make sure that the brushes bear on the commutator. Before reassembling, lubricate all linkage joints, shaft bearings and wiper arm joints. Note that plunger 5 is operated by a cam on the large gear at the other end of the motor and movement of the plunger operates the contacts 6 and 8 which form part of the parking switch.

Installation of wiper assembly:

Before fitting the assembly, check that the driving link is fitted with its angled end towards the righthand wiper bearing. The inner seal on the wiper arm bearing must be fitted so that the shoulder of the rubber moulding faces the wiper arm when installed. Move the wiper frame on its elongated hole so that the wiper spindles are at right-angles to the windscreen. The earthing cable on the securing screw must make good electrical contact.

11:14 The alternator

An alternator must never be run with the battery disconnected.

The battery earth cable must be disconnected before removing or installing the alternator or regulator.

The engine and alternator must never be started with a battery charger or booster still connected.

Check carefully that the cables are connected the right way round before coupling to the battery or starting the engine.

Disconnect the alternator before using electric welding apparatus on the car.

Testing:

1 With the engine stopped remove the positive battery cable, and fit a battery cut-out switch, reconnect the positive cable.
2 Fit a tachometer to the engine.
3 Fit a variable resistance between the positive terminal of the battery in series with an ammeter, and an earth on the chassis.
4 Connect the positive terminal of a voltmeter to the positive terminal of the battery and the negative side to an earth on the chassis.
5 With the battery in the circuit start the engine and run at 2500 to 3000 rev/min.
6 Adjust the variable resistance so that the ammeter gives a reading of 25 amps.
7 Cut the battery out of the circuit by means of the cut-out switch.
8 Re-adjust the variable resistance as necessary to maintain the ammeter reading of 25 amps.
9 Read off the voltage indicated on the voltmeter which should be 12.5 to 14.5 volts.

If the indicated reading is outside these values change the regulator and re-test.

If the reading is still outside the rated values change the alternator.

No repair parts are available for the alternator.

Removing and refitting:

The alternator is removed and refitted in a similar manner to DC generators, refer to the instructions in **Section 11:5.**

11:15 Fault diagnosis

(a) Battery discharged

1 Terminals loose or dirty
2 Battery internally defective
3 Short circuits
4 Generator not charging
5 Regulator defective

(b) Insufficient charging current

1 Check 1 and 4 in (a)
2 Generator driving belt slipping

(c) Battery will not hold charge

1 Low level of electrolyte
2 Battery plates sulphated
3 Electrolyte leaking from cracked casing or top seal
4 Plate separators ineffective

(d) Battery overcharged

1 Regulator defective

(e) Generator output low or nil

1 Belt broken or slipping
2 Faulty regulator unit
3 Shaft bent, worn bearings, loose polepieces
4 Commutator insulation proud, segments worn, burned or shorted
5 Brushes sticking, springs broken or weak
6 Field coils faulty

(f) Warning lamp not lighting with ignition on

1 Battery faults
2 Defective ignition switch
3 Bulb burned out
4 Generator brushes not contacting commutator

(g) Warning lamp stays on or brightens with engine speeding

1 Driving belt loose, generator faulty
2 Regulator faulty, charging cables loose or broken

(h) Warning lamp goes out only at high speed

1 Generator or regulator faulty

(j) Warning lamp stays on with ignition off

1 Contact points in regulator stuck

(k) Starter motor lacks power or will not operate

1 Battery discharged, loose connections
2 Solenoid switch contacts worn or dirty
3 Brushes worn or sticking, springs weak or broken
4 Commutator, armature or field coils defective
5 Armature shaft bent, engine abnormally stiff

(l) Starter motor runs but does not turn engine

1 Drive gear or flywheel gear defective

(m) Drive pinion stays in mesh

1 Armature shaft bent or dirty
2 Solenoid switch faulty

(n) Lamps inoperative or erratic

1 Battery low, bulbs burned out
2 Switch faulty, poor earthing, loose connections, broken wiring

(o) Wiper motor inoperative

1 Armature touching polepieces, windings faulty
2 Brush or commutator trouble
3 Tight bearings, bent linkage
4 Switch faulty, terminals 1 and 2 not connected
5 Wiring fault from terminal 1 to motor terminal 54

(p) Wiper motor runs with switch off, does not park blades

1 Contacts damaged, insulation broken
2 Contact 31b not touching contact 54d
3 Poor earthing of terminal 31b through wiper switch

(q) Wiper motor slow, armature burns out, squeaky operation

1 Lack of lubrication to linkage
2 Armature spindle presses on stop of brush-holder
3 Cover incorrectly positioned
4 Armature touches polepiece

NOTES

CHAPTER 12

THE BODYWORK

12:1 Body finish

The high standard of paintwork on VW vehicles is obtained by skilful application of special primers and finishing coats. These are exclusively available to VW Service Stations so that the repair and painting of any thing but minor damage must be left to them. Small scratches and tiny blemishes can be retouched by the owner, using the special touch-up paint which is supplied by VW. Before applying the paint it is essential to remove all traces of polish. This is done with white spirit, but in the case of silicone finishes, very gentle abrasion with the finest 'wet-or-dry' paper will be needed. If it is intended to retouch a small rusty spot or scratch, the rust must be removed with a gentle abrasive or a piece of wood. Leave each application of paint to dry before adding another coat and restore the brilliance of the abraded areas with a mild cutting compound. Repolish in the usual way.

12:2 Maintenance of bodywork

Apart from the normal cleaning and polishing there are a few places where lubrication is needed. With the exception of Karmann Ghia hinges, the door hinges should have a spot of general-purpose oil applied after dirt has been wiped away. On the edge of the door above the lock is a small hole through which a little oil should be injected to lubricate the lock, as shown in **FIG 12:1**. Lock cylinders must not be oiled, but graphite powder can be applied to the key, which is then inserted and operated a few times.

A tiny smear of universal grease should be applied to the door lock striker plates on the body. In the case of door locks be sparing with grease as it might otherwise come off on clothing.

Clean the seat runners of adhering dust and apply a thin smear of grease. Apply oil to the pivot points of convertible hood frames, being careful to keep it off the rubber seal on the top cover.

Other useful attention is to dust the rubber sealing strips round doors with French chalk. This helps to keep the seals flexible and prevents squeaks. Use the same technique on rubber buffers to eliminate noise.

Use universal grease on other contact surfaces such as bonnet and hood locks.

12:3 Servicing doors

To remove the door, release the check strap from the door pillar bracket by pressing the retaining ring off the

FIG 12:1   To lubricate the door lock, inject a few drops of oil through the hole above the latch

FIG 12:2   To remove an interior handle, press back the escutcheon plate and drive out the crosspin

Removing and installing door lock:

Early type:

To remove the lock, remove both interior handles by pressing in the escutcheon plates and drive out the securing pins as shown in **FIG 12:2**. Prise out the trim panel clips as shown in **FIG 12:3**. Undo the four screws adjacent to the window regulator spindle and remove the regulator. Remove the two screws concealed behind the weatherstrip and take off the outer door handle with rubber seal. From the door shut-face release the lock (four cross-head screws). Adjacent to the interior remote control spindle are two screws. Release these and then remove the screw which secures the rear glass-run channel. Lift up the glass and remove the lock and remote control assembly. Clean and then grease all moving parts. Refit in the reverse order, taking care that the rubber sleeve on the remote control rod is positioned where the rod is guided in the inner door panel. If the guide plate is slightly pre-loaded on the rod it will prevent rattles.

Later type:

Door trim panels:

Removal:

The plastic cover over the window regulator handle should be removed first, by prising it off from the shaft end. This will reveal a cross-headed centre lock screw which must be removed to free the handle assembly.

Prise out with a screwdriver the recessed plate behind the inner door handle lever to reveal a single retaining screw. Remove this and the assembly is freed.

The combined arm rest and door pull is retained by two screws which are unscrewed to release the door pull.

The door trim panel is held in position by a number of clips around its edge. These should be very carefully levered out of their holes in the metal door frame with a screwdriver or other similar tool and the trim panel lifted away.

Refitting:

This is a reversal of the removal procedure. Note that the spiral spring is fitted on the window winding shaft behind the trim panel with the wider end outwards. The large dished washer is fitted on the shaft between the trim panel and the handle.

Door locks:

Removal:

First remove the door trim panel as described to reveal the lock mechanism.

The interior handle can be removed by unscrewing the two retaining bolts and lifting it out together with the remote control and its packing piece. Unclip the interior lock mechanism.

Pull the rubber weather strip back and undo the screw securing the lock to the edge of the door, also the screw securing the outside handle which can now be removed.

The lock mechanism can now be withdrawn from inside the door. Unless the fault in the mechanism is very minor, it is unlikely that it can be repaired and a new lock will be necessary.

fixing screws. Unscrew them and pull the door out sideways complete with hinges. Do not use this procedure if the same door is to be refitted, but simply knock out the hinge pins. However, the lower sill panel must be removed before the bottom hinge pin can be driven out.

To install the door, first fit the weatherstrips if they need renewal. Use adhesive D12 to stick them in place. Having tightened the hinges so that the door does not seem to be far out, remove the lock striker plate from the door pillar and check the door for fit. The hinge fixings are moveable so that adjustment of their position is possible to correct jamming and to line up the door with the body aperture. Refit the striker plate and adjust it as outlined later, until the door shuts smoothly and lines up with the rear quarter panel.

Refitting:

This should present no difficulty if the procedure for removal is reversed, making sure that the lock is operating correctly before finally securing and replacing the trim.

Removing and installing window glass:

Remove the trim panel after taking off the interior handles as described earlier and illustrated in **FIGS 12 : 2** and **12 : 3**. On the passenger's side, pull the trim panel slightly away and then lift it in order to release the arm rest from its support. Release the check strap from the door pillar. Inside the triangular aperture in the door inner panel will be seen four screws securing the window lifting channel. Remove these and push the glass upwards. Release the window regulator from the inner panel and remove the single screw just above the remote control for the lock. Push the regulator inwards and pull the winder assembly downwards and out. Pull the glass down, tilt and remove from the door. If it is necessary to remove the trim moulding and weatherstrip, press out the securing clips from the rear. Remove the slot seal from the inner panel and, if necessary, pull the rear glass-run channel upwards out of the window slot. To remove the window guide channel release the single lower screw from inside the inner panel aperture.

To remove the ventilator, take out the cross-head screw from the upper window frame and lift out the assembly complete with window guide channel. Renew all defective channels.

The rear glass-run channel is supplied in a straight length. Bend it to shape and press into the clips in the door frame and rear guide channel. The lifting channel along the bottom edge of the sliding glass must be fitted 3.15 inch from the edge of the glass as indicated in **FIG 12 : 4**.

Install in the reverse order, greasing the lifting mechanism with universal grease. Fit the glass-run channel together with the ventilator and secure in place. When fitting the glass and the lifter mechanism, if the lifter cannot be pushed through the front guide channel near the remote control for the lock, lift the ventilator slightly.

Secure the window channel loosely to the lifting brackets, open and close the window a few times and then tighten the screws. Use adhesive D12 to stick a new sheet of plastic to the inner panel. Fit the rubber buffers and springs with the large ends of the springs touching the trim panel. Fit the handles at the correct angles.

Adjusting door lock striker plate (except later models):

The plate is shown in **FIG 12 : 5** and basic adjustment dimensions in **FIG 12 : 6**. To set the plate correctly, proceed as follows:

1 Remove the plate and check the fit of the door. The door should be flush with the body aperture with the waistline mouldings in line. The gaps at the top and side of the door should be approximately equal and the door must not rub either at the top or the bottom. The weatherstrip must bear evenly all round the door and be uniformly compressed. Adjust the door position by loosening the hinges.

2 Check the action of the lock by pulling on the door handle. The latch bolt on the underside of item 6 in **FIG 12 : 6** should retract completely into the housing

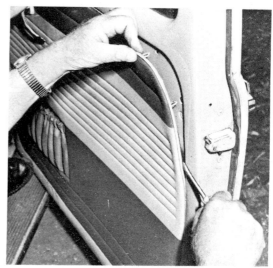

FIG 12 : 3 To remove a trim panel, prise out the spring clips with a screwdriver

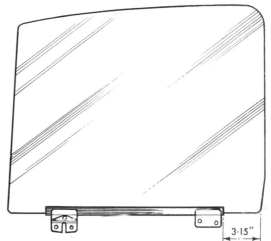

FIG 12 : 4 On front winding windows the lifting channel is positioned as shown

or there will be difficulty in opening and closing the door. The top and bottom surfaces of the housing must be quite flat and the latch bolt and safety catch openings must have no worn edges.

3 Check the striker plate 5. The lower contact surface for the latch housing must be in good condition, with little wear, and the plate must be renewed if the inner V-notch is badly worn. A damaged latch housing may score or wear the plastic wedge, in which case the wedge 4 must be renewed.

4 Fit the striker plate with the screws lightly tightened. Loosen the locknut 2 on the wedge adjusting screw 1 and turn the screw until the flange of the stop bush 3 contacts the inner face of the housing.

5 Adjust the plate sideways first. Shut the door and check that the door and rear quarter panels are flush,

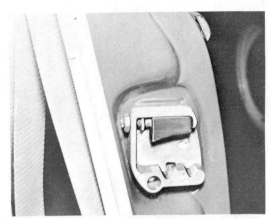

FIG 12:5 Early type of door striker plate, now super-seded by the rotary latch

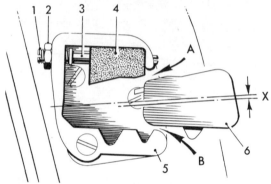

FIG 12:6 Components of early striker plate. Gap **B** should be less than gap **A** by about .08 inch as indicated at **X**.

Key to Fig 12:6
1 Adjusting screw	2 Locknut
3 Adjustable stop	4 Wedge	5 Striker plate
6 Latch housing	

moving the plate either in or out until this condition is reached. Now adjust the plate vertically. Refer to the illustration and set the plate so that the space at **A** is more than at **B.** When closing the door, the latch housing should ride on the lower surface of the plate and be lifted about .08 inch when the door is shut. The position of the plate can be seen if the weather-strip is pulled to one side just before the door is fully shut.

6 Open and close the door several times to check that the bearing faces of the housing and the plate are making even contact. Correct any errors by tilting the plate slightly. When satisfied that everything is working smoothly, tighten the plate screws fully.

7 It will be seen that the flange of adjustable stop 3 can limit the travel of the wedge. To adjust the position correctly, hold the screw by the outer slot and release the locknut. Turn the screw anticlockwise so that the stop moves outwards. Test by shutting the door. Continue to adjust and test until the closing pressure is felt to increase when the closed door is reopened. If this resistance seems to be excessive, or if the door

springs open when an attempt is made to close it, reduce the pressure on the wedge by turning the screw inwards. Tighten the locknut when satisfied.

8 Some readjustment of the wedge may be necessary after a new vehicle has been in use for some time. To complete the work on the door lock, lightly coat the contact surfaces of the latch housing and the wedge with petroleum jelly or molybdenum-disulphide paste.

Adjusting door locks (later models):

These locks have a rotary latch and the striker plate on the door pillar has a rubber wedge bonded to it to prevent rattling, as can be seen in **FIG 12:7.**

To check the adjustment of the striker plate, see that the door is correctly aligned with the rear quarter panel. Using the outer handle, force the door in and out to check for play between the latch and the striker plate. The door must also open without excessive effort, using either handle.

If the door springs open to the safety position when slammed, loosen the striker plate screws and move the top of the plate inwards a small amount until a cure is effected. **FIG 12:8** shows the operation.

If the door is difficult to open with the press button and drops when it is opened, loosen the striker plate and move it downwards.

If the door springs out of the locked position and engages only in the safety position, move the striker plate up slightly.

Sometimes it may be difficult to cure rattles, even by adjusting the striker plate. In this case try the effect of fitting a shim, up to $\frac{1}{64}$ inch thick in the position marked **X** in the illustration. This may cure the trouble without the need to renew the wedge or the striker plate.

12:4 Removing and installing windscreen

These instructions will apply to all vehicles, and to the renewal of other fixed glass windows. It is important to know whether the glass is laminated or of the safety type. Safety glass can be removed and refitted with blows of

FIG 12:7 Loosening striker plate screws to adjust position (latest rotary latch door locks)

the fist or a rubber hammer, but it is dangerous to use this method with the other type of glass. For these, hand pressure most suffice, and in all cases it is wise to protect the hands with cloth.

1 Remove the wiper arms. With laminated glass, use a wooden wedge to loosen the weatherstrip from the body. Start at one of the upper corners and push the screen and weatherstrip outwards.

2 The decorative finisher moulding fitted to the outer face of the rubber surround is secured by two sleeves. Drive these off and remove the moulding halves, followed by the rubber weatherstrip.

3 Remove old sealing compound from the body aperture and check the flange edges. These must be flat and smooth to ensure a leaktight seal.

4 Work the weatherstrip round the edge of the new glass, letting the ends meet halfway along the top edge. Prepare to fit the finisher moulding by inserting some strong cord in the slot in the weatherstrip shown in **FIG 12:9**. This is most readily done by using two or three inches of $\frac{5}{16}$ inch tubing flattened at one end for insertion into the slot. The cord is fed through the tube, which is then drawn round the slot, leaving the cord in position. Cross the cord ends in the centre of the lower edge and leave enough hanging out for handholds.

5 Push one half of the moulding into the slot, followed by the other. Slowly pull on the cord while pushing

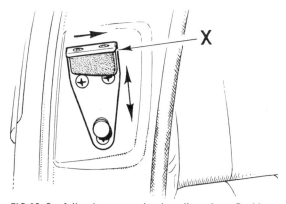

FIG 12:8 Adjusting rotary latch striker plate. Packing inserted at **X** may cure rattles

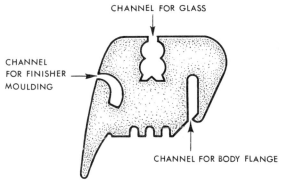

FIG 12:9 Section of windscreen moulding showing slots for glass, finisher moulding and body flange

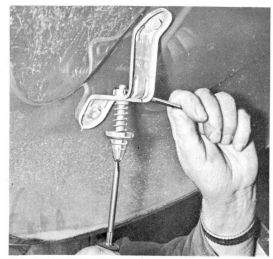

FIG 12:10 Adjusting the position of the bolt for the bonnet lock. Slacken locknut and turn bolt with screwdriver

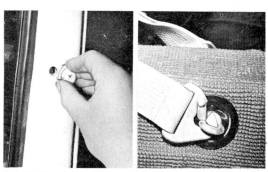

FIG 12:11 Front seat belt fixings. On the left, a plastic screw is removed from the door pillar to provide a top fixing point. The righthand view shows the fixings on the sides of the floor tunnel

the moulding into place, until the operation is completed. Fit the two cover sleeves over the joins.

6 Fit the cord into the slot in the weatherstrip which fits the body aperture, in the manner just described. Apply sealing compound to the outer surface of the weatherstrip and to the bottom corners of the aperture. Secure the services of an assistant.

7 Offer the screen to the outside of the frame with the cord ends inside. Press on the glass and pull at one end of the cable, keeping parallel to the glass. This should draw the lip of the weatherstrip over the body aperture. Continue pulling and pressing until the screen is in place. Safety-glass screens can be helped into place with modest blows from the fist. At all times avoid concentrated pressure in one place.

8 When the glass is properly seated, clean away all surplus sealing compound with petrol or white spirit.

12:5 Bonnet and hood locks

If the bonnet cable breaks, the latch bolt is free and the bonnet can be opened. To renew a cable, remove the lock

FIG 12:12 The location of front and rear seat belt fixings

and the coverplate of the assembly and release the cable from the latch. Pull the cable out of the guide tube. Grease a new cable and insert it in the tube. Press the latch against the spring until it projects into the locking bolt opening and secure the cable with the clamping screw.

To adjust the locking bolt, refer to **FIG 12:10**. Loosen the locknut and turn the bolt in the required direction. Check the action by opening and closing the bonnet several times. If the bolt does not register correctly in the latch opening, slacken the latch fixings and move the assembly in the slotted holes.

The rear hood lock can be removed after unscrewing three crosshead screws from inside. Install the handle from above and the lock from inside and secure with the screws. Operate the hood and lock several times to check the action. If necessary the striker plate can be moved in the slotted holes in order to correct any errors in alignment.

12:6 Removing and installing wings and sills

The wings and sills are bolted in place. To remove front wings, first detach the headlamps and direction indicators. Pull the cable out of the headlamp housing and the grommet from the hole in the wing. Remove one screw securing the wing to the sill and nine screws from the wing flange. Lift the wing and beading off the body.

Renew the beading if faulty. Stick it to the wing flange to ensure correct location. Clean out the body threads with a tap and apply grease to the securing screws. Fit the wing, place a new rubber washer between the wing and the sill. Check headlamp setting when installation is complete.

To remove rear wings, remove the rear lamp assembly and pull out the cables. Remove the bumper and brackets together with the seals. Remove the nut and screw

between the wing and the sill. Remove nine screws and one nut to release the wing. When installing a rear wing, fit a new length of beading if necessary. Use a tap to clean out the threads and oil the screws. Fit a new rubber washer between the wing and the sill. Fit the seals for the bumper bracket into the hole in the wing. Install the lamp, but check the gasket before fixing the lens.

The sill is attached by bolts underneath and by bolts and nuts to the wings. When refitting the sill, tighten the sidemember screws first and then the nuts and screws at the ends. The slots in the sill fit over the washers on the mounting bolts. Do not forget the rubber washers between the sill and the wings.

12:7 Trim and headlining

To remove the rear quarter trim, remove the rear seat and squab. Prise the panel from the inner panel of the body and squab. Prise the panel from the inner panel of the body. On De Luxe models there is a moulding which can be removed by bending up the spring clips. If required, the insulating padding can be stripped off. When fitting the padding, remove all traces of the old adhesive with benzine, and then stick the new padding in place with fresh adhesive. Remove broken moulding clips and fit new ones, bending all clips down after fitting the moulding. Before pressing the trim panel into place, make sure that the waterproof sheeting is correctly fitted so that it overlaps the inner panel and allows water to drain away.

To remove the headlining, remove the rear view mirror. Push forward the cardboard strip at the front end of the lining so that a tool can be inserted between the roof member and the lining. Do this with a finger in the hole in the roof member. Move the tool along, at the same time lifting the front edge of the lining. Insert the tool behind the corner of the front door pillar and work it back to the first support bow. Lift the bow and work the tool right back to the rear. With the lining released on one side, the bows can be pulled out from that side. Repeat the operation on the other side. The tool must then be used to release the rear of the lining and this will allow the lining and bows to be removed as a unit. If necessary, strip off the roof insulation.

Reverse the proceedings to install the headlining. Before sticking a new insulation pad into place, remove old adhesive with benzine. Start refitting at the rear. Fit the tool between the finishing strip and the headlining material and press on the cardboard strip until it is held by the flange of the roof member.

12:8 Sliding or folding roof

Sliding roof:

To remove the Golde sliding roof panel, open the roof halfway. Remove the front trim panel by levering out the five clips with a screwdriver between the panel and the roof. Push the trim panel rearwards as far as it will go. Set the roof about two inches open and unscrew both front guides. Close the roof and unhook the leaf springs from the rear guides, turning them round to face the front. Pull out both rear guide brackets from the supports and lift the roof panel evenly to avoid damage to the seal.

To install the roof panel, press down on the trim panel and slide the roof into the rear opening at an angle.

Lower the front end carefully so that the seal is not damaged and pull the roof to the front. Insert the rear guide brackets and fit the two front guides. Open the roof halfway and pull the trim panel to the front, securing it by pressing the clips into place.

Folding roof:

Rattling of the Golde folding roof can be eliminated by attention to the roller brackets at the ends of the centre bow. Bend the bracket until the roller touches the lower edge of the runner channel without play. If the handle rattles, make sure the spring under the escutcheon or the rubber plug in the tensioner spindle are not missing. Rattling can be cured by fitting a felt washer between the bow and the spring.

A folding roof may be difficult to lock due to too much tension on the rear bow. Slacken the tensioner screw in the centre of the bow. Excessive tension may also lead to trouble with leakage at the front. Alternatively, the seal under the header may be out of place. Sometimes, excessive force when trying to close the roof may bend the locking bow, in which case it must be straightened. If adhesive is required on the top cover use only D11.

Convertible top:

The folding convertible top will operate smoothly if the various joints in the linkage are given a few drops of oil.

Top catches may not hold the top firmly, in which case they must be straightened or renewed. In order to make the catches line up with the retaining lugs on the windscreen frame, leave the catches undone and pull the frame sideways until a cure is effected. Guide tongues which do not enter properly can be set, or small washers can be inserted under the locks. If the roof sidemembers rest on the window frames, the sidemembers may be set cold.

The door gap on a convertible may widen towards the top. This can be rectified by putting hard rubber packing under the body at the support points found just to the rear of the front edge of the rear wings and the bracket bolted to the rear suspension frame.

12:9 Seat belts

These are obtainable from VW Dealers and can be fitted to cars from Chassis No. 4/010/995. On all models the front belts are secured to the door lock pillar and the sides of the frame tunnel as shown in **FIGS 12:11** and **12:12**. For the rear passengers, the fixings are to the side panels under the seat and to the centre of the luggage compartment. Two more points are provided in the roof pillars behind the quarter windows. The fixing points are shown by arrows in **FIG 12:12**.

NOTES

APPENDIX

TECHNICAL DATA

Engine   Fuel system   Ignition system   Clutch
Transmission   Steering   Front suspension
Rear suspension   Brakes   Electrical equipment
Capacities   Torque wrench settings   Wiring diagrams

HINTS ON MAINTENANCE AND OVERHAUL

GLOSSARY OF TERMS

INDEX

Inches	Decimals	Milli-metres	Inches to Millimetres — Inches	Inches to Millimetres — mm	Millimetres to Inches — mm	Millimetres to Inches — Inches
1/64	.015625	.3969	.001	.0254	.01	.00039
1/32	.03125	.7937	.002	.0508	.02	.00079
3/64	.046875	1.1906	.003	.0762	.03	.00118
1/16	.0625	1.5875	.004	.1016	.04	.00157
5/64	.078125	1.9844	.005	.1270	.05	.00197
3/32	.09375	2.3812	.006	.1524	.06	.00236
7/64	.109375	2.7781	.007	.1778	.07	.00276
1/8	.125	3.1750	.008	.2032	.08	.00315
9/64	.140625	3.5719	.009	.2286	.09	.00354
5/32	.15625	3.9687	.01	.254	.1	.00394
11/64	.171875	4.3656	.02	.508	.2	.00787
3/16	.1875	4.7625	.03	.762	.3	.01181
13/64	.203125	5.1594	.04	1.016	.4	.01575
7/32	.21875	5.5562	.05	1.270	.5	.01969
15/64	.234375	5.9531	.06	1.524	.6	.02362
1/4	.25	6.3500	.07	1.778	.7	.02756
17/64	.265625	6.7469	.08	2.032	.8	.03150
9/32	.28125	7.1437	.09	2.286	.9	.03543
19/64	.296875	7.5406	.1	2.54	1	.03937
5/16	.3125	7.9375	.2	5.08	2	.07874
21/64	.328125	8.3344	.3	7.62	3	.11811
11/32	.34375	8.7312	.4	10.16	4	.15748
23/64	.359375	9.1281	.5	12.70	5	.19685
3/8	.375	9.5250	.6	15.24	6	.23622
25/64	.390625	9.9219	.7	17.78	7	.27559
13/32	.40625	10.3187	.8	20.32	8	.31496
27/64	.421875	10.7156	.9	22.86	9	.35433
7/16	.4375	11.1125	1	25.4	10	.39370
29/64	.453125	11.5094	2	50.8	11	.43307
15/32	.46875	11.9062	3	76.2	12	.47244
31/64	.484375	12.3031	4	101.6	13	.51181
1/2	.5	12.7000	5	127.0	14	.55118
33/64	.515625	13.0969	6	152.4	15	.59055
17/32	.53125	13.4937	7	177.8	16	.62992
35/64	.546875	13.8906	8	203.2	17	.66929
9/16	.5625	14.2875	9	228.6	18	.70866
37/64	.578125	14.6844	10	254.0	19	.74803
19/32	.59375	15.0812	11	279.4	20	.78740
39/64	.609375	15.4781	12	304.8	21	.82677
5/8	.625	15.8750	13	330.2	22	.86614
41/64	.640625	16.2719	14	355.6	23	.90551
21/32	.65625	16.6687	15	381.0	24	.94488
43/64	.671875	17.0656	16	406.4	25	.98425
11/16	.6875	17.4625	17	431.8	26	1.02362
45/64	.703125	17.8594	18	457.2	27	1.06299
23/32	.71875	18.2562	19	482.6	28	1.10236
47/64	.734375	18.6531	20	508.0	29	1.14173
3/4	.75	19.0500	21	533.4	30	1.18110
49/64	.765625	19.4469	22	558.8	31	1.22047
25/32	.78125	19.8437	23	584.2	32	1.25984
51/64	.796875	20.2406	24	609.6	33	1.29921
13/16	.8125	20.6375	25	635.0	34	1.33858
53/64	.828125	21.0344	26	660.4	35	1.37795
27/32	.84375	21.4312	27	685.8	36	1.41732
55/64	.859375	21.8281	28	711.2	37	1.4567
7/8	.875	22.2250	29	736.6	38	1.4961
57/64	.890625	22.6219	30	762.0	39	1.5354
29/32	.90625	23.0187	31	787.4	40	1.5748
59/64	.921875	23.4156	32	812.8	41	1.6142
15/16	.9375	23.8125	33	838.2	42	1.6535
61/64	.953125	24.2094	34	863.6	43	1.6929
31/32	.96875	24.6062	35	889.0	44	1.7323
63/64	.984375	25.0031	36	914.4	45	1.7717

UNITS	Pints to Litres	Gallons to Litres	Litres to Pints	Litres to Gallons	Miles to Kilometres	Kilometres to Miles	Lbs. per sq. In. to Kg. per sq. Cm.	Kg. per sq. Cm. to Lbs. per sq. In.
1	.57	4.55	1.76	.22	1.61	.62	.07	14.22
2	1.14	9.09	3.52	.44	3.22	1.24	.14	28.50
3	1.70	13.64	5.28	.66	4.83	1.86	.21	42.67
4	2.27	18.18	7.04	.88	6.44	2.49	.28	56.89
5	2.84	22.73	8.80	1.10	8.05	3.11	.35	71.12
6	3.41	27.28	10.56	1.32	9.66	3.73	.42	85.34
7	3.98	31.82	12.32	1.54	11.27	4.35	.49	99.56
8	4.55	36.37	14.08	1.76	12.88	4.97	.56	113.79
9		40.91	15.84	1.98	14.48	5.59	.63	128.00
10		45.46	17.60	2.20	16.09	6.21	.70	142.23
20				4.40	32.19	12.43	1.41	284.47
30				6.60	48.28	18.64	2.11	426.70
40				8.80	64.37	24.85		
50					80.47	31.07		
60					96.56	37.28		
70					112.65	43.50		
80					128.75	49.71		
90					144.84	55.92		
100					160.93	62.14		

UNITS	Lb ft to kgm	Kgm to lb ft	UNITS	Lb ft to kgm	Kgm to lb ft
1	.138	7.233	7	.967	50.631
2	.276	14.466	8	1.106	57.864
3	.414	21.699	9	1.244	65.097
4	.553	28.932	10	1.382	72.330
5	.691	36.165	20	2.765	144.660
6	.829	43.398	30	4.147	216.990

TECHNICAL DATA

Dimensions are in inches unless otherwise stated. The word 'limit' indicates the maximum permissible wear or clearance

ENGINE

Bore and stroke:
1192 cc ('1200')	77 x 64 mm
1285 cc ('1300' '1302', '1303')	77 x 69 mm
1493 cc ('1500')	83 x 69 mm
1584 cc ('1302S', '1303S')	85.5 x 69 mm

Compression ratio:
1192 cc	7.0:1
1285 cc	7.3:1 (7.5:1 after August 1970)
1493 cc	7.5:1
1584 cc	7.5:1

Crankshaft (all models):
Main journal diameters:	
Nos. 1, 2 and 3	2.1654
No. 4	1.5748
Main bearings:	
Nos. 1, 3 and 4	Sleeve type, aluminium alloy
No. 2	Split shells, aluminium alloy
Main bearing running clearance:	
Nos. 1, 2 and 3	.0016 to .004 (limit .0072)
No. 4	.002 to .004 (limit .0075)
Regrind undersizes	—.25, —.50 and —.75 mm
End float	.0027 to .005 (limit .006)
Crankpin diameter	2.1654
Crankpin regrind undersizes	—.25, —.50 and —.75 mm

Connecting rods (all models): ...
Running clearance, big-end	.0008 to .003 (limit .006)
End float, big-end	.004 to .016 (limit .028)
Maximum permissible weight variation	.18 oz

Pistons (all models):
Type	Aluminium alloy with steel strut
Running clearance (½ inch from skirt bottom at right angles to gudgeon pin)	.0015 to .002 (.0024 on '1500') (limit .008)
Weight tolerance, maximum	.18 oz
Piston rings (all models)	2 compression, 1 oil scraper
Side clearance, top compression	.0027 to .0035 (limit .005)
Side clearance, second compression	.002 to .0027 (limit .004)
Side clearance, oil control	.0012 to .002 (limit .004)
Compression ring gap	.012 to .018 (limit .035)
Oil control ring gap	.010 to .016 (limit .037)
Gudgeon pin type	Fully floating, located by cir-clips
Gudgeon pin bush	Bronze, pressed into connecting rod
Gudgeon pin clearance in bush	.0004 to .0008 (limit .0016)

Camshaft:
    Type (all models) ... ...   Cast iron, three bearings
    Bearings ... ...   Split, steel-backed, whitemetal
        lined

    Running clearance (all models) ... ...   .0008 to .002 (limit .0047)
    End float ... ...   .0016 to .005 (limit .0056)
    Backlash between timing gears ... ...   .0005 to .002

Tappets:
    Diameter ... ...   .7466 to .7472 (limit .7452)
    Working clearance ... ...   .0008 to .0024 (limit .0047)

Rocker shaft:
    Diameter ... ...   .7073 to .7080 (limit .7069)
    Running clearance of rocker ... ...   .0006 to .002 (limit .0031)

Valves:
    Head diameter, inlet:
        1192 cc 1.24
        1285 cc 1.3
        1493 cc, 1584 cc 1.4
    Head diameter, exhaust:
        1192 cc and 1285 cc 1.18
        1493 cc and 1584 cc 1.26
    Seat angle (all models) ... ...   45 deg.
    Stem diameter, inlet:
        1192 cc 1285 cc, 1493 cc and 1584 cc... ... ...   .3126 to .3130
    Stem diameter, exhaust:
        1192 cc, 1285 cc, 1493 cc and 1584 cc ... ...   .3114 to .3118
    Stem to guide clearance, inlet ... ...   .0020 to .0030
    Stem to guide clearance, exhaust ... ...   .0031 to .0041

Valve springs:
    Free length:
        1192 cc and 1285 cc 1.89
    Loaded length:
        1192 cc ... ...   1.32 at 96.5 ±7 lb
        1285 cc, 1493 cc and 1584 cc ... ...   1.22 at 126 ±8 lb

Valve timing (with rocker clearance of .040):
    Inlet opens and closes:
        1192 cc ... ...   6 deg. BTDC, $35\frac{1}{2}$ deg. ABDC
        1285 cc, 1493 cc and 1584 cc ... ... $7\frac{1}{2}$ deg. BTDC, 37 deg. ABDC
    Exhaust opens and closes:
        1192 cc ... ... $42\frac{1}{2}$ deg. BBDC, 3 deg. ATDC
        1285 cc, 1493 cc and 1584 cc ... ... $44\frac{1}{2}$ deg. BBDC, 4 deg. ATDC

Rocker clearance (cold):
    Inlet and exhaust... ... ...   .004 (.1 mm) till 1971 .006
        (.15 mm) after 1971

Oil pump:
    End float in housing (with gasket) ... ...   .003 to .007
    Backlash between gears ... ...   .001 to .003
    Pressure (hot, with SAE.30 oil) ... ...   7 lb/sq inch (idling)
    Pressure (hot, with SAE.30 oil) ... ...   42 lb/sq inch (at 2500 rev/min)
    Relief valve spring free length ... ...   2.480 ± .040
    Load when compressed to .930 ... ...   17 lb

Fan—clearance between fan and fan housing 065

FUEL SYSTEM

Carburetters:

Make ... ... Solex

Type:

1192 cc to 1969	28 PICT-2
1285 cc to 1969, 1493 cc	30 PICT-2
1192 cc 1970 on	30 PICT-3
1285 cc 1970 on	31 PICT-3, 31 PICT-4
1584 cc	34 PICT-3

Solex 28 PICT-2:

Venturi ... ... 22.5 mm
Main jet 122.5
Air correction jet ... ... 140Z (135Z 1969 on)
Pilot jet 55
Pilot air bleed ... ... 2.00 1969 on
Pump injector 50
Enrichment calibration ... ... 75 (85 August 1969)
Float weight ... ... 5.7 grams

Solex 30 PICT-2:

Venturi ... ... 24 mm
Main jet 125
Air correction jet 125Z
Pilot jet 155
Pilot jet air bleed 140
Pump injector 50
Float weight ... ... 8.5 grams

Solex 30 PICT-3:

Venturi 24
Main jet ... ... 112.5 (x 112.5 August 1971)
Air correction jet 170Z
Pilot jet 55
Pilot jet air bleed ... ... 150 August 1971 on
Pump injector ... ... 50 (40 August 1971)
Enrichment calibration 85
Float weight ... ... 8.5 grams

Solex 31-PICT 3:

Venturi ... ... 25.5 mm
Main jet ... ... 145 (x 130 August 1971)
Air correction jet ... ... 170Z (110Z August 1971)
Pilot jet ... ... 60 (52.5 August 1971)
Pilot jet air bleed ... ... 120 (100 August 1971)
Pump injector 50
Enrichment calibration 100
Float weight ... ... 8.5 grams

Solex 34 PICT-3:

Venturi ... ... 26 mm
Main jet ... ... 145 (x 130 August 1971)
Air correction jet ... ... 130Z (60Z August 1971)
Pilot jet ... ... 65 (55 August 1971)
Pilot jet air bleed ... ... 120 August 1971
Pump injector 60
Enrichment calibration ... ... 100 (85 August 1971)
Float weight ... ... 8.5 grams

Solex 31 PICT-4:
Venturi	25.5 mm
Main jet	130
Air correction jet	110Z
Pilot jet	52.5
Pump injector	50
Enrichment calibration	100
Float weight	8.5 grams

IGNITION SYSTEM

Sparking plugs:
Type:

Bosch	W145 T1
Champion	L10, later L85, L87Y, L95Y or L88
KLG	F70
AC	43L
Lodge	HBN
Also any other make with similar values	
Gap	.028

Distributor:

Contact breaker gap	.016

Ignition timing:

1192 cc:

August 1970 to August 1974	TDC
Others	7½ deg. BTDC

1285 cc:

August 1970 to June 1971	5 deg. ATDC
Others	7½ deg. BTDC

1493 cc:

Semi-auto transmission, before August 1969	TDC
USA models	TDC
Others	7½ deg. BTDC

1584 cc, Europe:

Before August 1971	5 deg. ATDC
After August 1971	7½ deg. BTDC

1584 cc, USA:

1970	TDC
Early 1973 to late 1974, except California	7½ deg. BTDC
Fuel injection with semi-auto transmission	TDC
All other models	5 deg. ATDC
Firing order	1–4–3–2

CLUTCH

Type	Single dry plate

Pressure plate springs (loaded length):

'1200'	1.16
'1300' and '1500'	1.48
Automatic clutch	Inner .86, outer .78
Pedal free play	.40 to .80

TRANSMISSION

Gearbox casing:

Type	1-piece, tunnel

Gear selection:

All models	Synchromesh on all four forward gears

Gear ratios:
  All models:
    1st 3.80:1
    2nd 2.06:1
    3rd 1.26:1
    4th ... ... .89:1
    Reverse 3.61:1
  Automatic transmission:
    1st 2.06:1
    2nd 1.26:1
    3rd ... ... .89:1
    Reverse 3.07:1
Differential ratio:
  '1200', '1300' and cars with automatic transmission ... 4.375:1
  '1500', '1600' 4.125:1

STEERING

Wheel alignment (unladen):
  '1200' and '1300':
    Camber angle ... ... 0° 30' ± 20'
    Kingpin inclination ... ... 4° 20'
    Castor angle ... ... 3° 20' ± 1°
    Toe-in ... ... 30' ± 15'
    Toe-out on turns (inside wheel) ... ... 34° ± 2°
    Toe-out on turns (outside wheel) ... ... 28° ± 1°
  '1500':
    Camber angle ... ... 0° 30' ± 20'
    Kingpin inclination ... ... 4° 20'
    Castor angle ... ... 3° 20' ± 1°
    Toe-in (10 angular minutes equals .047 with 15 inch
      tyres) ... 30' ± 15'
  '1600':
    Camber angle ... ... 40' ± 30'
    Toe-in ... ... 30' ± 15' or .03 to .01 (.8 to .4)
    Kingpin inclination ... ... 12° 30'
MacPherson strut type:
  Camber ... ... 1° + 20' − 40' positive (no
                                         more than 30' variation be-
                                         tween sides)
  Toe-in ... ... 30' ± 15' ($\frac{1}{16}$ to $\frac{7}{32}$, greater at
                                         rear than at front)

FRONT SUSPENSION

Torsion bars:
  Number of leaves 10
1302, 1303 ... ... Macpherson struts, coil springs,
                                         radius link, anti-roll bar

REAR SUSPENSION

Spring type ... ... One round torsion bar each side
Spring plate inclination:
  Models before chassis No. 116 1021 297 ... ... 17° 30' ± 50'
  Others without equalizer spring ... ... 18° 30' + 50'
  With equalizer spring ... ... 20° + 50'
  With double-jointed axle ... ... 21° 20' + 50'
Some special equipment models for rough roads vary from these figures; if in doubt consult a
                  VW agent

Rear wheel toe-out:

'1200A' and '1300'	5' ± 15'
'1500'	10' ± 10'
'1300' and '1600' (1971)	0 ± 15'

Rear wheel camber angle:

All cars	Many variations (consult dealer)

BRAKES

System:

All models	Hydraulic front and rear

Handbrake:

All models	Cable operation on rear wheels only
Dual circuit braking	'1500' and '1600'; also later '1200' and '1300'

Brake types:

All except '1500' and '1600'	Drum, 9 inch diameter
'1500', '1600', optionally late '1300'	Disc front, drum rear

Lining width:

Front:

All models (except disc)	1.570

Rear:

All models	1.180

Lining thickness:

Front and rear (except disc)	.15 to .157

ELECTRICAL EQUIPMENT

Battery:

Early '1200'	6V, 66 amp/hr
'1300', '1500' and later '1200'	12V, 36 amp/hr

Generator:

'1200A' Bosch (6-volt)	111/903/021H
Alternative VW (6-volt)	111/903/021J
'1300' and '1500' (12-volt) Bosch	G(L)14V/30A/20

Regulator:

'1200A' (6-volt) Bosch	113/903/801F
Alternative (6-volt), VW	113/903/801G
Test voltage with load of 45 amps	6 to 7$\frac{1}{4}$ at 4000 generator rev/min
'1300' and '1500' (12-volt) Bosch	VA/14V/30A

(Generators and regulators must be of the same make when installed.)

Starter:

'1200A' (6-volt) Bosch	113/911/021B
Alternative (6-volt) VW	113/911/021A
'1300' and '1500' (12-volt) Bosch	EF(L)12VO/7PS

CAPACITIES

Fuel tank (all except '1302' and '1303')	8.8 Imperial gallons
Fuel tank ('1302' and '1303')	9.2 Imperial gallons
Engine sump	4.4 Imperial pints
Transmission	5.2 Imperial pints initially (4.4 pints on refilling)
Brakes	.44 Imperial pint

VW Automatic:

Converter	6.3 Imperial pints
Transmission and final drive	5.3 Imperial pints

TORQUE WRENCH SETTINGS

Figures are in lb ft unless otherwise specified

Engine:

Crankcase nuts (8 mm)	14
Crankcase nuts (12 mm)	24 to 26
Cylinder head nuts	22 to 23
Flywheel gland nut	253
Connecting rod bolt	24
Fan nut	40 to 47
Generator pulley nut	40 to 47
Sparking plug	22 to 29
Oil drain plug	22
Copper-plated rocker shaft nuts	18

Transmission:

Bolts/nuts for casing	14
Nuts for differential side cover	22
Crownwheel bolts	43
Selector fork screws	18
Reverse selector fork screw	14
Drive pinion nut (tunnel casing)	43 (tighten to 87, release and then to 43)
Main drive shaft nut (tunnel casing)	43 (tighten to 87, release and then to 43)
Rear axle shaft nut	217
Bolts/nuts for spring plate mounting	72 to 87

Brakes and wheels:

Backplate bolts	30
Hose and pipe unions	10 to 14
Wheel bolts (oiled)	90

Steering:

Steering wheel nut	36
Drop arm bolt	47 to 54
Mounting nuts (worm and roller)	18 to 25
Nuts for ball joints	18 to 25

Front axle:

Axle to frame	36 to 43
Steering knuckle ball joints	29 to 36 (10 mm) and 36 to 50 (12 mm)

Automatic transmission:

Temperature switch (clutch housing)	18
Selector switch (transmission housing)	18
Drive plate (converter)	18
Retaining ring (double taper bearing)	101 to 115
Gear carrier (transmission housing)	14
Gearshift housing	11
Converter housing	14
Transmission housing cover	7
Rubber mounting (converter housing)	14
Rubber mounting (transmission housing)	14
Shift fork	18
Drive pinion nut (35 mm)	130 to 145

Ring gear... 32
Rubber mounting (gearshift housing) 25
Clutch carrier plate 11
ATF supply pipe 7
ATF return pipe ... ... 22 to 29
Clutch lever clamp screw 18
Constant velocity joint flange 25
Diagonal arm to spring plate 87
Diagonal arm to cross tube 87
Torsion bar cover... 22
Shock absorber to frame 44
Shock absorber to bearing housing 51
Transmission mounting to frame 167

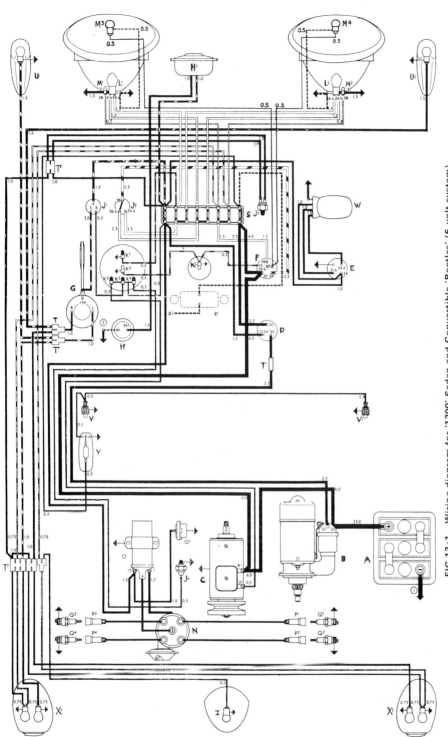

FIG 13:1 Wiring diagram for '1200' Sedan and Convertible 'Beetles' (6-volt system)

Key to Fig 13:1 **A** Battery **B** Starter motor **C** Generator **D** Ignition/starter switch **E** Windscreen wiper switch **F** Light switch **G** Direction indicator switch with dimmer switch **G1** Emergency light switch **H1** Horn ring **H2** Steering column connector **H3** Horn **J1** Flasher and emergency light relay **J2** Dipper relay **J3** Stoplight switch **J4** Oil pressure switch **K1** High beam warning light **K2** Generator warning light **K3** Direction indicator warning light **K4** Oil pressure warning light **K5** Speedometer light **K6** Fuel gauge light **L1** Sealed-beam unit (lefthand) **L2** Sealed-beam unit (righthand) **M1** Parking light (lefthand) **M2** Parking light (righthand) **N** Distributor **O** Ignition coil **O1** Automatic choke **O2** Electro-magnetic pilot jet **P1** Spark plug connector **P2** Spark plug connector **P3** Spark plug connector **P4** Spark plug connector **Q1** Spark plug **Q2** Spark plug **Q3** Spark plug **Q4** Spark plug **R1** Radio (optional) **R2** Aerial connection **S** Fuse box **T** Cable adaptor **T1** Cable connector (single) **T2** Cable connector (double) **T3** Cable connector (triple) **U1** Flasher light (lefthand) **U2** Flasher light (righthand) **V1** Courtesy light switch (lefthand) **V2** Courtesy light switch (righthand) **W** Windscreen wiper motor **X1** Stop, turn and tail lights (lefthand) **X2** Stop, turn and tail lights (righthand) **Y** Interior light **Z** Number plate light **1** Battery to frame earth **2** Horn ring to steering coupling earth connection

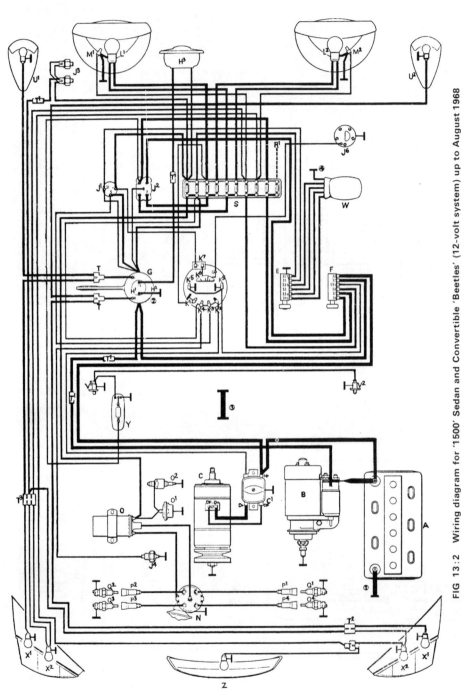

FIG 13:2 Wiring diagram for '1500' Sedan and Convertible 'Beetles' (12-volt system) up to August 1968

Key to Fig 13:2   A Battery   B Starter   C Generator   C1 Regulator   D Ignition/starter switch   E Windshield wiper switch   F Lighting switch
G Turn signal switch with automatic cancelling, hand dimmer button and steering/starter lock   H1 Horn half ring   H2 Steering column connection   H3 Horn
J1 Flasher relay   J2 Combi-relay for headlight flasher and dimming   J3 Brake light switch (2)   J4 Oil pressure switch   J6 Fuel gauge sender unit
K1 High beam warning lamp   K2 Generator warning lamp   K3 Turn signal warning lamp   K4 Oil pressure warning lamp   K5 Speedometer light
K6 Fuel gauge light   K7 Resistance for fuel gauge   L1 Twin-filament bulb (left headlight)   L2 Twin-filament bulb (right headlight)   M1 Parking light (lefthand)
M2 Parking light (righthand)   N Distributor   O Ignition coil   O1 Automatic choke   O2 Electro-magnetic pilot jet   P1 Spark plug connector (cylinder 1)
P2 Spark plug connector (cylinder 2)   P3 Spark plug connector (cylinder 4)   O2 Spark plug connector (cylinder 4)   P4 Spark plug connector (cylinder 3)   Q1 Spark plug for cylinder 1
Q2 Spark plug for cylinder 2   Q3 Spark plug for cylinder 3   Q4 Spark plug for cylinder 3   R1 Radio   S Fuse box   T Cable adaptor
T1 Cable connector (single)   T2 Cable connector (double)   T3 Cable connector (triple)   U1 Turn signal (lefthand)   U2 Turn signal (righthand)
Y1 Door contact switch (lefthand)   V2 Door contact switch (righthand)   W Windshield wiper motor   X1 Turn signal lights   X2 Brake and tail lights
Y Interior light   Z Licence plate light   1 Battery to frame earthing strap   2 Horn half ring to steering coupling earth connection   3 Transmission to frame earthing strap
4 Wiper motor to body earthing strap

158

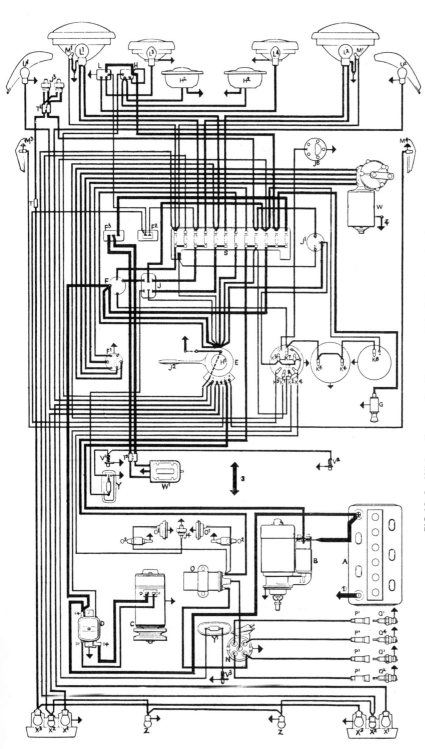

FIG 13:3   Wiring diagram for Karmann-Ghia (12-volt system)

Key to Fig 13:3
A Battery B Starter C Generator D Regulator E Turn signal switch with steering/ignition lock F Light switch
F1 Windshield wiper switch F2 Fog light switch F3 Sun roof switch G Cigar lighter H Twin-tone horn relay H1 Horn lever H2 Twin-tone horn
J Hand dimmer relay J1 Turn signal relay J2 Headlamp flasher button J3 Brake light switch J4 Oil pressure switch J5 Fuel gauge sender unit
K1 High beam warning lamp K2 Generator warning lamp K3 Turn signal warning lamp K4 Oil pressure warning lamp K5 Parking light warning lamp
K6 Speedometer light K7 Fuel gauge light K8 Clock light L Foglight relay L1 Twin-filament bulb for headlight (lefthand) L2 Twin-filament bulb
for headlight (righthand) L3 Foglight bulb (lefthand) L4 Foglight bulb (righthand) M1 Parking light (lefthand) M2 Parking light (righthand)
M3 Side parking light (lefthand) M4 Side parking light (righthand) N Distributor O Ignition coil O1 Automatic chokes O2 Electro-magnetic pilot jets
P1 Spark plug connector (cylinder 1) P2 Spark plug connector (cylinder 2) P3 Spark plug for cylinder 3 P4 Spark plug connector (cylinder 4) R1 Radio
Q1 Spark plug for cylinder 1 Q2 Spark plug for cylinder 2 Q3 Spark plug for cylinder 3 Q4 Spark plug for cylinder 4 R2 Aerial connection
R2 Aerial connection S Fuse box (10 fuses) S1 Cigar lighter fuse S2 Foglight and twin-tone horn fuse T Cable adaptor
T1 Cable connector (single) T2 Cable connector (double) U1 Turn signal (front lefthand) U2 Turn signal (front righthand) V1 Door switch (lefthand)
V2 Door switch (righthand) V3 Luggage compartment light switch W Windshield wiper motor W1 Sun roof motor X1 Turn signal lights (rear)
X2 Tail lights X3 Brake lights Y Interior light Y1 Luggage compartment light Z Licence plate light 1 Battery to frame earthing strap
2 Horn lever to steering coupling earth connection 3 Transmission to frame earth connection 4 Windshield wiper motor to body earthing strap
5 Front axle to frame earthing strap

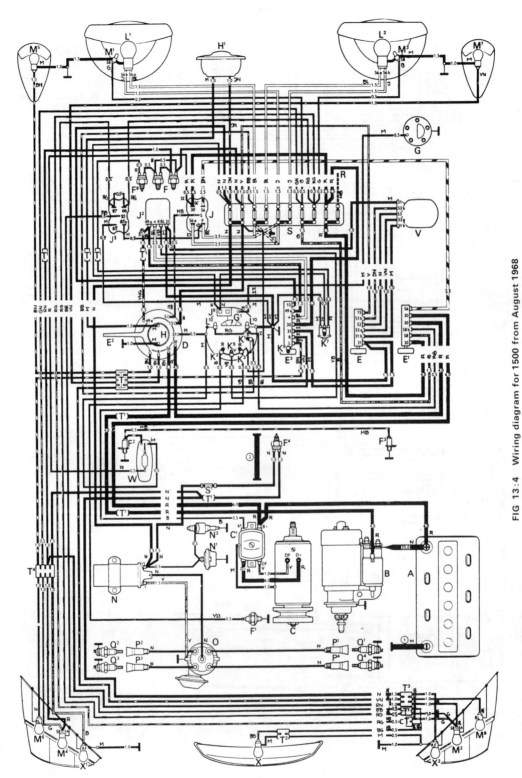

FIG 13:4 Wiring diagram for 1500 from August 1968

Colour code: B Blue BL White G Grey J Yellow M Brown N Black R Red Vi Violet Y Green

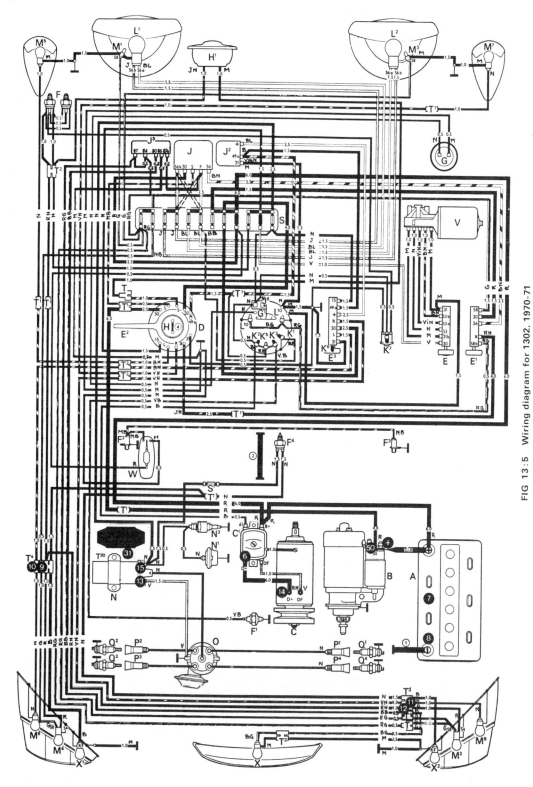

FIG 13:5   Wiring diagram for 1302, 1970-71

For colour code, see FIG 13:4

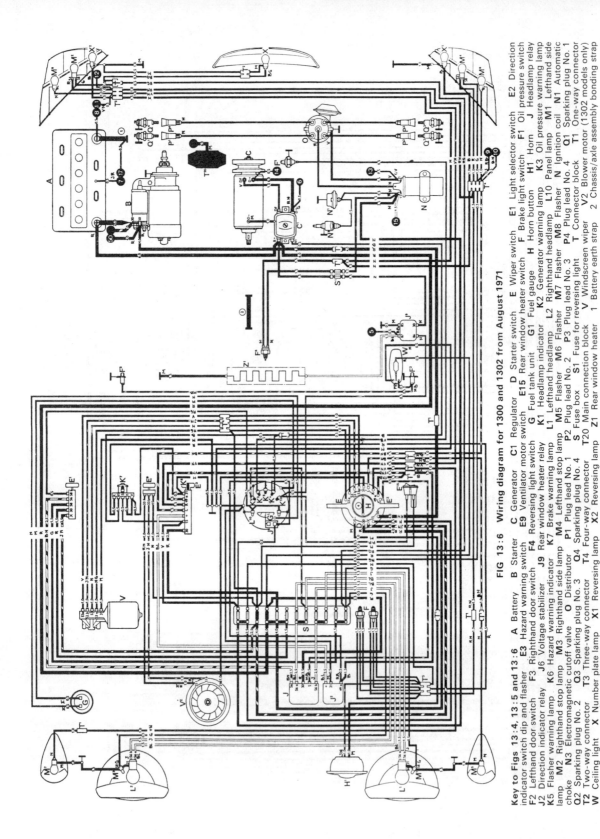

FIG 13 : 6   Wiring diagram for 1300 and 1302 from August 1971

Key to Figs 13 : 4, 13 : 5 and 13 : 6   A Battery   B Starter   C Generator   C1 Regulator   D Starter switch   E Wiper switch   E1 Light selector switch   E2 Direction indicator switch dip and flasher   E3 Hazard warning switch   E9 Ventilator motor switch   E15 Rear window heater switch   F Brake light switch   F1 Oil pressure switch   F2 Lefthand door switch   F3 Righthand door switch   F4 Reversing light switch   G Fuel tank unit   G1 Fuel gauge   H Horn button   H1 Horn   J Headlamp relay   J2 Direction indicator relay   J6 Voltage stabilizer   J9 Rear window heater relay   K1 Headlamp indicator   K2 Generator warning lamp   K3 Oil pressure warning lamp   K5 Flasher warning lamp   K6 Hazard warning indicator   K7 Brake warning lamp   L1 Lefthand headlamp   L2 Righthand headlamp   L10 Panel lamp   M1 Lefthand side lamp   M2 Righthand stop lamp   M3 Righthand side lamp   M4 Lefthand stop lamp   M5 Flasher   M6 Flasher   M7 Flasher   M8 Flasher   N Ignition coil   N1 Automatic choke   N3 Electromagnetic cutoff valve   O Distributor   P1 Plug lead No. 1   P2 Plug lead No. 2   P3 Plug lead No. 3   P4 Plug lead No. 4   Q1 Sparking plug No. 1   Q2 Sparking plug No. 2   Q3 Sparking plug No. 3   Q4 Sparking plug No. 4   S Fuse box   S1 Fuse for reversing light   T Connector block   T1 One-way connector   T2 Two-way connector   T3 Three-way connector   T4 Four-way connector   T20 Main connection block   V Windscreen wiper   V2 Blower motor (1302 models only)   W Ceiling light   X Number plate lamp   X1 Reversing lamp   X2 Reversing lamp   Z1 Rear window heater   1 Battery earth strap   2 Chassis/axle assembly bonding strap

For colour code, see FIG 13 : 4

162

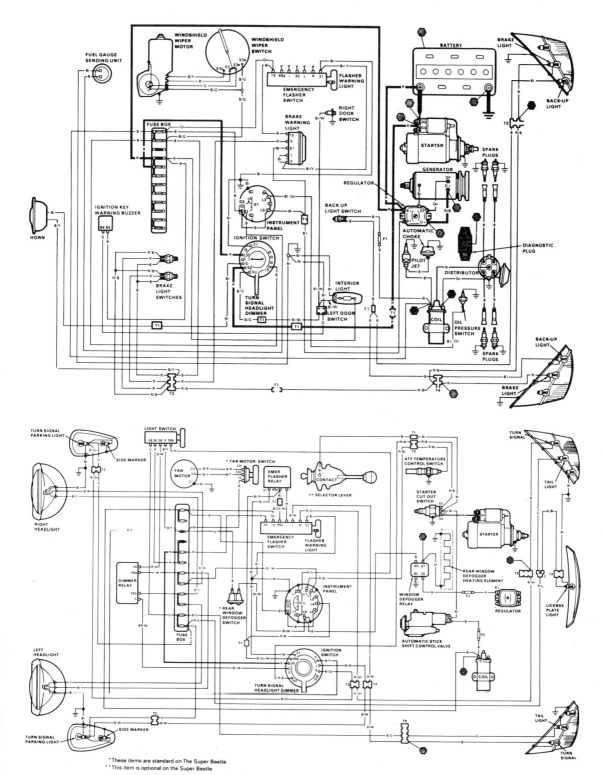

FIG 13:7 Wiring diagram for 1972 (US models). This diagram is presented in two parts for easier use. Some components appear in both since they may be used in more than one circuit. See page 165 for key

* These items are standard on The Super Beetle.
** This item is optional on the Super Beetle.

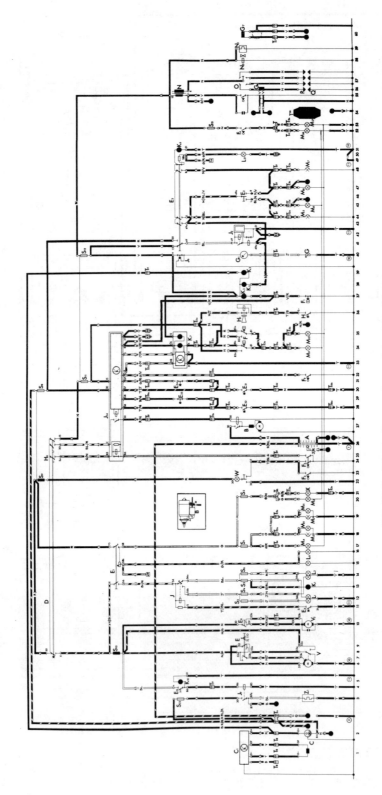

FIG 13:8 Wiring diagram for models with alternator

Key to Fig 13:7

F1 Back-up light in-line fuse   F2 Fuse for rear window defogger   F3 Fuse for automatic stick shift control valve   G1 Fuel gauge   G2 Fuel gauge vibrator   H Horn button   H1 ATF Temperature warning light   L1 High beam warning light   L2 High beam warning light   L3 Oil pressure warning light   L4 Turn signal warning light   L5 Generator charging warning light   L6 Rear window defogger warning light   L7 Instrument panel light   ◆ Diagnostic plug connection

Connector code: T Cable adapter   T1 Cable connector, single   T2 Cable connector, double   T3 Cable connector, triple   T4 Cable connector, quadruple

Colour Code: B Black   Bl Blue   Br Brown   G Grey   Gn Green   R Red   W White   Y Yellow

Key to Fig 13:8 (the numbers on the right relate to those on the diagram base line and will assist in locating items)

A	Battery	26
B	Starter	27
C	Alternator	1, 2
C1	Regulator	8, 25, 26
D	Ignition/starter switch	7, 9
E	Windscreen wiper switch	13, 15, 17
E1	Light switch	46
E2	Turn signal switch	41, 43, 44, 48, 50
E3	Emergency flasher switch	
E4	Headlight dip switch	11
E9	Fresh air fan motor switch	10
E15	Rear window heater switch	4, 5
E24	Safety belt lock left	31
E25	Safety belt lock right	29
E31	Contact strip in driver seat	30
E32	Contact strip in passenger seat	28
F	Brake light switch	34, 35
F1	Oil pressure switch	37
F2	Door contact and buzzer alarm switch, left	24, 25
F3	Door contact switch, right	23
F4	Reversing light switch	52
F9	Handbrake light switch	32
G	Fuel gauge sending unit	40
G1	Fuel gauge	40
G4	Ignition timing sensor	56
G7	TDC marker unit	60
H	Horn button	36
H1	Horn	36
H6	Contact in ignition/starter switch for buzzer	25
J	Headlamp relay	11, 13, 14
J2	Emergency flasher relay	41, 42
J6	Voltage vibrator	40
J9	Rear window heater relay	3, 4
J34	Safety belt warning system relay	25, 26, 27, 28, 29, 30, 31, 32, 33, 34, 35

K1	High beam warning light	13
K2	Alternator charging warning light	39
K3	Oil pressure warning light	37
K5	Turn signal warning light	38
K6	Emergency flasher warning light	51
K7	Dual circuit brake warning and safety belt interlock warning system	33, 34, 35
L1	Sealed beam unit, left headlight	12
L2	Sealed beam unit, right headlight	14
L6	Speedometer light	15, 16
L21	Light for heater lever illumination	50
M2	Tail light, right	20
M4	Tail light, left	17
M5	Parking light front, left	18
M5	Turn signal, front, left	44
M6	Turn signal, rear, left	45
M7	Parking light, front, right	19
M7	Turn signal, front, right	48
M8	Turn signal, rear, right	47
M9	Brake light, left	34
M10	Brake light, right	35
M11	Sidemarker light, front, left and right	18, 19
M16	Reversing light, left	52
M17	Reversing light, right	53
N	Ignition coil	55
N1	Automatic choke	59
N3	Electro-magnetic cut-off valve	58
O	Ignition distributor	55, 56, 57
P	Spark plug connectors	55, 56, 57
Q	Spark plugs	
S1 to S12	Fuses in fuse box	8, 12, 14, 17, 20, 22, 30, 31, 40

S21	Fuse for reversing lights (8 amp)	52
S22	Fuse for rear window heater (8 amp)	3
T	Cable adaptor, behind insulation in engine compartment	
	a Under rear seat bench	
T1	Wire connector, single	
	a Behind instrument panel	
	b Under rear seat bench	
T2	Wire connector, double	
	a In luggage compartment, left	
	b In luggage compartment, right	
	c Under passenger seat	
	d Under driver's seat	
	e In hood of engine compartment	
T3	Wire connector, 3 point	
	a In luggage compartment, left	
	b Behind insulation in engine compartment, right	
T4	Wire connector, 4 point behind insulation in engine compartment, left	
T5	Wire connector, single	
	a Behind instrument panel	
	b On passenger seat rail	
T6	Wire connector, double	
	a Under passenger seat	
	b Under driver's seat	
T7	Wire connector, 3 point, in engine compartment	
T8	Wire connector, 4 point, under rear seat bench	
T9	Wire connector, 8 point, behind instrument panel	
T20	Test network, test socket	54
V	Windscreen wiper motor	6, 7, 8
V2	Fresh air motor	10
W	Interior light	22
X	Number plate light	21
Z1	Rear window heating element	3
1	Earth strap, battery to frame	
2	Earth strap, transmission to frame	
10	Instrument panel earth connection	
11	Speedometer earth connection	

Key to colour code   B Blue   BL White   G Grey   J Yellow   M Maroon   N Black   R Red   T Brown   V Green   Vi Violet

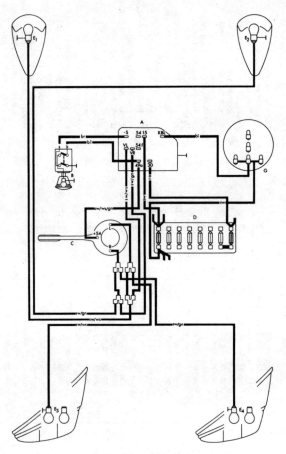

FIG 13:9   Hazard warning light system

Key to Fig 13:9   **A** Flasher and hazard warning light relay
B Warning light switch   **C** Indicator switch   **D** Fuse box
E1 Lefthand indicator, front   **E2** Righthand indicator, front
E3 Lefthand indicator, rear   **E4** Righthand indicator, rear
G Indicator warning light

HINTS ON MAINTENANCE AND OVERHAUL

There are few things more rewarding than the restoration of a vehicle's original peak of efficiency and smooth performance.

The following notes are intended to help the owner to reach that state of perfection. Providing that he possesses the basic manual skills he should have no difficulty in performing most of the operations detailed in this manual. It must be stressed, however, that where recommended in the manual, highly-skilled operations ought to be entrusted to experts, who have the necessary equipment, to carry out the work satisfactorily.

Quality of workmanship:

The hazardous driving conditions on the roads to-day demand that vehicles should be as nearly perfect, mechanically, as possible. It is therefore most important that amateur work be carried out with care, bearing in mind the often inadequate working conditions, and also the inferior tools which may have to be used. It is easy to counsel perfection in all things, and we recognise that it may be setting an impossibly high standard. We do, however, suggest that every care should be taken to ensure that a vehicle is as safe to take on the road as it is humanly possible to make it.

Safe working conditions:

Even though a vehicle may be stationary, it is still potentially dangerous if certain sensible precautions are not taken when working on it while it is supported on jacks or blocks. It is indeed preferable not to use jacks alone, but to supplement them with carefully placed blocks, so that there will be plenty of support if the car rolls off the jacks during a strenuous manoeuvre. Axle stands are an excellent way of providing a rigid base which is not readily disturbed. Piles of bricks are a dangerous substitute. Be careful not to get under heavy loads on lifting tackle, the load could fall. It is preferable not to work alone when lifting an engine, or when working underneath a vehicle which is supported well off the ground. To be trapped, particularly under the vehicle, may have unpleasant results if help is not quickly forthcoming. Make some provision, however humble, to deal with fires. Always disconnect a battery if there is a likelihood of electrical shorts. These may start a fire if there is leaking fuel about. This applies particularly to leads which can carry a heavy current, like those in the starter circuit. While on the subject of electricity, we must also stress the danger of using equipment which is run off the mains and which has no earth or has faulty wiring or connections. So many workshops have damp floors, and electrical shocks are of such a nature that it is sometimes impossible to let go of a live lead or piece of equipment due to the muscular spasms which take place.

Work demanding special care:

This involves the servicing of braking, steering and suspension systems. On the road, failure of the braking system may be disastrous. Make quite sure that there can be no possibility of failure through the bursting of rusty brake pipes or rotten hoses, nor to a sudden loss of pressure due to defective seals or valves.

Problems:

The chief problems which may face an operator are:
1. External dirt.
2. Difficulty in undoing tight fixings.
3. Dismantling unfamiliar mechanisms.
4. Deciding in what respect parts are defective.
5. Confusion about the correct order for reassembly.
6. Adjusting running clearance.
7. Road testing.
8. Final tuning.

Practical suggestions to solve the problems:

1. Preliminary cleaning of large parts—engines, transmissions, steering, suspensions, etc.—should be carried out before removal from the car. Where road dirt and mud alone are present, wash clean with a high-pressure water jet, brushing to remove stubborn adhesions, and allow to drain and dry. Where oil or grease is also present, wash down with a proprietary compound (Gunk, Teepol etc,) applying with a stiff brush—an old paint brush is suitable—into all crevices. Cover the distributor and ignition coils with a polythene bag and then apply a strong water jet to clear the loosened deposits. Allow to drain and dry. The assemblies will then be sufficiently clean to remove and transfer to the bench for the next stage.

   On the bench, further cleaning can be carried out, first wiping the parts as free as possible from grease with old newspaper. Avoid using rag or cotton waste which can leave clogging fibres behind. Any remaining grease can be removed with a brush dipped in paraffin. If necessary, traces of paraffin can be removed by carbon tetrachloride. Avoid using paraffin or petrol in large quantities for cleaning in enclosed areas, such as garages, on account of the high fire risk.

   When all exteriors have been cleaned, and not before, dismantling can be commenced. This ensures that dirt will not enter into interiors and orifices revealed by dismantling. In the next phases, where components have to be cleaned, use carbon tetrachloride in preference to petrol and keep the containers covered except when in use. After the components have been cleaned, plug small holes with tapered hard wood plugs cut to size and blank off larger orifices with greaseproof paper and masking tape. Do not use soft wood plugs or matchsticks as they may break.

2. It is not advisable to hammer on the end of a screw thread, but if it must be done, first screw on a nut to protect the thread, and use a lead hammer. This applies particularly to the removal of tapered cotters. Nuts and bolts seem to 'grow' together, especially in exhaust systems. If penetrating oil does not work, try the judicious application of heat, but be careful of starting a fire. Asbestos sheet or cloth is useful to isolate heat.

   Tight bushes or pieces of tail-pipe rusted into a silencer can be removed by splitting them with an open-ended hacksaw. Tight screws can sometimes be started by a tap from a hammer on the end of a suitable screwdriver. Many tight fittings will yield to the judicious use of a hammer, but it must be a soft-faced hammer if damage is to be avoided, use a heavy block on the opposite side to absorb shock. Any parts of the steering system which have been damaged should be renewed, as attempts to repair them may lead to cracking and subsequent failure, and steering ball joints should be disconnected using a recommended tool to prevent damage.

3 If often happens that an owner is baffled when trying to dismantle an unfamiliar piece of equipment. So many modern devices are pressed together or assembled by spinning-over flanges, that they must be sawn apart. The intention is that the whole assembly must be renewed. However, parts which appear to be in one piece to the naked eye, may reveal close-fitting joint lines when inspected with a magnifying glass, and, this may provide the necessary clue to dismantling. Left-handed screw threads are used where rotational forces would tend to unscrew a right-handed screw thread.

Be very careful when dismantling mechanisms which may come apart suddenly. Work in an enclosed space where the parts will be contained, and drape a piece of cloth over the device if springs are likely to fly in all directions. Mark everything which might be reassembled in the wrong position, scratched symbols may be used on unstressed parts, or a sequence of tiny dots from a centre punch can be useful. Stressed parts should never be scratched or centre-popped as this may lead to cracking under working conditions. Store parts which look alike in the correct order for reassembly. Never rely upon memory to assist in the assembly of complicated mechanisms, especially when they will be dismantled for a long time, but make notes, and drawings to supplement the diagrams in the manual, and put labels on detached wires. Rust stains may indicate unlubricated wear. This can sometimes be seen round the outside edge of a bearing cup in a universal joint. Look for bright rubbing marks on parts which normally should not make heavy contact. These might prove that something is bent or running out of true. For example, there might be bright marks on one side of a piston, at the top near the ring grooves, and others at the bottom of the skirt on the other side. This could well be the clue to a bent connecting rod. Suspected cracks can be proved by heating the component in a light oil to approximately 100°C, removing, drying off, and dusting with french chalk, if a crack is present the oil retained in the crack will stain the french chalk.

4 In determining wear, and the degree, against the permissible limits set in the manual, accurate measurement can only be achieved by the use of a micrometer. In many cases, the wear is given to the fourth place of decimals; that is in ten-thousandths of an inch. This can be read by the vernier scale on the barrel of a good micrometer. Bore diameters are more difficult to determine. If, however, the matching shaft is accurately measured, the degree of play in the bore can be felt as a guide to its suitability. In other cases, the shank of a twist drill of known diameter is a handy check.

Many methods have been devised for determining the clearance between bearing surfaces. To-day the best and simplest is by the use of Plastigage, obtainable from most garages. A thin plastic thread is laid between the two surfaces and the bearing is tightened, flattening the thread. On removal, the width of the thread is compared with a scale supplied with the thread and the clearance is read off directly. Sometimes joint faces leak persistently, even after gasket renewal. The fault will then be traceable to distortion, dirt or burrs. Studs which are screwed into soft metal frequently raise burrs at the point of entry. A quick cure for this is to chamfer the edge of the hole in the part which fits over the stud.

5 **Always check a replacement part with the original one before it is fitted.**

If parts are not marked, and the order for reassembly is not known, a little detective work will help. Look for marks which are due to wear to see if they can be mated. Joint faces may not be identical due to manufacturing errors, and parts which overlap may be stained, giving a clue to the correct position. Most fixings leave identifying marks especially if they were painted over on assembly. It is then easier to decide whether a nut, for instance, has a plain, a spring, or a shakeproof washer under it. All running surfaces become 'bedded' together after long spells of work and tiny imperfections on one part will be found to have left corresponding marks on the other. This is particularly true of shafts and bearings and even a score on a cylinder wall will show on the piston.

6 Checking end float or rocker clearances by feeler gauge may not always give accurate results because of wear. For instance, the rocker tip which bears on a valve stem may be deeply pitted, in which case the feeler will simply be bridging a depression. Thrust washers may also wear depressions in opposing faces to make accurate measurement difficult. End float is then easier to check by using a dial gauge. It is common practice to adjust end play in bearing assemblies. like front hubs with taper rollers, by doing up the axle nut until the hub becomes stiff to turn and then backing it off a little. Do not use this method with ballbearing hubs as the assembly is often preloaded by tightening the axle nut to its fullest extent. If the splitpin hole will not line up, file the base of the nut a little.

Steering assemblies often wear in the straight-ahead position. If any part is adjusted, make sure that it remains free when moved from lock to lock. Do not be surprised if an assembly like a steering gearbox, which is known to be carefully adjusted outside the car, becomes stiff when it is bolted in place. This will be due to distortion of the case by the pull of the mounting bolts, particularly if the mounting points are not all touching together. This problem may be met in other equipment and is cured by careful attention to the alignment of mounting points.

When a spanner is stamped with a size and A/F it means that the dimension is the width between the jaws and has no connection with ANF, which is the designation for the American National Fine thread. Coarse threads like Whitworth are rarely used on cars to-day except for studs which screw into soft aluminium or cast iron. For this reason it might be found that the top end of a cylinder head stud has a fine thread and the lower end a coarse thread to screw into the cylinder block. If the car has mainly UNF threads then it is likely that any coarse threads will be UNC, which are not the same as Whitworth. Small sizes have the same number of threads in Whitworth and UNC, but in the $\frac{1}{2}$ inch size for example, there are twelve threads to the inch in the former and thirteen in the latter.

7 After a major overhaul, particularly if a great deal of work has been done on the braking, steering and suspension systems, it is advisable to approach the problem of testing with care. If the braking system has been overhauled, apply heavy pressure to the brake pedal and get a second operator to check every possible source of leakage. The brakes may work extremely well, but a leak could cause complete failure after a few miles.

Do not fit the hub caps until every wheel nut has been checked for tightness, and make sure the tyre pressures are correct. Check the levels of coolant, lubricants and hydraulic fluids. Being satisfied that all is well, take the car on the road and test the brakes at once. Check the steering and the action of the handbrake. Do all this at moderate speeds on quiet roads, and make sure there is no other vehicle behind you when you try a rapid stop.

Finally, remember that many parts settle down after a time, so check for tightness of all fixings after the car has been on the road for a hundred miles or so.

8 It is useless to tune an engine which has not reached its normal running temperature. In the same way, the tune of an engine which is stiff after a rebore will be different when the engine is again running free. Remember too, that rocker clearances on pushrod operated valve gear will change when the cylinder head nuts are tightened after an initial period of running with a new head gasket.

Trouble may not always be due to what seems the obvious cause. Ignition, carburation and mechanical condition are interdependent and spitting back through the carburetter, which might be attributed to a weak mixture, can be caused by a sticking inlet valve.

For one final hint on tuning, never adjust more than one thing at a time or it will be impossible to tell which adjustment produced the desired result.

NOTES

GLOSSARY OF TERMS

Allen key — Cranked wrench of hexagonal section for use with socket head screws.

Alternator — Electrical generator producing alternating current. Rectified to direct current for battery charging.

Ambient temperature — Surrounding atmospheric temperature.

Annulus — Used in engineering to indicate the outer ring gear of an epicyclic gear train.

Armature — The shaft carrying the windings, which rotates in the magnetic field of a generator or starter motor. That part of a solenoid or relay which is activated by the magnetic field.

Axial — In line with, or pertaining to, an axis.

Backlash — Play in meshing gears.

Balance lever — A bar where force applied at the centre is equally divided between connections at the ends.

Banjo axle — Axle casing with large diameter housing for the crownwheel and differential.

Bendix pinion — A self-engaging and self-disengaging drive on a starter motor shaft.

Bevel pinion — A conical shaped gearwheel, designed to mesh with a similar gear with an axis usually at 90 deg. to its own.

bhp — Brake horse power, measured on a dynamometer.

bmep — Brake mean effective pressure. Average pressure on a piston during the working stroke.

Brake cylinder — Cylinder with hydraulically operated piston(s) acting on brake shoes or pad(s).

Brake regulator — Control valve fitted in hydraulic braking system which limits brake pressure to rear brakes during heavy braking to prevent rear wheel locking.

Camber — Angle at which a wheel is tilted from the vertical.

Capacitor — Modern term for an electrical condenser. Part of distributor assembly, connected across contact breaker points, acts as an interference suppressor.

Castellated — Top face of a nut, slotted across the flats, to take a locking splitpin.

Castor — Angle at which the kingpin or swivel pin is tilted when viewed from the side.

cc — Cubic centimetres. Engine capacity is arrived at by multiplying the area of the bore in sq cm by the stroke in cm by the number of cylinders.

Clevis — U-shaped forked connector used with a clevis pin, usually at handbrake connections.

Collet — A type of collar, usually split and located in a groove in a shaft, and held in place by a retainer. The arrangement used to retain the spring(s) on a valve stem in most cases.

Commutator — Rotating segmented current distributor between armature windings and brushes in generator or motor.

Compression ratio — The ratio, or quantitative relation, of the total volume (piston at bottom of stroke) to the unswept volume (piston at top of stroke) in an engine cylinder.

Condenser — See capacitor.

Core plug — Plug for blanking off a manufacturing hole in a casting.

Crownwheel — Large bevel gear in rear axle, driven by a bevel pinion attached to the propeller shaft. Sometimes called a 'ring gear'.

'C'-spanner — Like a 'C' with a handle. For use on screwed collars without flats, but with slots or holes.

Damper — Modern term for shock-absorber, used in vehicle suspension systems to damp out spring oscillations.

Depression — The lowering of atmospheric pressure as in the inlet manifold and carburetter.

Dowel — Close tolerance pin, peg, tube, or bolt, which accurately locates mating parts.

Drag link — Rod connecting steering box drop arm (pitman arm) to nearest front wheel steering arm in certain types of steering systems.

Dry liner — Thinwall tube pressed into cylinder bore

Dry sump — Lubrication system where all oil is scavenged from the sump, and returned to a separate tank.

Dynamo — See Generator.

Electrode — Terminal, part of an electrical component, such as the points or 'Electrodes' of a sparking plug.

Electrolyte — In lead-acid car batteries a solution of sulphuric acid and distilled water.

End float — The axial movement between associated parts, end play.

EP — Extreme pressure. In lubricants, special grades for heavily loaded bearing surfaces, such as gear teeth in a gearbox, or crownwheel and pinion in a rear axle.

Fade	Of brakes. Reduced efficiency due to overheating.
Field coils	Windings on the polepieces of motors and generators.
Fillets	Narrow finishing strips usually applied to interior bodywork.
First motion shaft	Input shaft from clutch to gearbox.
Fullflow filter	Filters in which all the oil is pumped to the engine. If the element becomes clogged, a bypass valve operates to pass unfiltered oil to the engine.
FWD	Front wheel drive.
Gear pump	Two meshing gears in a close fitting casing. Oil is carried from the inlet round the outside of both gears in the spaces between the gear teeth and casing to the outlet, the meshing gear teeth prevent oil passing back to the inlet, and the oil is forced through the outlet port.
Generator	Modern term for 'Dynamo'. When rotated produces electrical current.
Grommet	A ring of protective or sealing material. Can be used to protect pipes or leads passing through bulkheads.
Grubscrew	Fully threaded headless screw with screwdriver slot. Used for locking, or alignment purposes.
Gudgeon pin	Shaft which connects a piston to its connecting rod. Sometimes called 'wrist pin', or 'piston pin'.
Halfshaft	One of a pair transmitting drive from the differential.
Helical	In spiral form. The teeth of helical gears are cut at a spiral angle to the side faces of the gearwheel.
Hot spot	Hot area that assists vapourisation of fuel on its way to cylinders. Often provided by close contact between inlet and exhaust manifolds.
HT	High Tension. Applied to electrical current produced by the ignition coil for the sparking plugs.
Hydrometer	A device for checking specific gravity of liquids. Used to check specific gravity of electrolyte.
Hypoid bevel gears	A form of bevel gear used in the rear axle drive gears. The bevel pinion meshes below the centre line of the crownwheel, giving a lower propeller shaft line.
Idler	A device for passing on movement. A free running gear between driving and driven gears. A lever transmitting track rod movement to a side rod in steering gear.
Impeller	A centrifugal pumping element. Used in water pumps to stimulate flow.
Journals	Those parts of a shaft that are in contact with the bearings.
Kingpin	The main vertical pin which carries the front wheel spindle, and permits steering movement. May be called 'steering pin' or 'swivel pin'.
Layshaft	The shaft which carries the laygear in the gearbox. The laygear is driven by the first motion shaft and drives the third motion shaft according to the gear selected. Sometimes called the 'countershaft' or 'second motion shaft.'
lb ft	A measure of twist or torque. A pull of 10 lb at a radius of 1 ft is a torque of 10 lb ft.
lb/sq in	Pounds per square inch.
Little-end	The small, or piston end of a connecting rod. Sometimes called the 'small-end'.
LT	Low Tension. The current output from the battery.
Mandrel	Accurately manufactured bar or rod used for test or centring purposes.
Manifold	A pipe, duct, or chamber, with several branches.
Needle rollers	Bearing rollers with a length many times their diameter.
Oil bath	Reservoir which lubricates parts by immersion. In air filters, a separate oil supply for wetting a wire mesh element to hold the dust.
Oil wetted	In air filters, a wire mesh element lightly oiled to trap and hold airborne dust.
Overlap	Period during which inlet and exhaust valves are open together.
Panhard rod	Bar connected between fixed point on chassis and another on axle to control sideways movement.
Pawl	Pivoted catch which engages in the teeth of a ratchet to permit movement in one direction only.
Peg spanner	Tool with pegs, or pins, to engage in holes or slots in the part to be turned.
Pendant pedals	Pedals with levers that are pivoted at the top end.
Phillips screwdriver	A cross-point screwdriver for use with the cross-slotted heads of Phillips screws.
Pinion	A small gear, usually in relation to another gear.
Piston-type damper	Shock absorber in which damping is controlled by a piston working in a closed oil-filled cylinder.
Preloading	Preset static pressure on ball or roller bearings not due to working loads.
Radial	Radiating from a centre, like the spokes of a wheel.

Radius rod	Pivoted arm confining movement of a part to an arc of fixed radius.
Ratchet	Toothed wheel or rack which can move in one direction only, movement in the other being prevented by a pawl.
Ring gear	A gear tooth ring attached to outer periphery of flywheel. Starter pinion engages with it during starting.
Runout	Amount by which rotating part is out of true.
Semi-floating axle	Outer end of rear axle halfshaft is carried on bearing inside axle casing. Wheel hub is secured to end of shaft.
Servo	A hydraulic or pneumatic system for assisting, or, augmenting a physical effort. See 'Vacuum Servo'.
Setscrew	One which is threaded for the full length of the shank.
Shackle	A coupling link, used in the form of two parallel pins connected by side plates to secure the end of the master suspension spring and absorb the effects of deflection.
Shell bearing	Thinwalled steel shell lined with anti-friction metal. Usually semi-circular and used in pairs for main and big-end bearings.
Shock absorber	See 'Damper'.
Silentbloc	Rubber bush bonded to inner and outer metal sleeves.
Socket-head screw	Screw with hexagonal socket for an Allen key.
Solenoid	A coil of wire creating a magnetic field when electric current passes through it. Used with a soft iron core to operate contacts or a mechanical device.
Spur gear	A gear with teeth cut axially across the periphery.
Stub axle	Short axle fixed at one end only.
Tachometer	An instrument for accurate measurement of rotating speed. Usually indicates in revolutions per minute.

TDC	Top Dead Centre. The highest point reached by a piston in a cylinder, with the crank and connecting rod in line.
Thermostat	Automatic device for regulating temperature. Used in vehicle coolant systems to open a valve which restricts circulation at low temperature.
Third motion shaft	Output shaft of gearbox.
Threequarter floating axle	Outer end of rear axle halfshaft flanged and bolted to wheel hub, which runs on bearing mounted on outside of axle casing. Vehicle weight is not carried by the axle shaft.
Thrust bearing or washer	Used to reduce friction in rotating parts subject to axial loads.
Torque	Turning or twisting effort. See 'lb ft'.
Track rod	The bar(s) across the vehicle which connect the steering arms and maintain the front wheels in their correct alignment.
UJ	Universal joint. A coupling between shafts which permits angular movement.
UNF	Unified National Fine screw thread.
Vacuum servo	Device used in brake system, using difference between atmospheric pressure and inlet manifold depression to operate a piston which acts to augment brake pressure as required. See 'Servo'.
Venturi	A restriction or 'choke' in a tube, as in a carburetter, used to increase velocity to obtain a reduction in pressure.
Vernier	A sliding scale for obtaining fractional readings of the graduations of an adjacent scale.
Welch plug	A domed thin metal disc which is partially flattened to lock in a recess. Used to plug core holes in castings.
Wet liner	Removable cylinder barrel, sealed against coolant leakage, where the coolant is in direct contact with the outer surface.
Wet sump	A reservoir attached to the crankcase to hold the lubricating oil.

NOTES

INDEX